The Guns of Lattimer

PREFACE

THE GUNS

of

LATTIMER

The true story of a massacre and a trial August 1897–March 1898

by MICHAEL NOVAK

BASIC BOOKS, INC., PUBLISHERS

NEW YORK

Library of Congress Cataloging in Publication Data

Novak, Michael.
   The guns of Lattimer.

   Bibliography: p. 265
   Includes index.
   1. Anthracite Coal Strike, 1897. I. Title.
HD5325.M62N68   33.89'282'233509756775   78-54500
ISBN: 0-465-02793-8

LATTIMER MASSACRE

September 10, 1897

"It was not a battle because they were not aggressive, nor were they defensive because they had no weapons of any kind and were simply shot down like so many worthless objects, each of the licensed life-takers trying to outdo the others in butchery."

The Hazleton *Daily Standard*
September 11, 1897

Inscription on the monument erected
at Lattimer in 1972

DEDICATION

This book is intended as a
partial repayment for the gifts America gave
—work, freedom, and flawed but
idealistic justice

CONTENTS

BALLAD OF THE DEPUTIES

How proud the deputies must feel
    Who took so brave a part
In that conflict where their rifles
    Have pierced the manly hearts
Of honest fellow workmen
    Without pistol, gun or knife,
Without the smallest weapon
    To defend their sacred life.

We cannot forget the bravery
    Of those noble warlike men,
Who after shooting victims down
    Took aim and fired again.
Oh, noble, noble, deputies
    Our heads are bent with shame,
We shake with fear and blush to hear
    The list of cowards' names.

Though the press of Philadelphia
    May uphold the Sheriff's name,
It makes the crime no lighter
    And it lessens not the shame.
The crime you have committed
    Leaves a stain forever more
On the fair name of Hazleton
    Such as was never known before.

The region is in mourning
  For the victims who have died,
In trying to maintain their rights,
  The rights they were denied.

Beneath the starry banner
  Though they came from foreign lands,
They died the death of martyrs
  For the noble rights of man.
Oh, noble, noble, deputies
  We will shout the news aloud,
The Sheriff was a coward
  And he led a cowardly crowd.

Can you still live here and witness
  The destruction you have wrought,
Where you'll hear the little orphans
  Mourning o'er their fateful lot?
And hear their widowed mothers
  Crying for the ones they loved,
And praying prayers of vengeance
  To the Mighty One above.

If the courts of justice shield you
  And your freedom you should gain,
Remember that your brows are marked
  With the burning brand of Cain.
Oh, noble, noble, deputies
  We always will remember,
Your bloody work at Lattimer
  On the 10th day of September.

The Hazleton *Daily Standard*, Sept. 17, 1897

Ballad of the Deputies   *ix*

INTRODUCTION: THE TRAGEDY

AT LATTIMER MINES

THE AMERICAN PEOPLE derive from peoples who on other continents have warred against each other. Yet here they have been mainly peaceful. This nation is diverse and energetic and from the beginning has trusted its citizens with guns. Its peoples are restless, they are ambitious, and the social system draws upon cupidity. Yet out of such unpromising materials have grown wealth, serenity, and placid suburbs. This sleepy surface, however, has frequently been broken by sudden convulsions, strikes, riots, and armed skirmishes. This is the story of a sudden flash of bloodshed that erupted near Hazleton, Pennsylvania, at about 3:46 on the hot afternoon of September 10, 1897. Nineteen men died and at least thirty-nine were wounded. The date was, to the day, seventy-four years before the riot at Attica prison.

The story of the guns of Lattimer has been strangely neglected in history books, even in histories of violence in America, even in labor histories. Why such amnesia? How can so distinguished a collection like *American Violence, A Documentary History* (1970), by Richard Hofstadter and Michael Wallace, amply document 107 instances of riot, slaughter, and assassination, while totally omitting even a mention of Lattimer, the most bloody of all but a half dozen others? The reasons may be that Lattimer's victims did not speak English and, more than others, have lacked a public voice. They were Slavs— a word which the Germans suggest derives from the Latin *slavus*, slave. (Slavs say it derives from the Slavic *slava*, glory.) Louis Adamic, one of the few literate and, in America, widely published of the early Slavic immigrants, wrote bitterly in *Laughing in the Jungle* of the "dungheap" onto which Slavic laborers were thrown in America. He wrote about the scores of thousands who lost their lives in the mines, factories, dams, and tunnels of the early industrial era. Many disappeared from sight, he wrote, never to be heard from by their families in Europe, as though they had been swallowed up by darkness. The reputation of America in eastern Europe was not at that time bright.

Today the United States is the third largest eastern European nation in the world. Nearly one in ten Americans has at least one eastern European grandparent, Catholic, Jewish, Protestant, Orthodox, or atheist.* Yet, few American scholars or journalists in 1897 spoke eastern European languages, could interview eastern European immigrants, or read eastern European newspapers. The primary historical sources of the eastern European immigration have been closed to the public. Some of these peoples—the Lithuanians, the Hungarians, the Jews—are not Slavs. Yet it is probably true that the most silent, and most invisible, Americans have been the Slavs. Books about their experience in America have been few indeed.

Although I am a philosopher and theologian rather than a historian, the story of Lattimer attracted my imagination. In the hope of telling it accurately—to serve truth, that value which Alexander Solzhenitsyn says is the most powerful in the world (lacking success in democratic freedoms, the Slavic peoples have necessarily cherished a more spiritual ideal)—I have tried to meet the standards of historians. No sentence in this book, I trust, is factually, in tone or in context, at variance with recorded evidence.

The historical record came to fascinate me—the young John Nemeth riding breathlessly on horseback at midnight after the fatal march; the handsome John Eagler, having acted as translator for the district organizer of the often rebuffed United Mine Workers, at the head of the line; and the whole body of four hundred marching men, unarmed, incompetent in English,

---

* In *Ethnic Diversity in Catholic America* (1973), Harold J. Abramson counts some 10 million Roman Catholic Poles, Lithuanians, and other eastern Europeans. The U.S. Census reported that American Jews in 1977 numbered some 5.7 million. A conservative estimate of Russian Orthodox, Greek Orthodox, Lutheran, and other Christians of eastern European background would appear to be 4 million. The number of the unchurched is unknown.

carefully carrying two American flags, and painfully aware that in the Austro-Hungarian Empire they could conduct no such open and peaceful protest as they did here. That their march should have ended in brutal bloodshed—the worst labor massacre in the history of Pennsylvania and in the nation until that time—deepened in them and in other Slavic communities around the nation a familiar sense of tragedy and injustice. It did not tempt them in the least to believe that life under the Emperor of Austria and King of Hungary was more civil or more just. Their tragic sense is something precious in America, and it deserves to be recorded. They were good men, of admirable spirit, and what they added to the American character and to the nation's self-understanding is as necessary now as then, and as overlooked. Whoever says "work ethic" speaks also of theirs. Whoever speaks of the "American character" must include theirs, for in significant ways they expanded its range and depth.

It will be obvious to the discerning student that a major difficulty in a work of this sort is to "get inside" the leading agents on the strikers' side. For reasons easily comprehended, both the newspaper records and the accessible books and archives tell us much about the reasoning, motives, and feelings of the owners, superintendents, generals, officers of the law, deputies, and soldiers of the Pennsylvania National Guard. Those who speak with authority leave records. In this case, communion in the English language was also on their side. Few strikers were asked for interviews or were sought out for their reflections on America or were requested to deposit their recollections. Many of the victims did not leave a family, and of those who did, most families (so far as I could discover) have by this generation erased the trauma—and the stigma—from memory. Very few are the live oral traditions a researcher is able to tap.

Partly for this reason, I have sought out novels and memoirs among Slavic peoples in Pennsylvania from that period, in order to discover such patterns of thought, emotion, and daily ritual as these might reveal. I did not find the classic literary novels of this period—Willa Cather's novels of the Czechs in Nebraska—of as much help as I would have liked. Many Moravians and Bohemians settled in rural areas in Illinois, Iowa, Nebraska, and Texas; whereas the Slovaks, the Lithuanians, and the Poles, the chief protagonists in this story, turned in far greater proportions to the northern cities and bore the brunt of industrial labor. The rural experience was so qualitatively different from the urban that aspects of character vital to the story of Lattimer Mines do not much appear in Cather's work. Secondly, for all her talent, Miss Cather describes the Slavic world from outside—in and through a sensibility already foreign to it, so that its distinctive edges are not illuminated.

The novel *Hordubal*, written in Czech (and translated in Great Britain) by Karel Čapek, however, was of tremendous help to me; it tells the story of a miner who came to America, saved some money, and went back to Europe, to find that his wife was living with another man. Of even greater help was the novel by Thomas Bell (Tomaš Belejčák), *Out of this Furnace* (1941). When I began this research, the latter was out-of-print, and a secondhand copy was one of my most precious possessions; but it has now been made available in paperback by the University of Pittsburgh Press. I have also relied heavily on the sympathetic and vivid books on the Slav miners by that marvelous Protestant missionary of the period, Peter Roberts. Roberts did not much like the cultures or personal qualities of the immigrants, but he did care about their well-being as he saw it. The microfilm files of *Jednota*, the Slovak newspaper, were also helpful, through the assistance of Joseph Krajsa, Sr., and Sister M. Martina Tybor. The latter's translation from the Slovak of Konštantín Čulen's chapter on Lattimer, which as the editor of *Slovakia* 1977 I was privileged to publish, is of special historical value.

The technical problem posed by the imbalance of intimate evidence I have attempted to solve by creating some brief fictional sections whose intent is to reveal the feeling, fantasies, and inner lives of at least one miner who marched on Lattimer under the brilliant sun of September 10, 1897. These sections are set off from the rest of the text in separate chapters. Here, too, I have taken pains to be exactly faithful. I believe that every sentence in these clearly marked sections of fiction rings true in fact, sentiment, and image. But these are, just the same, imaginative reconstructions. Their realism may be checked against the sources just mentioned and others like them. What I cannot claim is that the specific Slavic miner I have invented —Benedikt Sakmar—is to be found in the historical records.

In selecting the name "Benedikt Sakmar" I have been perhaps too daring. It is the name of my maternal grandfather, now dead for many years. I have endowed this fictional person with the birthplace of my grandfather, Brutovce in county Spiš, eastern Slovakia. One reason for this choice is that I visited that village in 1974; it is clear in my mind's eye. Another is that as a point of departure it is entirely typical: one of every three Slovaks from that and the adjoining two counties were driven from their homeland between 1880 and 1914, chiefly by hunger and basic demographic changes.* Most voyaged by way of Bremen, Germany, seeking work in American factories and mines, from Connecticut to Minnesota, although a few went to other nations on other continents. I know very little about my grandfather directly. He never worked in the mines. He settled in western rather than in eastern Pennsylvania. The "Ben Sakmar" in the specially set-off pages below, then, is not my grandfather but a creature of my imagination, a literary device to tell an essential part of the story that otherwise could not be told. Similarly, I placed the date of the Jurich wedding— which is narrated in the Sakmar sections—in August 1897; although the actual date is unknown, some evidence suggests that it may have been earlier. The story Jurich tells Ben about the Klondike was reported in the Hazleton paper. So these fictional pages, too, have a base in historical evidence.

Outside of these separate fiction sections, however, every assertion is based either directly or by inference on sources listed in the appendices. The historical record has gaps, but it is vivid. Almost everything needed by an historian and even by a novelist is there, not in abundance and not at every place one

* Mark Stolarik's thesis, "Immigration and Urbanization: The Slovak Experience, 1870–1918," University of Minnesota (1974), has been of great help to me in understanding the historical background in Slovakia. His criticism of my present text is also deeply appreciated. I have relied on his experience in northeastern Pennsylvania for the most reliable spelling of eastern European names.

would desire, but quite enough to make the times, the events, and the people come to life.

At times, particularly in the case of Sheriff Martin, I have attempted to reconstruct thinking or feeling. In every case, these reconstructions are based on written evidence or on inferences from recorded behavior. In order to present a full story, some interpretation of motives can scarcely be avoided. The autobiography of Henry W. Palmer allowed me to reconstruct his own thoughts almost verbatim, and the official report of Sheriff Martin to Governor Hastings and other published sources closely guided my interpretations of the sheriff's thoughts. For other protagonists, many details about the style and quality of their actions are known. From these I have attempted an interpretation of the character of the agents. I hope such efforts have been discreet and accurate.

One other point. It will be obvious that I came to love the persons that research has introduced me to, and that I feel a certain kinship with the miners. My eye, I hope the evidence will show, is realistic nonetheless. That generation of Slavic immigrants did not seek affection and was not easy to like. If you met some of the survivors even today, you would see that with strangers they tend to be suspicious, stolid, sometimes ingratiatingly polite, but always somewhere deep a little hostile. Some of the descendants of the Lattimer victims did not trust me with memories or memorabilia. To them, I represented the big and distant world of officials. The outside world has not been kind to middle-European Slavs. For a thousand years, strangers have almost always brought them harm. Family could be trusted, but even in the family various systems of repression bred deep discontents and lack of trust. However friendly an individual might be—and extroversion is not the most frequent Slavic trait—an inner reserve bordering upon opposition is almost always present. Slavic women are unusually strong in personality. Among the peasants, they commanded the budget and ran home and family with an iron hand, by right and by tradition. Both in the economic world and in the domestic world, men who had been serfs and only recently emancipated peasants had a certain meekness, which at its best represented a kind of peacefulness and sweetness and at its worst hid deep reservoirs of thunderous anger and resentment. Among the Slavs, both men and women, anger is not a much inhibited emotion. Slavic endurance is almost superhuman, but its costs in repression and resentment are profound. Explosive fits of temper and sullen moodiness are in daily evidence. Alcohol in large quantities has been a ransom paid to demons.

In the gregarious, informal, quick-talking America described by Tocqueville, the Slavs were not as articulate and sociable as many other immigrants. As their clothes were dark and their demeanor dour, so their manners were also somewhat forbidding. As newcomers, they were strange enough. Their personal style was stiff, formal, distant. Their languages were more distant from English than were Latin or Germanic tongues. Taught by life to be thoroughly suspicious of authorities but outwardly deferential, they were hard to flatter, cajole, amuse, or kid. The wit of the Irish did not penetrate their defenses. The wink and elbow of the con man and the regular guy made those defenses tighten. The signals they received and those they gave were not easy to recognize. They lived in poverty so extreme it scandalized their neighbors. Their capacity for saving was prodigious.

These immigrants were not, then, a wholly attractive people. If one places oneself in the shoes of those who experienced their coming, one sees how frictions and misunderstandings must have festered. Sheer verbal communication was, for the most part, out of the question, and the rituals and gestures of nonverbal expression must have been so skewed that great feelings of hopelessness and frustration had to well up. Among some of the Slavs, it was considered rude and impolite to smile on formal occasions or in the presence of superiors. Even to look superiors straight in the eye was considered an impudent and rebellious act. On this point alone, conflict with Anglo-American mores was assured, as one might surmise from Ralph Waldo Emerson's praise in *English Traits* for the candor and directness recorded in English portraiture. The groundwork for the by-now-infamous "Polish jokes" was perhaps laid in America's first experience with the stolidity and formality of the Slavic peasants.

I do not, in a word, wish to romanticize the Slavic immigrants. In the present context, of course, even to show them in the roles of carriers of conscience and justice will be regarded as showing them in a more romantic light than American literature has often shed on them. The story I have encountered in the newspapers and other contemporary accounts is not romantic. It is, perhaps, a bit brutal, as working-class struggles have tended to be.

In 1946, the novelist Thomas Bell explained in an interview for a Slovak newspaper why he had written *Out of this Furnace*, the best piece of fiction yet produced by an American of Slavic background:

My conscience dictated that I write it. I saw a people brought here by steel magnates from the old country and then exploited, ridiculed, and oppressed. None of my books contains such a slice of life as this book about my people. The life of a Slovak boy in Braddock 30–40 years ago was a bitter one. As a small boy I could not understand why I should be ashamed of the fact that I was Slovak. While Irish and German kids could boast of the history of their ancestors, I did not know anything about the history of my people. I made up my mind to write a history of the Braddock Slovaks . . . I wanted to make sure that the hardships my grandfather, my father, my mother, and my brother, sisters, and other relatives lived through would not be forgotten. [Afterword, *Out of this Furnace*, p. 418]

My own purpose is only in part like Bell's. It is true that I want my children to have a history. Though not a historian, I found a gap in history. There was nothing to do but to fill the gap myself. Confronting painful daily evidence that one of America's largest minorities—the family of the Slavic peoples —needs creative stimulation and intellectual encouragement, I could not evade a sense of obligation.

But my interest in this task transcends ethnic interests. I wanted to make a present to the entire American people. This historical record is now part of the mutual history of all of us. In it, one sees a closer connection between the many struggling peoples of America than we usually are conscious of. I hope that this book has caught the facts truly, and that this truth is, in the end, healing.

I realize full well that the classic American mythos within whose boundaries of expectation and plausibility such stories as this are usually told is in the mode of pathos: helpless victims are exploited and then destroyed by cruel and powerful interests. I do not think that in this instance (or in others) pathos does justice to the facts. Because life always demands that we make decisions before we have all the knowledge we would like, before, that is, we quite know what we are doing, history always includes tragedy. The shock of flowing blood is often required of human beings before they can recognize where they are heading. The guns of Lattimer may be seen as a lesson in the tragic sense of life. Those who fired the guns did evil. In the trial, justice was not done. Rather than curse America on that account, one may learn a law of life: good and evil come intermixed. American history is far more tragic than a widespread belief in the perfectability of man permits most Americans to note. To understand this nation's history, a tragic sense of life is plainly necessary. A tragic sense is common sense. Perhaps now the nation is mature enough to complement its simple optimism and insupportable innocence with the cleansing release that comes from facing life's tragedies with a clear and steady eye.

In any case, the present story is a tragic one, in the classic sense that its actions grew out of flaws carried by each of the participants and out of the social structure of that time and place. Granted that this social structure was perhaps the most favorable that working people—not least, the Slavic miners—had in 1897 ever encountered; its structural blindness and rigidities made bloodshed like that of Lattimer Mines all too probable, provided only that the workers had the bravery and the solidarity to march against them. They did so in the name, eventually, of all of us. We learn from them a tragic sense and owe them thanks.

> Syracuse, New York
> September 10, 1977,
> the eightieth anniversary of the massacre
> at Lattimer

A NOTE ON SOURCES

ASIDE from the books, articles, and reports listed in the bibliography, the author has found the files of several newspapers to be indispensable resources: the Hazleton *Daily Standard*, the Wilkes-Barre *Times*, the New York *Times*, the Pottsville *Republican*, the United Mine Workers *Journal*, the Pottsville *Daily Miners' Journal*; and from Philadelphia, the *Inquirer*, the *Press*, the *Public Ledger*, the *North American*, and the *Evening Bulletin*. In addition, individual articles have been consulted in the New York *Sun*, the New York *Journal*, the Hazleton *Sentinel*, the Hazleton *Plain Speaker*, the Wilkes-Barre *Record* and also the *Leader*, the Utica *Illustrated Weekly*, and others.

The Hazleton *Daily Standard* sympathized slightly with the strikers, the Wilkes-Barre *Times* with the coal operators. The Pottsville *Republican*—at a safer distance from events—seemed evenhanded. These three sources supplied my most frequently used accounts.

In reconciling the many contradictions, minor but nagging, that are to be found in any two newspapers' accounts, I usually waited until some third or fourth source indicated which was the more reliable version. Often the decisive source gave convincing concrete detail which ruled out other versions. Often several newspapers reprinted without attribution the same story by the same writer while adding detail from other stories. It was usually possible to determine quickly which writers were eyewitnesses and which merely repeated what others had said or written. When two versions of equal weight did remain in conflict, my principle was either to retain the contradiction, if that thickened the story, or to follow the version most consistent with other evidence.

I must also mention the two most useful primary sources: there are 110 pages on the massacre and the trial in *Papers*

relating to the Foreign Relations of the United States, De-
cember 5, 1898 (Washington, D.C.: U.S. Government Printing
Office, 1901); and 214 pages of newspaper cuttings, documents,
and comments on the trial in *Fifty Years at the Bar and in
Politics, Henry W. Palmer, His Book,* (Williamsport, Penna.:
Snyder & Bischof, 1913).

A Note on Sources

PART ONE

August, 1897

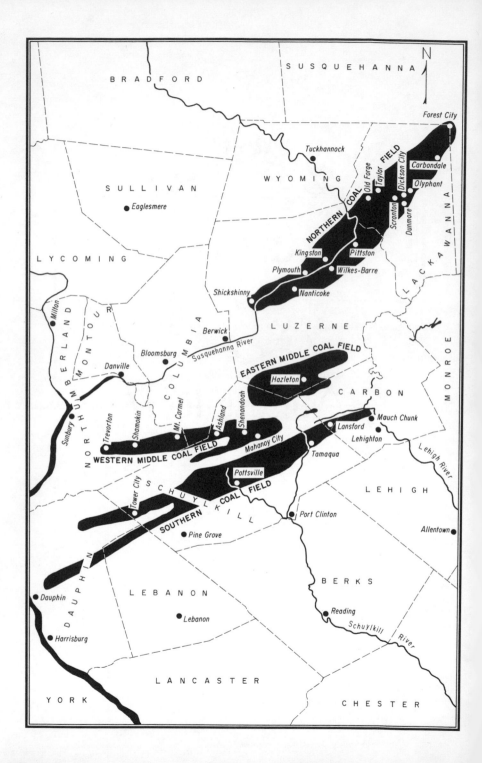

August, 1897

THE DEFENSE ATTORNEY

THE HONORABLE Henry W. Palmer ceased rocking for a moment and slapped at his balding forehead. The day was sweltering and his hand came away wet, innocent of the blood of the pesky mosquito. He wished he had a lemonade and thought of summoning the servants. But for a moment he settled back in his white wicker chair and listened, rocking on the well-painted porch. Across the white railing he could see the rolling fields and pastures of the farm in Clifford, Susquehanna County, where he had been born fifty-eight years before, on July 10, 1839. He took satisfaction in those two-hundred rolling acres, purchased by his grandfather, and thought there was no place in the world that gave him such peace. He took satisfaction in the Palmer family name, too, noting that it figured in Shakespeare and in Sir Walter Scott. He knew the precise references. The name referred to pilgrims who returned from the Holy Land with palms in their hands. He traced his lineage to William Palmer, who sailed on the *Fortune*, the ship next after the *Mayflower* to plunge its anchor in Plymouth Bay, Massachusetts; and to William's wife Frances, who crossed on the next ship, *Anne*, called "the Brides' Ship." Henry Palmer's grandfather had bought the land in Pennsylvania, but his father Gideon Wilbur Palmer was the first in the line to immigrate into the Keystone State. In later years, Henry was to be elected to three terms in the U.S. Congress.

Rocking on his porch, the air still and heavy with heat, Henry W. Palmer had a right to feel content. He could remember the raising of Henry Clay's flag in 1844, when he was only five, and could reflect in his maturity that since that time he could not remember a day when he had not been interested in politics.

Even the boyish sports in Carbondale were in a sense political. Race and religion had much to do with baseball, he was amused to recall: the uptowners were all Protestants and Americans and the downtowners were Irish and Catholics. His side had won its share.

Gideon Wilbur Palmer, his father, had been elected sheriff of Luzerne County as a Democrat (and founded a newspaper called the *True Democrat*), of the Copperhead faction after the Civil War. Later, he was elected to the Pennsylvania Legislature on the Know-Nothing ticket.

In 1856, at the age of seventeen, young Henry was working as an engineer building a railroad line from Scranton to Catawissa. His father committed him to the guardianship of Frank Stewart, a lawyer in Berwick, not far up the river from Catawissa, and a staunch Republican, who took young Henry on the campaign trail of 1858, speaking out about Freemont and "Bleeding Kansas." Henry became an enthusiastic Republican. His eloquence as a lawyer became renowned in northeastern Pennsylvania.

Yes, good years. A good life. An honorable man. Why, then, did he feel newly alert and vigorous? He knew the answer well. The papers were full of it. War was gathering in the mine fields. He swatted again at the mosquito in the air near his ear. A cow mooed heavily in the distance. Just at this moment, no doubt, somewhere in the county foreigners were again causing mischief. They hadn't yet taken up guns like the Molly Maguires. But it would come to that. Henry Palmer knew a thing or two about human nature. It would come to guns. Inevitably. A lesson would have to be taught, as every sensible man knew. In the sweltering heat of August 1897, as the editorialists were darkly suggesting, blood was in the air.

It is not known whether Attorney Palmer read these words

of Henry Rood, in *Forum* Magazine for September 1892, but the represent rather well the sentiments of many of his class:

Already the stream of immigration from Southern Europe is sweeping toward the Northwest and the South; but it began to pour into the mining regions of Pennsylvania over a dozen years ago . . . one of the richest regions of the earth overrun with a horde of Hungarians, Slavs, Polanders, Bohemians, Arabs, Italians, Sicilians, Russians, and Tyrolese of the lowest class; a section almost denationalized by the scum of the Continent, where women hesitate to drive about the country roads by day, where unarmed men are not safe after the sinking of the sun. There he will see prosperous little cities like Hazleton, Mahoney, Ashland, Shenandoah, with fine business houses and educated people of fortune, and surrounding these towns great wastes of the Commonwealth diseased by thousands and tens of thousands of foreigners who have no desire to become Americans, who emigrate to the United States for a few years to make money, who have driven to the cities and to the West the great army of English, Scotch, Irish, Welsh, Germans, and Americans who once gave stability to the coal regions. . . .

August, 1897

THE STAGE

UNDERNEATH a small section of northeastern Pennsylvania, in an area covered by rustling trees, far underground, lie three long seams of hardened black coal. On a map, they look like three long lakes. Three-quarters of the world's known anthracite lay waiting there long before men walked the earth, waiting to tempt, to trap, to enrich, to kill. During the 150 years after 1800, 9 billion tons of coal came out of Pennsylvania, much of it from those three seams. From the upper tip of the northernmost seam to the lower tip of the southernmost is a little less than one hundred miles. The lakes lie slantwise, from southwest to northeast. They are enclosed within a rectangle hardly more than thirty miles wide.

It is about events over the middle seam—an irregular cluster of nearly continuous coal beds—that the present story is concerned. At some places, deep underground, the bed of glinting black coal is more than thirty feet deep. These coal beds go by the name of the Lehigh region.

To the north is a long, regular seam, far larger and of far better quality coal, in a bed shaped like a long canoe, which at either end rises as close as six feet to the surface. This is the Wyoming region.

To the south, on the surface above another large and regular deposit, composed of coal of less consistent quality, lies the Schuylkill region.

Hundreds of centuries ago, the earth between Pittsburgh and Philadelphia buckled, and the distance between Philadelphia and Altoona was compressed by one hundred miles. In geological time, the Pennsylvania Period is the name that designates the era from 280,000,000 to 310,000,000 years ago. Deep underground swamps, under enormous new pressures during millions of silent years hardened into lignite, bituminous, and anthracite. Some of the veins heaved upward, describing shapes like an S or an N set at crazy angles. Pursuit of the contours of the beds was for the nineteenth century of our era an uncertain and a dangerous business.

One forgets, at times, how recently a civilization beyond the Stone Age came to these lush and quiet valleys. As late as 1778, General Washington called volunteers from this mountainous frontier into the Continental Army, and the British under Colonel John Butler marched with large Indian forces into the Wyoming Valley and massacred the outnumbered white defenders. A half-breed Indian, called Queen Esther because of her bearing and her role among the local Senecas—or, if not Queen Esther herself, her sister, also through marriage a tribal leader—entertained the victorious Indians by having twelve of the white prisoners marched before her in a clearing. Their heads were laid on a large flat rock. Raising a stone hammer, Queen Esther one by one crushed their skulls. Pulp rushed over the Rock of Massacre. Later in the war, Queen Esther's village was razed to the ground in retaliation. She and her tribe fled northward into upper New York State. Some claimed in later years she visited the region by stealth, but no record of her later life or death remains.

Twenty years later, a Welsh settler discovered a seam of coal near the earth's surface. In 1808, another showed how a draft of forced air could make the hard coal burn to produce little smoke and unusually efficient heat. In 1838, Ario Pardee watched a deer scratch in the soil near a hilltop rising from a plain and uncover glinting black coal. He began buying land. He laid out a plan for a future city—Hazleton. For the next ninety years the dimensions of the region's coal deposits were to become gradually mapped, and the anthracite industry became the leading passion of the countryside. Beautiful farmlands had stretched across the shimmering hills and valleys; but farms now gave way to mines. First Welsh miners fresh from Britain and then, in the 1850s, the Irish were manipulated by a dozen or more landholding families connected with the railroad trusts. Finally, about 1870, mine patches and immigrant communities made pictures of the valleys seem like daguerreotypes of central and southern Europe.

Law and order were slow to develop in the region. The largest cities, Wilkes-Barre and Scranton, lay to the extreme north. Hazleton in the center and Pottsville to the south were not as large. State government was not really effectual except in emergencies and then only because of the newly formed National Guard. The maintenance of order fell upon the counties and in particular upon the county sheriff. County government began in Pennsylvania in 1711 and remains even today the base of Pennsylvania politics. Sheriffs at that time were distinguished political leaders, in some ways more powerful than most mayors; indeed the decline of the sheriff's office dates from the Lattimer massacre and the subsequent trial. Town government of the New England type was difficult, because of the isolation of the towns, their cultural diversity, and the presence of huge interests whose scope was vaster than that of any town. In addition, the Lehigh coal region was particularly hard to govern, for although its center lay in Luzerne County, the underground lakes that absorbed its interests extended into Carbon and Schuylkill counties, not more than a half-dozen miles south of Hazleton. The sheriff of Luzerne

County, moreover, had important responsibilities in the Wyoming coal region twenty miles north of Hazleton, centered in the larger city of Wilkes-Barre.

By 1897, roads, railroads, and even a trolley system made travel over the region fairly easy. But the sheriff of Luzerne County, technically able to enforce the law through this rapid transportation system, would have his hands full when troubles arose in more than one place at once—as in the mine fields they were wont to do. Miners who worked at one site usually lived in settlements with men who worked at other sites. News was passed, on a daily basis, from colliery to colliery.

The economics of the anthracite industry, moreover, seem from the distance of the present day a little odd. In 1894, 140,000 miners in northeastern Pennsylvania produced 51,000,000 tons of anthracite, and 446 men were killed bringing it out of the earth. From 1870 until 1968, there were 31,047 known fatalities in the anthracite mines. Meanwhile, demand rose and fell. Yet the owners cared more about keeping their prices up than about the steady livelihood of their work force. Demand in the two major markets, New York City and Philadelphia, fluctuated wildly. The miners suffered boom and bust. By August of 1897, thousands of workers in the Lehigh field had had only 41 days of work that year. In 1896, the average number of days a miner worked was 178; in 1897, the mines were operating on an average of between 1 and 2 (out of 6) days a week.

The composition of the work force had changed dramatically by 1897. In 1880, only 1.7 percent (1,925) of the inhabitants of the region were immigrants from the Slavic lands and Italy; by 1900, the percentage was 46 and the exact number 89,328. The high percentage of foreigners was all the more remarkable because so many of the migrant workers were males without their families. Many intended to return to Europe. Others sent for their wives, sweethearts, relatives, or neighbors when they could.

Strange tongues were heard, strange manners seen. Abstemious English and Welsh Methodists were offended by the hard drinking of the newcomers. The bulb-shaped steeples of the Eastern rite, the Roman collars of the priests, the crosses

The Guns of Lattimer

and processions of the Catholic rites, gave troubling premonitions. The English-speaking Irish, too, although Catholic, had certain fears about the unknown and unintelligible "flat-faced" or "roundhead" newcomers in their midst. It was commonly believed, and often expressed in public speech and in the public press, that a lower type of human being was threatening the valleys, less intelligent, less democratic, unnaturally willing to endure conditions the more civilized "Americans" (among whom, too, the Irish were numbered) would no longer tolerate.

In recent times, the beauties of the region are celebrated in John Updike's stories about Olyphant in the northern Wyoming region, and in John O'Hara's stories about Pottsville (Gibbsville) in the Schuylkill region. To the east, the Poconos attract honeymooners, skiers, and vacationers, and to the south stretches the rolling, doll-like Pennsylvania Dutch country. In the center, in the mining and industrial cities like Hazleton, and in the mile upon mile of barren man-made canyons and culm banks, the brutality of the coal era still makes its presence felt, like welts and bruises left to scar the face of a fighter years and years after the clamor of the ringside has subsided. "Coal," writes journalist-historian Paul Beers in *Pennsylvania Sampler,* "brought employment to millions, death to thousands, riches to a few, poverty to many, blight to hundreds of acres of once lush landscape, acid-polluted rivers and streams which will take billions of dollars to purify, and a mining culture to Pennsylvania which is especially its own."

August 8, 1897

BEN'S STORY

ON THE HILL outside the mine, Benedikt Sakmar stretched in the sun. For a moment he thought he was asleep under a bush outside of faraway Brutovce.* Nostalgia filled his chest.

* Pronounced *Bru-tof'-seh*

He shook his head and watched a great white cumulus blow across the pale blue sky. Under that sky, somewhere, were his brothers and his sister. And his mother. He missed them. He reminded himself that he was too old to cry. Sometimes, he felt entirely alone, as though he would never see them again. He remembered the smell of hollyhocks and the brilliant red of poppy, and the smells of the densely crowded garden outside the kitchen. He could smell the *holubki* (stuffed cabbage) boiling in his mother's kitchen. His eyes burned.

He could not hope to see them again until 1903. It would take him that long, at least, to set aside the $3,000 he had set as his goal for taking back with him. How rich he would be! They would see, then, that he had become a man. He could see Anička's * eyes shine as she threw herself upon him. He loved her so, his little sister. She would be fifteen now. Of everything and everyone, Anička was the one he missed the most. She would be grown up now, without him—by 1903, when he hoped to return home, perhaps even married.

He had been in America two years. With a grimace, he recalled how Uncle Emil had tried to warn him not to leave. Uncle Emil described America in harsh and bitter terms. Young people might be fooled by its promises. He had seen too many go to America. He knew a man in Levoča † who had come back, coughing black blood until he died. Others came back without an arm or a leg. They brought back dollars, yes, but at what cost? Few could live in Slovakia again. Few believed their own stories about Cla-ve-land, or Brij-por, or Pitts-burgh. Uncle Emil did not like their eyes.

The young man pulled a round stem of flowering grass from its sheath and sucked its juice, bit off its end, spat it away. A lazy Sunday afternoon. He had not gone to church. The breeze was already cooling. He would squander a coin on a glass of beer at supper and go to bed. Tomorrow he would begin again his life underground. For six more days he would hardly see the sun. It didn't seem fair for a farmer's son to be in cold and damp darkness all day long, never to see the sun or hear the birds. He had always loved to count the clouds, to study them,

---

* Pronounced *A-nitch'-ka*
† Pronounced *Leh'-vo-cha'*

to sail with them across the Tatras.* His mother would be angry that he had not gone to church. Ever since his father's death, his mother's religiosity had intensified. In America, he felt free. Rather, he felt that all week long he was in prison. On Sundays, he could hardly bear to be in church. The turbulence he felt in church made the experience of going there a torment. He needed the sky, the clouds, his dreams. He needed them to keep alive.

He threw the blade of grass into the breeze. Sunlight flashed across the waving golden grass all along the hillside. He was young and strong. Once he had lifted one end of a coal cart by himself, after it had been derailed. He remembered how thin he had been at seventeen, and he could see himself clearly on the hillside far away, in Brutovce, in County Spiš,† in Hungary, which no one in the whole United States had ever heard of—see himself putting up the roadside grotto, a cross with a pitched roof over it, and on its fresh wooden base the carved letters of his own name, BENEDIKT, and ANNA, and the year, 1895. He had intended it as his monument, his mark. Later that summer, just before his eighteenth birthday, he had set off by night, on foot, a package of clothing and food under his arm, to escape from the agents of the emperor's army. He jumped from the train before it reached the river. He crossed by night, in a rowboat provided by an old woman and her suspicious son, who charged him more than his brothers had told him it would cost. Across the border, he boarded the train again, two days later. He made his way to Bremen, eyes observant all along the way. Not knowing any other language, well warned not to trust anybody, he kept silent. His silence seemed to him a form of power. Observe and say nothing. Who could know he was afraid? He felt free, brave, excited. To be eighteen and all alone in the world was to be a man and to see cities far beyond the mountains of Brutovce.

No one there would recognize him now, he smiled to think. His shoulders had broadened and his muscles were enormous. He knew the world.

Ben Sakmar arose from the grass, which began to spring back

* The Alp-like mountains of Central Slovakia
† Pronounced *Spish*

from where he had lain upon it, a dark patch in the brilliantly waving field. He brushed off his black trousers, hitched his suspenders, and slowly walked down across the field to the road back to Harwood. The road was rocky and hot. Grasshoppers leapt across it. The cries of birds and the buzz of insects filled the sweet air. He could smell the coolness of the creek.

Something reminded him of an August day when he was eight or nine. His father had had gout and consumption, and some days he couldn't work. One day, his father moved too slowly in the fields. The *gróf* * had ridden with his retinue up the road from the castle at Spišské Podhradie to visit the peasants in the field. The children ran along the route, hiding themselves in shyness, gawking at the splendid horses and the Magyar count. The horsemen clopped along the road and climbed up into the fields. Later, the children saw in the distance a commotion. A horse reared. One of the stewards was using a cudgel. Some of the girls began to cry. It was an hour later, after the gróf and his men were gone, that three neighbors carried Ben's father home. He had an open lump on the back of his head. Ben could still see the blood on his tunic and the blue welts on his arms. The little finger of the man's right hand had been broken. His father was motionless and avoided his son's eyes. His mother ordered the children out of the house.

The innocence of the sunlight and heat may have brought the memory back. Or perhaps a feeling of being eight again—always in the grip of forces larger than the self. He didn't like his own anger. He evaded it. He remembered the smell of fresh cut hay, the wooden rakes, the women gathering the hay in bundles carried by a band across their heads. The fields seemed so serene. He often wished to hug the earth.

He kicked a rock with his heavy shoe. The business of a man is to endure and to enjoy. He filled his lungs with the air of America—air with smells, and weight, and sounds, different from those of county Spiš, heavier, more humid, rougher and not so sweet. There the air of the mountains had been light and the earth always smelled wet and the poppy and the sunflowers made the air rich. Goldenrod and milkweed and sumac

* Although serfdom was legally abolished in 1848, its forms and residues persisted—especially in outlying areas—into the early twentieth century.

gave the air of Pennsylvania a different tang. He liked it. It was making him a man. But he missed Anička and longed for the nightly thunderstorms, the lightning and the thunder of the Tatras.

August, 1897

THE UNDERGROUND MEN

TO LIVE for ten hours in a mine, day after day, is to learn a special attitude toward life. It is not so much the isolation. It is the weight always overhead, the enormous dark stony weight of earth. The underground man is a fatalist, from living below earth where other men come only when buried, and from facing death on every descent. Miners believed that rats, able to sense any shift in the crushing weight overhead, began to run before a fall. They listened for loosened pebbles dropping from the roof. Sometimes no warning came at all. In the anthracite fields, three men died every two days, on the average. Nearly every miner bore external signs of injuries: a missing finger, stitches, scars, limps. Bluish specks of coal dust were implanted under the skin of their faces and arms from each blow of the pick and from the blast of explosives. All day long the men inhaled dust, fumes, and damp air. In their souls, they may have borne more wounds than in their flesh. Miners kidded each other often, as when they added after they had requested new equipment, "before I get killed."

The path toward the coal pit was normally of packed gravel, slate, and shattered coal. Footsteps crunched along it. The "cage" in 1897 was an elevator car, often of flimsy and virtually open sides. The cables by which the car hung suspended glistened oily and black overhead. Descent into pitch-blackness was normally rapid, after a warning bell was rung. Cool damp air rose to one's lungs. Fear gripped the heart of those on their first descent, an instinctive and involuntary constriction of stomach and lungs, as though like a turtle one needed to suck oneself inward to resist the dangerous weight above one's head. The thought of any accident—of being trapped—was almost unendurable. Under any collapse or cave-in, there was no place to flee. Any failure in the system of supports, any loss of air or any broken cable, could mean entombment. The novice faced fears of fancy. The experienced miner knew of dangers the novice did not dream of—of gases that built up in stagnant dampness or that gathered near the roof at one's bent-over head, gases without odor or color that could suffocate through carbon dioxide, gases that could explode.

The cage jarred to a sudden halt. The silence was total. The darkness was thicker than imagination can conceive. For the miner of the 1890s, little flames encased in glass (which would go out as a warning if oxygen diminished) gave only a flickering light. Walking cautiously along the narrow cuts of the passageways carved from rock and coal, miners watched constantly for low overhangs, rafters, or rock too solid to remove. Strangely altered drafts of air suggested passageways one could not see somewhere in the dark. Fear of losing one's way—and losing light—matched fears of losing air.

Other miners along the way appeared at first by the whites of their eyes and their gleaming teeth. Their hands and faces were black with dust. Mules looming in the dark showed mournful circles of white around their huge eyes. Some mules in the 1890s stayed underground as long as four years without ever seeing light. In an article about his own visit to a mine, published in *McClure's* in 1894, Stephen Crane described the delirious joy of a mule released after an extended period of pitch-darkness, released to air and sky and clouds and fresh grass. The sides of the animal heaved. He trembled at first with fear. And then the madness of life in air and light overcame him. Such mules could not be forced underground again. Even the mules who went in and out each day bitterly resisted the cage. Underground, they were so afraid of the darkness that the mule boys found the easiest way to lead them was to walk ahead with the light. The mules would follow mournfully.

Pillars of coal were supposed to be left standing to support the roof. Sometimes whole walls of coal were left standing along the boundary line separating the rights of two adjacent mining companies. Surveyors had marked out exactly where aboveground landmarks stood directly overhead. "Straight up," one's guide might say, "is the company office where we saw the pump," or "Remember the rock formation I pointed out on the mountain? Now we're under that." Thinking of the hundreds, or thousands of feet of intervening rock and earth, Crane found such words of orientation hardly reassuring.

The taste of coal dust was soon upon one's tongue. One heard trickling water and at times heard one's feet slapping puddles or sloshing through thin sheets of moving water. A light upon the water showed rust, or sulphur, or slicks of violet oil. Water underground seemed stale, metallic, and acidulous. Great fungi grew out of the timbers holding up the roof, or out of pools of stagnant water.

The miners dug into walls of coal with drills of various sorts and sometimes tamped small charges of powder behind the face on which they had been working. They retreated, blasted, and waited for dust and fumes to settle. Then with picks and shovels the loosened coal was loaded onto a car, tagged, and sent off toward the distant surface. The art of planning out the passageways, following the veins of coal, and maximizing the ease of getting out the coal while minimizing the amount of preparatory work was highly developed by 1897. Hundreds of men would be working simultaneously in parallel, multilevelled, honeycombed crevasses in total darkness.

Miners got paid for the coal they brought out, not for the time they put in. Often the miner's assistant was left to do all the hard, painful, and time-consuming work, while the miner —who kept two-thirds of their joint salary himself—merely pointed out the day's assignment and supervised the day's first cuts or blasts. Greatly feared were the explosives that failed to go off. All too often they went off precisely at the moment the miner and his assistant stepped forward to see what had gone wrong. Sometimes forgotten but unexploded blasting caps—Dooley caps—remained in the coal. Mike Adamiak in the Hauto Screen Building near Shamokin accidentally brushed a cap against a potbellied stove, and it exploded and blew his fingers off. His boss was furious and took him to old Doc

Kistler over at Lansford, who wore big whiskers, and the doctor "fixed him up pretty good."

Often one had to work for hours at a time on one's knees, or even on one's belly, because of the contours of the surrounding rock or the necessities of working around obstacles. Cuts on hands and knees were so frequent that the men hardly noticed them. In the daylight, caked blood was covered by black dust.

August 14, 1897

"GOMER JONES, SLAVE DRIVER"

IN HUMAN AFFAIRS, the one who sows evil does not always reap it. Nor does he always intend it. In the newspaper records of August 1897, there is no doubt about the original villain of the bitter and sudden strike. Even in defending him, his superiors made large admissions. His friends defended him because he had "come up the hard way." No one denied his own capacity for work and dedication.

On April 24, 1897, Gomer E. Jones had reached his forty-second birthday. He confided to a friend that he had already worked thirty-five years in the mines. For he entered the mines of his native Wales in 1862 while only seven years old, and when his father and mother, Evan and Mary, brought him to America at thirteen in 1868, he was already a six-year veteran. In Pennsylvania, Jones worked at almost every position in the mines and watched with cold eyes the bombings and burnings of the Molly Maguires until they were at last suppressed by the Pinkertons. He was married on the Centennial, July 4, 1876, to Ida Crouse of Wanamie, amid dramatic celebrations, bunting, and fireworks. Two years later, Jones was named a mine foreman for the Upper Lehigh Coal Company. Ida bore him nine children (the eldest of whom died) in fifteen years of marriage. When she died in the heat of August, 1891, Gomer and Ida had been living in Stockton for two years, and now he was general mine foreman with responsibility for six mines. For some months, Mr. Jones coaxed Isabella Brockmire of Upper Lehigh to become mother to his brood (the oldest being thirteen), and she gave her formal consent in the Methodist church in August 1892. The marriage to Isabella was just entering its fifth year when Gomer Jones was hired away from Linderman, Skeer and Company to become division superintendent of the Lehigh and Wilkes-Barre Coal Company near the new borough of McAdoo.

Gomer Jones was not fond of Irish laborers and liked the Slavs and Italians less. He was quoted in the papers as saying that the Slavs "moved too slow." His unpopularity among the miners was so intense that it reached the newspapers often. In 1897, Jones told a Wilkes-Barre reporter: "When I came here a year ago, I came to restore discipline in the mines and to operate them in such a manner that the company could continue in business. The discipline was certainly lax. The men did about as they pleased. The two superintendents who were here then associated with the men, mixed with them, drank with them, and were regarded as 'hail fellows well met' everywhere among the miners. Now I cannot do that. I'm not a drinking man, and I've never made it a practice to hobnob with the men. However, when I give orders I expect them to be obeyed and do not permit miners to do exactly as they please."

A headline in the Ashland *Advocate* read: GOMER JONES, SLAVE DRIVER. Jones, the paper said, "was once a poor miner; in fact, until quite recently. Power suddenly thrust upon him made the fellow a cruel master. It is generally the case. Put a beggar on horseback and nine times out of ten he makes an ass of himself. A prominent Shamokin mining official says of Jones that he is the worst slave-driver who ever set foot in the coal region." Gomer Jones was a strict, religious man, with a righteous and violent temper. He was hard on the men both in the rules he imposed and in the terrible swift flashing of his wrath. His voice often exuded contempt. "For weeks and months," the Hazleton *Daily Standard* wrote (August 19), the miners "tried to become accustomed to the despotic methods [of Gomer Jones]. Not only in the lowering of wages did he make himself odious, but by his frequent boisterous expressions about the workers."

Gomer Jones was hired to make the mine owners money. Ten hours a day the men were supposed to work; ten hours of production he wanted from them. Through the early, hot days of August, Jones scratched his whiskers and thought. He went from mine to mine in the new southwestern region of his operations, covering the mines around Harwood, Audenreid, Beaver Brook, Jeansville, and McAdoo. Usually, the miners worked in teams. By Pennsylvania law, only native-born and naturalized citizens could become miners. Foreigners needed at least a two-year apprenticeship and some familiarity with English, even to become a miner's assistant. Besides the miners and their men, there were carpenters, blacksmiths, weighers, air-boys, mule drivers, breaker boys, and others. These were the jobs foreigners began in. One place to cut back, Jones mused, was on the mule drivers. If he had a central stable, one crew could take care of watering and feeding. There would be a savings on pasturage, facilities, and deliveries. The men wouldn't like it. They'd have to go farther for their mules. That'd be their problem. Pay doesn't start till they get their mules to the mine.

Meanwhile, the foreign miners were already angry on other counts. First, the miners were only working about half-time. Secondly, the Pennsylvania legislature had just voted an alien tax of three percent a day, to be deducted from paychecks beginning late in August. Thirdly, the legislature had again decreed that only naturalized Americans could work in the mines even as miners' assistants. Even though the enforcement proceedings were a farce, the Slavs and the Italians were losing standing, money, opportunity, and equality. At a minimum, the new law meant one more bribe to pay, above the standard $8 in costs. Finally, earlier legislation obliging the companies to pay the miners every other week, rather than at the end of the month, was being ignored. In the monthly payroll period ending August 31, 1897, for example, one manager of a Hazleton colliery paid all his miners $8,000 out of a $26,000 payroll. The rest was owed to the company for debts in the company store, for rents on the company houses, for fees deducted to pay the company doctor, and for fees deducted to pay the priest. While the men waited for their monthly payments, choices over the uses of their own money could not be exercised. Immediate needs had to be met by debt. For the immigrants, this was excruciating, because over half of them worked only to save enough to bring their families over or to return to Europe. Savings were their reason for being. The legislature seemed to be driving them from the state.

The record is at first a little vague, but it appears that on August 11 or 12, Superintendent Jones announced his new decision to one small group of mule drivers, then another. The men grumbled. Some of them told Jones they should be paid for the extra work. He flatly refused. As a last resort, a few of the mule drivers at the Honey Brook Colliery asked for a clarification. Superintendent Jones agreed to see them on August 13, a Friday. It was early in the afternoon. The heat was stifling. Mr. Jones stood before them outside the supervisor's shed, a crowbar in his hands, the local supervisor at his side. He looked over their inexpressive faces until the noise abated and everyone stood in earshot. He explained again that at night they would take their mules to Audenreid, and pick them up there the next morning. The boys who understood English lifted their chins. The others watched Jones's face, but looked away when he flashed his dark eyes in their direction. A few murmurs arose, but Jones waited for effect until there was silence and then let them know it was an order. He turned on his heel and entered the shed.

When the wooden door swung upon its hinges and closed, the mule drivers gathered around the English-speakers. Two of the young men explained the new orders carefully, correcting each other to get every word exact. Hands were raised in angry gestures. The young men saw immediately that they would get home that night an hour later than usual, and that the next morning they would have to rise an hour earlier.

Some of the thirty-five mule drivers at Honey Brook went on strike on Friday the thirteenth. The next day, they set up a line to prevent anyone else from working. Most of them had earned only $300 in the whole preceding twelve months. Jones was laying off friends of theirs. What had they to lose? They were furious at being asked to do two hours of extra work every day. They were tired of being regarded as docile and stupid. They began to form a living fence, preventing anyone from going to the mine.

It took Gomer Jones a little while to notice the unexpected rebellion. When he emerged from the supervisor's shed, shading the sun from his eyes, the smile vanished from his face. He went back inside for a crowbar, then marched with fury to the nearest striker and began beating him upon his shoulders. The young boy's name was John Bodan, a tough, dogged youth, not easy to intimidate. Bodan doubled over, then sprang on Jones, while his fellow strikers ran to his assistance. Bodan pulled the crowbar from Jones's hands. Solid blows landed on Jones's back, and two of the men grabbed his arms, while others pulled at his clothes. At one point, they threw him to the ground. One man had a rock. They might have killed him had not Oliver Welsh, the local supervisor, shouted orders and pulled Jones from the hands of his assailants. White and shaken, waving his fist, shouting that all of them were fired, Jones retreated to the supervisor's shed. Welsh himself had his scalp cut by a stone, and red blood flowed from it; later, eight stitches were required to close it.

Raising a whoop, the young strikers raced to the whistle tower and sounded the call to cease work. Angrily, they passed the word about the crowbar. The whistle blew. Men poured from the slag heaps, the trains, the breakers, and the mines. The breaker boys, flashing grimy smiles, cheered. Release was in the air. Spreading out toward their homes, the workers shouted the news in many tongues. By evening, eight hundred miners were out on strike. That night, many went to bed with dread in their hearts. They knew only two keys to success: to stick together and to persevere.

On Monday the sixteenth, John Bodan swore out a warrant for the arrest of Gomer Jones, presented the crowbar to Squire Dailey in evidence, provided a list of witnesses, and agreed to appear at a hearing. Jones was arrested by Constable Gillespie of McAdoo on August 17 and entered bail in the sum of $500 for his appearance at the Schuylkill County Court. Before his trial could be held, far more serious violence would arise in the region. Gomer Jones would never be far from its emotional center. At critical moments, however, he was to show better judgment than some who thought themselves his betters.

August 14, 1897

BEN AND MAUREEN

AS HE WALKED WEARILY along the road toward Harwood, Ben rubbed his left arm. The Monday before, he had jarred something or torn something, and every time he used the pick a spasm ran from his hand to his shoulder. This morning, just after he began swinging his pick, a sliver of flying coal dug into his forearm and left a blue welt. When he had tried to compensate for the pain in his shoulder, the cut in his arm had throbbed. The day underground had not passed swiftly.

He had washed the cut under the water pump as soon as he came out. The cold water burned at first but its cleanliness was a comfort. His feet seemed to feel every pebble in the curving road, but the light and air, the calls of birds and the buzz of grasshoppers, made his walk the best part of every day. He now preferred to walk alone, thinking his own thoughts. For a time he had sought companionship, protection almost, and the pleasures of speech. He didn't know English enough to talk with any but Slovaks. Speaking Slovak filled him with ambivalence.

The pain in his arm, perhaps, made him think of a day almost two months before—the Fourth of July, to be exact. That was his second Fourth in America. There had been speeches, a picnic, races, and a homemade sort of carnival in McAdoo. Beer was cheap. Ben enjoyed the bunting. The colors were almost those of Slovakia. It made him homesick. He had watched a local team play baseball against visitors from Honey Brook. Ben admired the game, even though it made him feel foolish.

His arms and legs had never learned American movements. He felt clumsy the few times he had tired to catch or throw—stiff, ragged, jerky. He could see how awful he must have looked when he watched other greenhorns cup their fingers to catch or bend their arms to throw; they thought they were doing well, but it wasn't at all like the Americans. The gracefulness of the true player made him envious. Standing with his chin upon his hand, his elbow on a post at the side of the field, Ben was trying to imagine what it would have been like for him if he had been born American, spoke English, lived in a big house, not had to fear insults.

He became aware of furtive looks from one of the girls sitting on a blanket on the grass not far away. They were Irish girls. The father of one of them ran a saloon in McAdoo. Another's father was an undertaker. There was an Irish parish in McAdoo, and not a few of the better sort of miners were Irish. He didn't know the name of the black-haired girl whose eyes, he felt, had been studying him. He thought she had a brother in the field, because one of the young men had brought over a wallet or something of the sort to keep for him, and his manner was peremptory, that of a brother rather than a friend. He had noticed, because he could see himself acting so to Anička.

The girl had black hair and a beautiful, pale, aquiline face. She *couldn't* be looking at him in a friendly fashion. Usually, girls giggled and moved away, as though driven off by magnetic forces. They avoided foreigners. Don't they know we can feel what they are doing? he sometimes thought. Just because they don't understand our words, or we theirs, do they think their gestures and manners are invisible? There was a heavy, thick wall between him and America, and no matter how strong he was he would never move it. He would never speak as fast as Americans.

Still, the girl's eyes met his again.

Ben took his chin off his hand and fumbled with his fingers at his shirt just above the trousers. He looked unconcernedly at the distant sky. Was his moustache crooked? Was there a smudge on his face? He remembered how ragged his Sunday clothes had become after two years. He grew so uncomfortable he could think of nothing except to walk away.

Then he saw her again when he was tossing horseshoes. This was something he was pretty good at. She looked beautiful in a flouncing white dress. Her ankles were tied in black bands from her shoes. He held a horseshoe to the level of his eyes, swept his right arm back steadily, stepped as smoothly as a dance step, and let his fingers unfold crisply from the heavy metal. As he had hoped, metal clanged on metal; he hit the stake. As he had not wished, the shoe spun over five times, and rolled nearly five feet away. It moved, however, in the direction of the girl's feet. Almost like his thoughts. Their eyes met. He shrugged. She laughed and turned away.

Ben felt he had nothing if not courage. What could he lose? He didn't seek her out immediately, but he followed from a distance. At the sausage stand, they stood close enough for him to be aware that she was conscious of him, might want him close.

Not knowing English, he knew no way to approach her. The crowd seemed suddenly hostile and frustrating. Without the crowd—on an ordinary day—he would have no way to see her. In the crowd, how could he approach her? His hands rubbed the sides of his legs.

As the chill of evening came on, he carried over a gift to her, impulsively, and thrust it before her. She was alone. The gift was his effort at speech rather than what he held in his hand: "Hot dog," he said carefully. Then he repeated it. She hesitated and his courage fled. Then, impulsively, she seized it and set her little black foot toward the baseball field, as if she knew he wished to walk with her. He followed as a dancer follows. They walked silently together.

She pointed. "Grass."

"Grass," he said solemnly.

"Sky."

It was a wonderful hour. It seemed like forever. They walked all around the edge of the field.

A small band of boys near the backstop watched them angrily.

As the young couple neared the infield, Ben could feel the menace.

"Maureen!" The voice of her brother was full of meanness. "Maureen! You think you're shanty Irish? Whatta you walking with a hunky? Whatta you walkin' with an ape?"

The girl barely touched Ben's hand and then ran.

Five boys rushed Ben. He didn't understand the words. Except "hunky." They kept calling him "ape" as they pounded him. He couldn't forget the sound or the emotion. He fought as well as he could and cut some lips and raised some bruises. But they pounded him and left him only when he was exhausted, his clothes torn and bloody, with aches and throbs all over his body.

The next day, he wanted to ask some of his friends the meaning of the word, but he couldn't. After his bruises healed, he asked John Eagler one day what it meant, "Ay-pp?" When he learned, he could feel the flush rising to his ears again. His blood boiled. He knew a pure, clean hatred.

That was almost two months ago. Ben still felt anger as he walked the long way home from work, listening to the bullfrogs down in one of the shaded bottoms.

As he approached Harwood, on the outskirts of Hazleton, Ben realized that something was different. The men who worked at Honey Brook were agitated and uneasy. Steve Jurich met him at the boardinghouse. Steve recounted the fight with Gomer Jones. The men used the name Jones—which they pronounced Yones—almost in a generic way. As Andrew Moye, an Irish breaker boy later explained, the name sounded like a superintendent's name.

"We'll all be on strike by Monday," Jurich told him with a troubled face. "Everybody must go out. Yones has already fired eighty men."

Ben knew that Jurich was getting married on the twenty-second, a week away. Jurich needed the work, and he didn't need the trouble.

"It will be all right," he told his friend. The pain in his left arm was sharp again.

Jurich told him that there was to be a massive meeting at McAdoo the next afternoon. They were all supposed to gather

The Guns of Lattimer

at the baseball field. Ben blushed at the memory of the baseball field.

The clang of the beer wagon filled the air. Every door down the narrow main street of Harwood seemed to open. Buckets of frothy beer were carried to every household.

Ben had a sudden inspiration. "I buy you beer."

"No, no," Steve protested.

"Dust head to toes. Drink!" Ben said. "After your wedding, maybe we don't work for a week. It will be like St. Lawrence Day. We will burn fires every night. Come on, for your wedding."

The two lads with their clumsy gait, covered with coal dust, approached the sweating green wagon, from whose rear corners rivulets of cold water dripped from melting blocks of ice.

August 16, 1897

THE MEETING AT MCADOO

SUNDAY, AUGUST 15, the Feast of the Assumption of the Blessed Virgin Mary, an important holiday in southern and eastern Europe, and Monday, the young Italians and "Hungarians" of Audenried and the surrounding towns circulated word of Gomer Jones's use of the crowbar. Since the failure of the many strikes of the preceding decade, desperation had grown in the mine fields. Many of the new immigrants had now been in America ten years. Some were buying land, despite an average income among the workers of $300 annually. The immigrants had begun to be Americanized. Some spoke English. Many knew their way around. The new alien tax infuriated them. The foreigners were being singled out for being foreign. That united them.

By Monday morning, walking from breaker to breaker, patch to patch, the three hundred and fifty or so miners most inflamed persuaded three thousand others in the Lehigh and Wilkes-Barre mines to stay out of work. Their demeanor was grim. Some of the roughest miners used guns and clubs to make their point. Those who wished to be left alone, who wanted desperately to work in order to pay off their debts or to attain their strict savings goals, were not tolerated. The southern and eastern Europeans did not believe in too much individualism. One by one, every single one of them could be laid off, blacklisted, and eliminated from employment. The only safe path was to force everyone to act as one. Many were afraid. Some hid. Others sneaked to work by unwatched routes. The strikers knew that they were taking their livelihood into their hands.

John Fahy, the pragmatic young organizer sent into the region by the United Mine Workers, had spent several weeks in the area with almost no success. In midsummer, he gave up his face-to-face work in the field. The foreign miners did not much trust outsiders and would not surrender the coins he demanded as dues. Fahy therefore retreated to lobbying in the state capitol at Harrisburg and tried to win the support of the English-speaking miners first by promoting a tax on alien workers.* Fahy knew that the foreigners were not organizers, they needed him as a guide in negotiations. They may have been ignorant of Fahy's support of the alien tax, or they may have overlooked it out of necessity. He was a quiet, modest man, peaceful and moderate in his dealings. He knew that violence would bring down the wrath of the Coal and Iron Police.

The Lehigh and Wilkes-Barre mining company issued orders on August 16 dismissing several clerks and foremen sympathetic to the strikers. Rumors that eighty workers had been fired at Honey Brook were printed in the papers. Two squads of Coal and Iron Police, Winchester rifles over their arms, were sent to make a show of force by traveling through the patches systematically.

---

* Fahy was at this time hyperbolic in his lobbying for the 3 percent tax. He wrote in the *United Mine Workers Journal* (July 1): "What a world of good this law would do the American citizens who try to earn their living in the coal mines, if the tax were one dollar a day." [i.e., virtually 100 percent]

Late in the afternoon and early evening of August 16, hundreds of miners began gathering in McAdoo. Some stood and talked—some shouting, some describing the events of the weekend—and visiting reporters overheard a babel of languages. A few hundred crowded into Michalchik's Hall in McAdoo. Windows were opened, but even so the air was humid. In a spirited election, the men elected Jozef Kinchila [Kinčila], a Slovak, to be their president, and Nille Duse [sic], an Italian, to be vice-president. The newest state laws were directed at the aliens, and the aliens were the ones who called the strike. They concentrated at first on stopping work among their own. The Welsh, Germans, Irish, and other Americans refused to participate. Reporters noted with surprise the sudden end to docility among the foreigners. "Never in all our experience have we met a more determined body of strikers than was found in the several patches," wrote the correspondent for the Hazleton *Evening Standard* in the next day's edition. "The strike now in progress on the South Side has furnished an object lesson that it will be well for the operators in this section to make note of. The day of the slave driver is past and the once ignorant foreigner will no longer tolerate it," the same paper editorialized three days later.

Jozef Kinchila led the miners at McAdoo to formulate two grievances, which were then telegraphed to Lehigh and Wilkes Barre supervisor Lawall. They demanded (1) a wage increase; and (2) the removal of Gomer Jones for "tyrannical methods of ruling." The miners must have been unusually upset by Jones; or perhaps they were just beginning to gain self-respect. For tyrannical methods of ruling were common in the mine fields. "They treated us like dogs," John Moye recalls.* "The mules got better treatment," others told the press.

Cold beer was much enjoyed during the strike. Men spent the days doing extra work in their gardens or homes, talking excitedly and grimly with one another, patrolling the streets. Taking power into one's own hands is a heady and risky business.

---

* John Moye was born in Lattimer just after the massacre. His clear memories of the era added vivid detail to a reconstruction of Lattimer and its atmosphere. See interview, cited in appendix.

Young men like John Eagler, only nineteen but already nine years in America, watched and listened closely. He was an immigrant from Zemplin in Slovakia, tall, good-looking, and intelligent. He much admired John Fahy, and the latter had already marked him out from the others, partly because his English was good and his presence commanded respect.

Steve Jurich was hoping that the strike would not disrupt the coming wedding. He was nervous. He attributed his premonitions of disaster to the great step he was about to take. It was not easy, at nineteen, to be certain he could support a family; he wasn't sure yet where he and his bride would find a place to live.

Some of the men were quite religious, and they prayed with special intensity. Others were rather hostile to religion, or simply irreligious. Among some groups traditions of anticlericalism ran deep, modified in America by the fact that the local parishes were cultural centers, where contact with the rituals, the language, and the ceremonies of birth and death that some had known all their lives offered a symbolic world in which to breathe. The Slovak Lutherans had already built a church in Freeland, and the Slovak Catholics went into Hazleton; the Poles had St. Stanislaus.

The Reverend Richard Aust, a Benedictine from Poland, administered to the Slovak Catholics. He was a slender, tall man of thirty-two, of considerable dignity and poise. He worked closely with the union men, while keeping a place of honor among the leaders of Hazleton. He had been in America since 1882, the year of his ordination. His fifteenth anniversary as a priest was to be observed on August 24.

John Nemeth [Ján Németh] was thirty-five. He was a steamship agent in Hazleton, a Hungarian from Garadun, with good connections at the Austro-Hungarian consulate in Philadelphia. He had come to America in 1880, at the age of eighteen. Like others, he began by picking slate for over a year. Luckily, he then found employment as a clerk with Simon Miller, a general merchant. After five years Nemeth formed a new partnership, Martin and Nemeth, with another associate. Together, the two men added a brokerage business in foreign exchange and a steamship connection to their general mercantile trade. A Democrat, Nemeth was described thus in *The History of Luzerne County* (1893): "In politics he is very liberal, although in national issues he is a firm Democrat." The biographer also noted that Nemeth came to New York with thirty-four cents, and "is now worth about seven thousand dollars, which property he has accumulated in five years." Nemeth married Helen Deutch in 1889, and they had two children, John, Jr., and Ida.

To keep in touch with events, John Nemeth left the store in Hazleton on August 16, and circulated through Harwood, McAdoo, and Audenried. He had learned about the incident with Gomer Jones on Sunday at mass, as had Father Aust. He was uneasy about the number of nonnaturalized miners, who faced special jeopardy if the strike grew violent or lasted too long. He knew even better than the others the contempt that many of the Americans in Hazleton had for the foreigners. His own line of comment to American business associates was to stress how reliable the Slavs were as business risks. "They always have money buried somewhere," he joked. "They will never trust it all to the banks." He cherished the notion that Slavs were always worth more than appearances suggested. They did not believe in spending freely. His business depended on amounts they cached away to mail back to Europe.

John Nemeth returned to Hazleton at night and told his partner that difficult times lay ahead. He did not think there was enough intelligence in the region to absorb the sight of an aroused peasantry. Long had he waited for his fellow eastern Europeans to awaken from their slumber. But they were now doing so with such suddenness, unanimity, and power that the future seemed ominous. Henry Palmer, Calvin Pardee, and all the other better people would not be amused. There were many hotheads like Gomer Jones who, given a sign of official forgiveness in advance, would willingly shoot to kill. A streak of murderous passion ruled the hearts of many in the mine fields. It was a raw land. Many resentments and unhealed hurts lay beneath the placid surface. He worried about the administration of law. Unlike Hungary, there was no national law covering the whole United States. Controls by central government were weak. In Hazleton, people of power were the law.

God protect us all, John Nemeth thought.

August 17, 1897

SHERIFF JAMES L. MARTIN

SHERIFF James L. Martin read the morning paper over coffee down at the Wilkes-Barre Cafe. He joshed with the men at the counter. One of them showed him the Hazleton morning paper, reading a sentence aloud: "Never in all our experience have we met a more determined body of strikers than was found in the several patches."

"Doesn't sound good, Sheriff," another said. He slapped the Wilkes-Barre *Evening Leader* from the night before and read from it: "The Eye-talians and Hungarians, who are very aggressive, cannot be controlled."

"Don't worry, boys!" The sheriff laughed self-mockingly. "Sheriff Martin's on his way."

The sheriff set down his coffee cup, let the front legs of his chair down on the floor, pulled himself up to his full height, and walked across the room. The men shouted their encouragement. He was deferential, good-humored, a regular fellow.

The sheriff figured to make a tour of the southern end of the county, just to see what was up. He knew he should call on Mr. Lathrop, and maybe Mr. Lawall and Mr. Pardee, as well.

A strapping six foot-four, large of build, handsome, debonair in manner, the sheriff was a great favorite in Luzerne. His idea of a perfect day was to bet a buck or two on the bicycle races—and win. He liked to walk around with his badge and pistol, and to sign proclamations, "JAMES L. MARTIN, HIGH SHERIFF OF LUZERNE COUNTY." He *was* the law in the county. It was his to run his way, so long as he minded his p's and q's. He loved politics: in just a week or two, the county Republican convention was coming up in Wilkes-Barre, and he had a head or two he hoped to knock. He had worked hard for President McKinley in the last election, although mostly of course, he had worked for himself. Before the summer was out, he hoped to sneak in a week at Atlantic City, "taking in the sights," especially of women out from under all those skirts.

James Martin had been born on August 26, 1851, and he was hoping to spend his forty-sixth birthday in Atlantic City. His parents, George and Mary (née Maysmith) Martin were natives of England. A breaker boy at nine, he was a miner by the third year of the Civil War, when he was only twelve. At the age of twenty-two, he married Catherine Stark. They attended the German Lutheran church. For more than a year, around 1880, and again for four months in 1882, then in his thirtieth year, he tried to find silver in Colorado. He was a mine foreman in Luzerne for awhile after 1884, but in 1887 he wandered down to Texas to pick cotton. He got elected sheriff in November 1895 and took office in January 1896. He had built Catherine and himself a stunning large residence in the borough of Plains, just outside of Wilkes-Barre. Despite his long absences in Colorado and Texas, they had raised seven children.

The sheriff had a force of a thousand men if he wanted it; he hadn't had to call them yet. The owners didn't want conflict. They wanted work. Miners couldn't afford not to work. Even the organizer they had had up here was back in Harrisburg, disgusted; he couldn't get anything going among the hunkies. The sheriff had heard he'd managed to collect only thirty-six dollars in dues. Jim Martin hitched his belt, which was weighted down with a silver-handled six-shooter. The strike would last two or three days, at most. The newspapers were screaming for a settlement. Gomer Jones should've known better than to bash a head. The company would give the men ten cents a day raise. Just so the sheriff could slip out of town for the weekend and maybe take a whole week, sitting on the beach, doing nothing.

He called to his deputy, George Wall, on the telephone and told him that he was going down to Hazleton. Wall told him that Superintendent Lawall was at the Lehigh Valley Coal

Company offices, waiting to meet with a delegation of the miners. They could settle the thing any day now. The argument was how tough to be, so as not to encourage the bastards. The sheriff grunted his approval, hung up the phone, and idled over to the barbershop. He had an Italian barber who really knew how to give a shave; who patted his cheeks, extravagantly applied the warm lather, clipped his moustache and long sideburns like an artist. He had more than an hour before the train, and Angelo could sometimes take that long if he divined that the sheriff was in the mood.

On the train up the mountain to Hazleton, the sheriff saw from the window a squad of boys working on a breaker. They sat astride the trays of coal that moved beneath them on a conveyor, smartly spotting dull pieces of slate and heaving them away. He himself had started on the breakers when he was nine. He remembered not a few beatings about the shoulders for assing off and missing slates. If there was one thing he was glad of, gladder than not being poor and not being hungry, it was to be out of the mines. He swore when he was ten that he would never end up in the mines. He saw too many fellows stay too long, until they couldn't get away.

He had a certain sympathy for miners. He was an open, friendly fellow—that had helped him a lot in politics. People like a smile, a manner they can approach. He practiced waving at people and noticing their existence. To be recognized by the sheriff meant a lot to people; it surprised him how much it meant, and since recognition was for free he gave away lots of it. He meant to keep his paycheck for a long time. "It certainly beats heavy lifting," he would say when folks asked how he liked the job. It always got a laugh.

If he didn't like the Hungarians, Polanders, Eye-talians, and the other foreigners, it wasn't because he was prejudiced. He wasn't. He just couldn't tell what was going on in their heads. They wouldn't look you in the eye. He couldn't understand their jabbering. It made him feel, sometimes, like a keeper in a zoo. The way they lived, in houses no American would live in, crowded twelve or sixteen in a room. It wasn't human.

He half-admired their bravery. Most of them were loners, no women, no family, didn't care much what happened to them. He never saw men like them for taking chances. It was easy to get them to volunteer for dynamiting, or to go down in the shafts no one wanted to take a chance on. Americans hesitated. Invariably, one of the hunkies would go. Martin had seen arms severed, legs crushed. Once he saw an eye dangling by a string. Dumb hunky had wanted to watch a blast and a hunk of metal crushed his skull. Never a week without two or three hauled out on canvas.

The year James Martin became a foreman, 1884, nineteen men were killed in a gas explosion when a miner went back inside to recover some rails and forgot to cover the light-flame on his helmet. Later that year, fourteen more died in a gas explosion at Youngstown. In 1891, one hundred nine were killed in Mammouth Mine near Pottsville in a mine that was supposed to be "nongassy." Six months after the sheriff took office, on June 18, 1896, a roof-fall entombed fifty-eight men, all of whom died. The men were paid for the coal they dug out, not for the time they spent putting up or replacing safety beams every five or six feet or so. Sometimes no one wanted to stop to go fetch more timbers. The immigrants were especially impatient. Some Americans didn't like to work with them. The sheriff remembered many a battle between his own impatience and his fear. One of his best friends, for instance, aged eleven, was jumping across the breaker chutes after a toilet break, missed a step, got his foot caught in the conveyor. Before they got the machinery turned off, the lad's leg had been pulled in over the knee. They cut it off to pull him out. He still remembered the boy's screams.

Sheriff Martin watched the wooded hills flash by as the train chugged down from Wilkes-Barre to Hazleton. The greenness of the hills soothed him. It seemed a beautiful place to live. He marvelled at the railroads, the elaborate trolley network, the telegraph, the telephone, the daily papers—things that hadn't existed when he was a boy. It was satisfying to think how well-respected he was by the people who owned these things. The newspaper people, the mining people, the railroaders, they knew a good man when they saw one. They didn't much like his womanizing and his fondness for bicycle races, and more or less let him know that a scandal could hurt him.

One of the bankers in town had said, "Jim Martin was born to be a sheriff." The sheriff was glad for such backing. No sheriff in this county was any stronger than his backing at Lehigh and Wilkes-Barre, at Coxe and Company, Pardee, and the others. The mining companies buttered the bread in the Wyoming and Lehigh valleys. Jim Martin was not dumb.

But he was worried. He had a theory that the Huns might prove to be the most dangerous strikers. The Eye-talians were more talkative, more excitable, more expressive, and he liked that better. The story running around the countryside was that every Eye-talian carried a hidden stiletto, and that they were mean fellows in a fight. Personally, he had seen some fellows cut pretty bad after a fight at a wedding or in a bar Saturday nights. The Eye-talians got things off their chests. The damn Hunkies just kept silent, and looked at you so you couldn't read a thing. They would obey, however angry they might be. He saw it happen dozens of times. Ignorance, fear, whatever it was, they kept their place. He had heard that in Europe the troops took no lip from peasants. Mr. Pardee had explained over drinks why the owners didn't like the limits on foreign laborers the legislature was considering, and why they were fighting the United Mine Workers on the issue. John Fahy was the one who wanted the foreigners taxed. The owners didn't want it. They preferred the Slavs (Mr. Pardee pronounced it "Sclavs") for their strong, docile backs. The owners didn't complain, like some others, about all the property the Slavs were buying, and the large savings accounts they held. Even the state banking acts had been changed, to let women keep accounts, because the Slavic women minded the budget. The owners ran the banks too.

The sheriff worried, though, about driving the Slavs too far. He wouldn't want to deal with them if the whole region erupted in a strike. Fatalists worried him. A man has a price, you can deal with him; if he feels he has nothing to lose, watch out. The sheriff wasn't sure whether it would be better to teach the hunkies a good hard lesson early. Or whether to count on their basic love for money: no work, no savings.

Keep the peace, they'll fall into line. Never failed, too many eager fellows out of work—fire the foreigners, there are two or three Americans to take every place. Well, not quite. Trouble with Americans, they want out of the lowest jobs. The Hunkies push everybody else up. They can't stay ignorant forever. We'll just have to nudge them into line until the last coal is shovelled from the last pit. He was smiling out the window as the train rounded a bend.

August, 1897

THE MARKLES AND THE PARDEES

IN 1884, an illustrated map of Hazleton was published by Bailey and Company of Boston. Almost in the center of the map, occupying a whole block on Broad Street between Church and Laurel, surrounded by trees, the map clearly shows the spacious lawn and the tall white mansion of the Pardee family. To the back of the mansion, on Green Street, the twin spires of the Methodist Episcopal church tower above neighboring residences. To the left stands the stately Presbyterian church and behind it another smaller church. To the right, across the lawns, begin several blocks of the most important real estate in Hazleton, including the Markle and Brothers Bank Building, Hazle Hall, and the Hazleton House. Old-timers from the surrounding mine patches recall as an overwhelming fact of life: "In those days, the Pardee family ran Hazleton. The Markles and the Coxes and Van Wickles were the other big names." J. Gillingham Fell was the founder of another clan. The name appears on fewer properties, but the Fells invested wisely. The grandfather had prosecuted the Molly Maguires in the 1870s; in 1897, the grandson served as district attorney for Luzerne County. The mining companies, landholding trusts, railroads, banks, flour and powder mills, and other industries of the region were nearly all in the hands of a few families, joined in commingled interests, interlocking boards of directors, and intermarriages. From their homes on the top of the great hill on which Hazleton was built, these favored few overlooked a panoramic kingdom of farms and mining patches. They were a remarkable breed. Smokestacks and breakers reared above the trees. Church spires pierced the sky. All these (they might be forgiven the conceit) sprang from their imagination and their industry.

Ariovistus Pardee was born in Chatham, New York, on November 19, 1810, but grew up on his father's farm in Rensselaer County, New York, until his twentieth year. Self-taught at his own fireside, but stimulated in his fifteenth year by the Presbyterian Reverend Moses Hunter, an unusual teacher in the local district school, Ario Pardee later remembered himself as "an industrious worker at my books in my leisure time at home." Before daylight one Monday in the summer of 1830, he left home on foot to go to work as a rodman with a townsman who had known him since childhood, Edwin A. Douglass, an engineer with the canal company, then surveying between Trenton and Princeton, New Jersey. In May 1833, Douglass sent the young man to Beaver Meadow, Pennsylvania, to make a survey for a railroad to connect local mines to the Lehigh Canal at Mauch Chunk. Soon, Ario Pardee, barely twenty-three, had charge of the entire project. He stayed until the first shipment of coal clanged down the new line, and then in February of 1837 he settled in Hazleton, working as a superintendent for the Hazleton Railroad and Coal Company. He was ready to quit and actually headed for New Jersey, but a man he met along the way told him to stay, and he went back. It was the turning point. That year, Pardee made the first investment of his own money near the present Lafayette College which, in later years, was to be the object of his munificence. In 1840, he went into business for himself as an independent coal operator. In time, he and J. Gillingham Fell formed A. Pardee and Company, which became the largest individual shipper of anthracite in Pennsylvania, with mines in Hazleton and in a large surrounding circle: Cranberry, Harwood, Sugar Loaf, Crystal Ridge, Jeddo, Highland, Lattimer, Hollywood, and Mount Pleasant. Later, Pardee built ironworks in Allentown and Stanhope, Pennsylvania, Secaucus, New Jersey, Buffalo, New York, and Longdale, Virginia; lumber operations in Pennsylvania, Michigan, the Carolinas, West Virginia, and Canada; and large business interests in Florida. His holdings were vast and national in scope.

His friends called Pardee "the silent man," and at his death in Florida, on March 26, 1892, the Hazleton *Plain Speaker* wrote: "This was our master man. For more than fifty years he has been foremost in the development of the community. . . . His was a master mind that could grasp easily every detail of even the greatest plans. His force of character was such that energetic action followed upon his planning as day follows night. And he worked as giants worked. Back of all was an iron will that brooked no contradiction. The secret of his success was the concentration of purpose, he swerved not a hair's breadth from the direct line of his business interests. . . . Of the men closely associated with him in business, his counsel was always given the highest value."

In his long life, Pardee suffered many reversals. The financial upheaval of 1837 wiped out his first investments and forced him to borrow heavily. He lost one fortune in Canada, another at Allentown. Yet in 1864, he testified in court that in the preceding single year (the year of the battle of Gettysburg) his personal income had been over a million dollars. His children by Elizabeth Jacobs of Butler Valley were General Ario Pardee, Jr., of Philadelphia; Calvin (who succeeded his father as president of A. Pardee and Company); Alice; and Ella (who died in Paris). By Anna M. Robison of Bloomsburg, his second wife, he had Israel (President of the Hazleton National Bank from 1894–1934), Anne, Barton, Frank (who worked with Calvin in Hazleton), Bessie (who married A. S. Van Wickle), Edith, and Gertrude. In Florida for his wife's health, Pardee at eighty-two forced himself against his doctor's wishes to take strenuous exercise, refusing to stop and rest. "A slight cold," comments *The History of Luzerne County,* "and then a chill, and in a few hours he peacefully passed away." His friends in Hazleton refused to believe that he had died. "The silent man," says the *History,* was of "the kind that builds nations. . . . His fortune and life-work for years hung in the balance between success and failure; his close friends feared utter failure and ruin, but he never wavered."

Pardee's contributions to the anthracite industry were both conceptual and organizational. He grasped early the superiority of anthracite and helped to develop methods to make it burn efficiently. Above all, he solved the problem of transportation: "Without transportation the finest coal in the world at the mouth of the mine is only rubbish." But he also grasped quickly the way to organize far-flung companies and to make one asset contribute to another. His achievements helped to fuel the great leap forward of industrialization in America.

Ario's son, Calvin, who was fifty-one in 1892 when his father died, succeeded him as head of the firm. Calvin thought of himself as a good boss, firm but fair. He watched profit margins closely. The coal business was uncertain and, according to Professor Harold W. Aurand, author of *From the Molly Maguires to the United Mine Workers*, the owners employed a primitive economics in trying to regulate its flow to market, often contributing by their decisions to simultaneous shortages and falling prices. Like other tycoons of his time, Calvin Pardee understood better the internal organizational problems of his industries than the economic laws of the larger marketplace. He was prepared to make his laborers suffer for his own convictions about how to control supply. Demands for wage increases of ten percent or more, such as the strikers were demanding in August 1897, must have struck Calvin Pardee as an impossible load for the market to bear, and as a foolish lack of insight on the part of the laborers caught in a labor glut. He blamed the foreign miners for his troubles. He was sure that, thanks to his father's industry, the English-speaking miners had experienced a tangible rise in employment and income over the preceding twenty years. He had already arranged an ethnic split between the miners at his two main works in Harwood and Lattimer—predominantly Slavs at the former, predominantly Italians at the latter. On September 10, 1897, the climactic day of the strike, he was to send word that he would gladly meet with the English-speaking men—but not with the foreigners. His son was to stand with the deputies at Lattimer.

The destiny of the Pardee family had long been closely linked to that of the Markles. The families had risen in power and wealth together. The Markles traced their family back to

Heinrich Merklen of Friesland in 1430, but the name descends from antiquity as Marcus and has many regional variants. By 1593, Christian Merkel, descendent of Heinrich, was a merchant in Metz, and his three great-grandsons came to America in 1703, settling in Berks County. When George Bushar Markle was born in 1827, his branch of the family had lost its money (the decline of wealth is as typically American as its rise), and George could not finish school. He was injured in his work as a carpenter, and by the age of twenty was a leather worker in Bloomsburg. There he married into the Robison family, as had Ario Pardee, and in 1847, at twenty, became clerk in the Pardee store, and then general superintendent of the Pardee collieries. George Bushar Markle was a mechanical genius and rose rapidly in fame and wealth through dozens of inventions.

The most dramatic of these inventions was his design of a breaker. The anthracite operators wished to offer only the purest, highest quality coal, sorted by size. They achieved this purpose by constructing huge, tall buildings, in which the coal was lifted mechanically to the highest point, and then tumbled down long chutes and open troughs at various angles. Breaker boys sat astride the chutes, plucking out the slate and sorting out lumps of coal by size. The clanging noise inside as the chains and belts pushed the coal along was earsplitting. The entire building rattled and shook when the belts were in operation. Fine black dust covered all ledges, walls, and machinery. The boys shouted boisterously and swore like troopers, contemptuous of their bosses, fiercely independent, rebellious. Many lost limbs in the machinery. Several were known to have disappeared, to be found hours later mangled and crushed while caught bent around one of the turning wheels. Windows were broken, icy air swept in during the winter, and in the stifling summers the fine dust on their bodies was caked with sweat. The boys were paid fifty-five cents a day. But the machinery was almost foolproof, a total improvement on the systems that had preceded it. Even the miners boasted about it.

Markle also invented the "Markle pump" for keeping water out of the mines, and new bearings and rollers, and scores of other mechanical improvements. By 1858, at the age of thirty-one, with the financial backing of Ario Pardee, J. Gillingham Fell, and General William Lilly, he organized G. B. Markle and Company and began his own independent operations at Jeddo and Highland. By 1868, he had founded the banking house of Pardee, Markle and Grier. He became a stockholder and director of the Lehigh Valley Railroad and many other companies in the business of coal, iron, land, and railroads. In 1874, he moved to Philadelphia, but after 1879 his health failed and trips abroad to seek European specialists were of no avail. He returned to Hazleton to die. He had barely turned sixty-one when death caught him at his home in 1888.

His son, John, who had been sent away to a military academy in White Plains, New York, at age eleven, was then thirty. John had taken a degree in mining engineering at Lafayette College in 1880. During his college years, he worked summers at every job in the mines and railroads, learning the two businesses from every practical perspective. On graduation, he took his father's place as general superintendent, so that by the time his father died he had already been running the family holdings for eight years. He bought out the large interest held in the G. B. Markle and Company by the Asa Packer estate and thus assumed financial as well as administrative control. He gained new leases or made new outright purchases, securing mines at Jeddo, Highland, Ebervale, and Harleigh. When underground floods forced the abandonment of the nearby Harleigh and Ebervale mines in 1886, and all efforts to clear the waters failed, John Markle purchased the properties and designed a system to salvage them. He formed the Jeddo Tunnel Company, invested a million dollars in an improbable engineering feat, and personally supervised the precise surveying required for underground work. Using compressed air drills and powerful explosives, his men labored for three years, at constant risk of their lives, one team driving north and the other south in underground darkness. On September 15, 1894, the two teams met and tore out the intervening wall. Their floors did not differ by as much as an inch. Esteem for Markle spread. When later strikes brought flooding to other unworked mines in the area, Markle's drainage tunnel kept his mines free of water damage. He worked hard at keeping his relationships with his workers personal and direct.

He reorganized the Sprague Electric Company, which he then sold advantageously to the General Electric Company; became director of the Industrial Finance Company, and of the Morris Plan Company in New York; and held farflung investments and directorships. After his marriage to May E. Robison of New York in 1884, he resided in New York City, keeping private offices there at 2 Rector Street, returning to Jeddo as a summer residence and for business purposes.

John Markle's younger brother, George B. Markle, Jr., tried to establish a new career in various businesses in Portland, Oregon, after his dying father designated John controller of the family firm. Six years later, he returned to Hazleton. "He was a charming host, loved to entertain his friends at home, and was very popular," writes his biographer. He enjoyed the Hazleton Country Club, the Theta Delta Chi college fraternity, and many other clubs throughout the county. His older brother inherited his father's genius and driving spirit, but George, Jr., enjoyed inherited wealth, and worked pleasantly in politics "to break the shackles fastened on Pennsylvania by what is politely termed 'the Organization.' "

John Markle used to give advice to young men "who are starting life's battle": "All you get out of life is a living, and that degree of living is evidenced by the condition of your mortal body and every dollar that you have in excess of the cost of that living is evidence of your success in the commercial world. With these funds in your possession, you become a trustee for your fellowmen for the proper use of them."

The immigrant miners employed by the Pardees and Markles would no doubt have found the vision of the world inherent in such advice breathtakingly novel, had they ever been in a position to hear it. Neither the peasants nor the landholders of central Europe spoke like that. Yet by 1897, the immigrants had already aroused common envy because by their prodigious savings they had demonstrated their own version of capitalist virtue. Each year, they mailed hundreds of thousands of dollars from the coalfields back to Europe. Each year, the numbers of properties they purchased in the mining region grew by alarming proportions. Those who began by saying that the foreigners could never learn American ways were saying, by 1897, that the foreigners were too willing to live meanly and to save money, living at standards far below those the Americans deemed human. It was, so they said, unfair.

The Pardees and the Markles sought foreign labor because it brought them—as they often said—excellent workers. They admired the workers' physical industry, but loathed their tendencies toward solidarity, and later opposed their unions. The Pardees and the Markles were determined to fulfill their "trusteeship" by carrying out the responsibilities they knew best. George F. Baer, the president of Reading Coal and Railroad, voiced their convictions pithily: "The rights and interests of the working man will be protected and cared for, not by the labor agitators, but by the Christian men to whom God in his infinite wisdom has given the control of the property interests in this country." * "A prominent feature of the lives of both George B. Markle and his son, John Markle," recounts the *Encyclopedia of Biography,* "was the strong stand taken by them in the labor troubles that have from time immemorial harassed the anthracite region. By common consent, both have been leaders among the independent operators: 'Whatever George Markle does, we will do.'" In 1877, in conjunction with the president of the Reading Railroad Company, George Markle had hired the Pinkertons to break the back of the Molly Maguires. That year, Markle's life had been threatened and a would-be assassin had fired on his buggy; George had leapt from the buggy in bold pursuit. From 1887 onward, the two Markles, father and eldest son, had an arbitration agreement with their men, broken only by the great strike of 1902, when John Markle spoke for the operators at a press conference with President Theodore Roosevelt, who sided with the miners. The Pardees and the Markles were secure in the superiority of their family and racial stock, and in the tangible record of their own

* Of this sentiment, Finley Peter Dunne had Mr. Hennessy ask: "What d'ye think iv th' man down in Pennsylvania who says th' Lord an' him is partners in a coal mine?" Of which Mr. Dooley archly inquired: "Has he divided th' profits?" [see Beers, p. 82]

spectacular achievements. They felt in touch with the inner meaning of history in a peculiarly powerful way.

These were intelligent, active, farseeing, admirable people, the Markles and Pardees, the Coxes and Van Wickles and Fells. In fewer than fifty years these few bold men and women transformed a wilderness into an enormous source of power and wealth, not only for themselves, but for the entire nation and the world. Their talent for abstract thinking, for organization, and for the execution of vast plans is one of the marvels of comparative culture. And yet they had their limits. There were serious differences between the immigrant miners and the English-speaking miners in the coalfields, differences of experience and outlook. Despite their many cosmopolitan advantages, or perhaps because of them, the Markles and the Pardees did not see the world as either group of miners did.

John Markle remained in New York for most of the period of the strike of 1897. Pardee remained at his home in Germantown, outside Philadelphia. They were prepared to close down their mines for the winter, if necessary—or at least to threaten so. They thought only irrational men would threaten to strike when labor was already in excess supply. Harsh reality, they felt, would give instruction. Only slowly did they come to recognize how serious the miners were.

August 17, 1897

ELMER LAWALL'S OFFICE

ON TUESDAY MORNING, August 17, a committee of miners went to meet Elmer H. Lawall at the Lehigh and Wilkes-Barre offices in Hazleton. Some of the girls and young men who served as clerks showed nervousness and faint disdain as the miners' delegation tromped heavily across the floor. The white-collar workers were unhappy about having miners in their own inner offices. Still, although the air was a little strained, it was clear that the miners were peaceable and their demands moderate. As usual, the company officials were determined to be firm. They dreaded nothing so much as a sign of weakness. The local newspapers and townspeople were pleading for peace. No one in a company town benefited by prolonged unemployment. Besides, fear of the unknown flitted through the "American" homes. Would "they" be violent? Would "they" come in darkness? There is a sense in all small towns that evil comes from outside-in. Newcomers are not soon trusted.

Wisely, the strikers included two "Americans" in the negotiating committee. The *Daily Standard* reported "A committee consisting of two representatives of each nationality met general superintendent Elmer H. Lawall during the forepart of the day. The popular official could not give any answer until higher authority could be consulted."

Lawall was courteous. He agreed to revoke the original work rule that Gomer Jones had imposed upon the mule drivers, but he refused to concede that Gomer Jones would be, or ought to be, disciplined. He urged that the men go back to work. If they did, then he would consider a wage boost. He would promise nothing, negotiate nothing, until work had been resumed.

The strikers' committee did not relish explaining their petty achievement to the men gathering at McAdoo. On their return, the scene was like a holiday. Some men pitched horseshoes. Hundreds milled around talking and arguing. Soon Michalchik's Hall was densely packed. More than half could not get inside and hundreds lined both sides of West Blaine Street. The workers expected a victory. When they heard the committee's report, they booed and groaned. The meeting was long and confused. The American miners wanted to get back to work. The foreigners refused. No raise, no work. The mood turned uglier.

BIG MARY SEPTAK, LATTIMER MINES

LATTIMER MINES was one of the most nondescript, humble, hidden little villages of the Hazleton region. It is found today only with difficulty, off the modern Route 309 to the northeast of Hazleton, tucked over the northern side of a rolling hill. Below it lie gray culm banks. In 1897, it consisted of two streets, with dirt roads running back over the hill to other clusters of shacks and shanties. Two large breakers rose in the valley to the north of the village, Lattimer Number One and Lattimer Number Three. The narrow asphalt road that leads into Lattimer today lies only approximately along the path of the dirt road of 1897. Just like the older road, however, it curves as it approaches the first homes in view and issues in a fork that becomes the two main streets of the village, the lower one to the north in those days called Main Street and the upper one, which passed below the jerry-built schoolhouse, Quality Row. There at the fork of the road today stands the "massacre tree" with the simple monument erected in 1972; and there in 1897 to the north lay the spot where so many men fell. A less romantic, more rigorously plain place could hardly be imagined. Underbrush grows now in a field of slag and slate. The space seems too small, the roads too unimportant, the modern homes that stand in the place of or alongside the homes of an earlier era seem modest, placid, and peaceful. No sign of grandeur is in evidence.

The Pardee coal company laid out the village in 1869. The first residents were "Americans" (Welsh, chiefly), who were mainly the managerial personnel and lived on Main Street or Quality Row, the street with big houses and quiet lawns. Near the end of the lower street was the mine superintendent's office, a general store, a mule barn and machine repair shop. Near that end of the street, it appears, there also stood a wooden frame boardinghouse, in which sixteen eastern European miners' assistants lived. Mary Septak (María Septaková)

—"Big Mary," as she was known—lived there with her husband and presided over the household. But few were the eastern Europeans in Lattimer Mines. Mostly, the Pardees had brought Italian families to Lattimer, settling the Poles, Lithuanians, Slovaks and other eastern Europeans in villages near the mines to the south of Hazleton like Harwood, Cranberry, Crystal Ridge, and others. By 1897, on the upper street in Lattimer and on the higher ground of Scotch Hill, several Irish and German families had homes. Several of the houses on Scotch Hill were painted red, but up a little higher the shacks were unpainted save for large red numerals on their doors (a device distinctive of Lattimer). Most of the residents in these were Italians. Scattered over the hill and off a mile or so away, in a settlement then known as Lattimer II, the same residential patterns were repeated, except that a few more Slavic families—Polish, Ukrainian, and Slovak—were in evidence.*

The shanties of the latest arrivals were made of scrap lumber of assorted sizes. As needs arose and materials allowed, new rooms were added to one side or another; the shanties were of irregular shape. The men nailed tar paper to them as soon as they could afford it. Narrow gardens, jagged with bean poles, filled every inch of ground space between the homes and their outhouses. Flowers and vegetables as close to those the immigrants had known in their old world villages—hollyhocks, sunflowers, poppies, plum trees, grapevines—were carefully tended. In size and comfort, although not perhaps in material and solidity, these homes were sometimes as comfortable as those the peasants had known in their homelands. Roads here were narrow, rutted, and muddy, just as they had been in Poland, Lithuania, or Italy. Some families kept chickens, or rabbits; an occasional family raised a pig or two. About half the families owned a cow, which the children milked. Between the houses, particularly along the roads, many families had built fences to protect their gardens, rough and irregular fences fashioned from inch-thick branches pushed into the earth, like the primitive stockades one sees from various regions of the

---

* Here the actor Jack Palance still maintains a home today.

world in *National Geographic*. Poles were used for carrying bundles, for walking sticks, for trellises, for grape arbors.

In one of these houses, altogether typical, the Moye house, lived six brothers and sisters, their father and mother, a grandmother and her stepsister. Ten persons shared two bedrooms and an attic. This luxurious space—the household was Irish—represented better living than that of the Poles and the Italians. The Moye children played with Irish and Protestant kids. The Italians and "Polacks" played by themselves.

Inside the Moye house, as in others from Scotch Hill up, there were no rugs, only broad floorboards. Cloth was nailed below the rafters and a kind of broad crepe paper was stretched over the cloth to keep the heat in. Every so often, old paper would be pulled off and fresh paper put up. Pipes from the kitchen stove or a coal heater "gave heat" to attics, where children slept. Mostly, families used multiple blankets. For light, coal-kerosene lamps might be carried from room to room.

Women and children went barefoot most of the time. Shoes, worn only to church, were made to last for ten years. Boys got their hair cut at the mule stable, across from the store. Until after dark, children played games and ran races, flashing their bare feet. They played "Lay Sheep Lay" and "Hide 'n Seek." They were taught to stay away from Quality Row and to cut through fields rather than to go down *their* street.

Two doctors toured the village regularly on horse and buggy. Doctor Harvey, a kindly man with a kindly wife, lived on Main Street. A dollar a month was deducted from paychecks to pay the doctors, and other fees were added. No one "went" to the doctors. Even teeth were pulled right in the home. The miners resented the automatic monthly deduction from their pay. They also resented the pressure they felt to make all their purchases in the company store. If they were seen carrying bags of food or clothing from Hazleton, where prices were cheaper, such disloyalty was brought to their attention. They felt watched.

Women were relatively few in number, since most of the foreign laborers had come to America as solitary migrant laborers who had every intention, at least at first, of returning to Europe. (About one in four did so return.) The women had virtually total responsibility for childcare. Since the women had little contact with the new world outside their homes, they were often anxious lest the training they gave their children at home might mis-prepare them for survival in a strange culture. As carriers of culture, the women were especially torn by conflicts between the old world and the new. On the other hand, women sometimes found it easier to learn English through their shopping and their contacts with other women, while the men in some occupations were almost totally isolated from conversation. The women were socially more active in the churches and other spheres; the men, following peasant traditions, sometimes knew no other world outside the home besides their jobs.

The women also carried the full burden of gardening, laundering, gathering food, cooking, and all manner of household tasks. They used ingenuity and skills in virtual small businesses of their own, taking in laundry, tailoring, sewing, cooking, cleaning. Often, they had full control over the budget. Husbands brought their pay home to their wives. Nearly everyone who could took in boarders. The women did all the boarders' washing by hand, wrestling with clothes that must be made to last even though caked with grime, dust, sweat, and blood. They set out rain barrels, because the only pump in the locality was on Red Hill, far from many of the shanties. The women collected lumps of coal and firewood. Every night, a beer wagon was pulled up the dusty roads. The women would go out to meet it to purchase buckets of beer and have it ready when the men came home. On arrival the men would strip and the women would pour water over them and sponge-bathe their backs outside, at the corner of the house, even in cold weather. The women bathed all of the men, not only their husbands, and ribald banter was not uncommon. Single men had no alternative except to board with others, and most of the younger married couples also boarded until they had saved money. Given illnesses, mortality rates, and migrating patterns, relationships in these homes were often complex. Widows, stepsisters, cousins, in-laws—many were alone in the world, many others tenuously or thickly related to those they lived with. Cabbage foods were staples for the Slavs, pasta for the Italians, potatoes for the Irish. Bunk beds and airlessness, darkness and crowding, simplicity and raw penury characterized their lives.

Only a few vivid details are known of Mary Septak, many of them from a feature article about her in the *Century Magazine* in 1898. After the massacre, she was to become (at least briefly) a dominant leader. It was said that the motormen on the trolleys were intimidated by her, as also the proprietor of the company store and local mining officials. Certainly her boarders heeded her directives. Mary Septak was a large woman, short and heavy. She had a formidable voice and flashing eyes. She was a woman of great force and good humor. She brooked no nonsense. She spoke her mind without uncertainty. She had a strong and immediate revulsion against injustice.

About her activities in August 1897, only surmises are possible. We may imagine that most of the sixteen men who slept in the crowded quarters of her home were Slavs. The newspapers referred to her as "Big Mary." Slavic women of her generation were not easily intimidated, and were no strangers to the giving of authoritative orders. The men, mere peasants in Europe and even less than that in America, were often docile and silent in manner. Some observers, perhaps unfairly, wrote that they were crueller to their women than men from other cultures in the mine patch were. They would sometimes strike their women or beat them. Yet most of the time, around the home, the voice of angry authority was the woman's. She upbraided her men—husband, relatives, sons, boarders—as though they were children. She often seemed disappointed that they did not fight back. The men seemed to come to life only when they were drinking. At weddings, they seemed suddenly transformed—animated, dancing, shouting, laughing. Almost every night, some men would drink too much beer. Especially on Saturday nights.

Mary Septak loved her husband with a remarkable love. She had lived with "her man" as she called him twenty-seven years. She had lost nine of her ten children to various diseases; year after year had brought sorrow. Living in an all-male world, she saw with her own eyes what work in the mines did to the newcomers, especially the young ones. Even at her own simple table, hunger threatened. Men fretted about having no money to send for their wives, or children, or sweethearts.

She had a special affection for the young boys, having lost her own. She watched them go into Lattimer's two breakers every day. Slate pickers sat bent over on a rough poke board, keeping their eyes on the never-ending stream of slate and coal that passed through the chute. The slate-picker boss would not hesitate to give a boy a stinging clout across the hands for putting coal in the slate box or slate in the coal chute. The slate was sharp, gloves were useless. Raw fingers were called "redtop." In winter, old men would sometimes find the path home from the breaker by the drops of blood in the snow. Some of the boys wrapped a long strand of copper wire around each finger, like a ring, to create an artificial grip. Mary Septak had watched one of her own boys go into the breaker, before he died. At night she had rubbed ointment into his raw fingers, saying, "*Synu môj,** someday things will be better."

News of the strikes to the south excited Mary Septak. But the two breakers at Lattimer Mines roared and clanged without letup. Lattimer was isolated and alone. Mary thought the men should strike. If they acted like sheep, nothing would change. She would lead them herself if necessary. She was ready to lead them out in August. By mid-September she could not be restrained.

At its appropriate place, we will return to the story of Big Mary Septak. But in one of the curiosities of history, it happens that a much more famous woman also passed through Lattimer Mines three summers after the exploits of Big Mary. This was a fiery Irish lass born in County Cork as Mary Harris but known in the mine fields from Illinois to Pennsylvania as Mother Jones. It seems that Mother Jones did not know of Big Mary, even though her own activities a few years later were to mirror Mary's so exactly. Just as the Molly Maguires found inspiration in a militant woman, and just as the strikers of 1897 were to cherish the exploits of Big Mary, so also Mother Jones put fire into the labor movement on many occasions and at many places. In *The Autobiography of Mother*

* Pronounced: *See-nu moy,* "my son."

Jones (1925),* she tells how on October 7, 1900, she tried to inspire the men of Lattimer and the Hazleton region to new courage.

Lattimer was an eye-sore to the miners. It seemed as if no one could break into it. Twenty-six organizers and union men had been killed in that coal camp in previous strikes. Some of them had been shot in the back. The blood of union men watered the highways. No one dared go in. . . .
The Lattimer miners and the mule drivers were afraid to quit work. They had been made cowards [by the earlier bloodshed]. . . .

Mother Jones went to Lattimer in 1900 to organize another strike. She and other women took up guard positions on the front step of every home, physically preventing any men from going to work. At one house, two women threw a hapless man over a fence, knocking him unconscious. Mother Jones described it in *The Autobiography*:

. . . Those that insisted on working and thus defeating their brothers were grabbed by the women and carried to their wives.
An old Irish woman had two sons who were scabs. The women threw one of them over the fence to his mother. He lay there still. His mother thought he was dead and she ran into the house for a bottle of holy water and shook it over Mike.
"Oh for God's sake, come back to life," she hollered. "Come back and join the union."

* The Third Edition, Revised (1976) includes an excellent introduction and guide by Fred Thompson, and adds a note from her testimony before the U.S. Senate in 1915 about her deeds in Lattimer in 1900:
"I got about 1500 women lined up, and we walked into Lattimer. It was dark, and we knocked on every door, and told them there was no work to do. . . . The drivers came along to take the mules to the mines, and I had all the women centered in front of the company's store, and we had 3,000 men down at the mines that the company or sheriff knew nothing about—they had come in on different roads, and I said when he ordered the boys to take the mules to the drivers, that the mules would not scab. I kept entertaining the sheriff and general manager and deputies, and the mules came back directly without the drivers. Of course we cheered the mules. We closed those mines in the anthracite and that really was the key to the situation. They had shot 23 men in the back just three years before. I served notice on the sheriff that no 23 workers would be shot that day; that he had just as well make up his mind those mines were going to be closed, and we had no pistols or guns, nothing but just our hands." [The exact number of the dead was cited loosely at the time.]

He opened his eyes and saw our women standing around him. "Shure, I'll go to hell before I'll scab again," says he.

Mother Jones went with a band of 150 women on an all-night, all-day march covering more than thirty miles, from McAdoo to Coaldale, closing down mines as they marched.

I went to a nearby mining town that was thoroughly organized and asked the women if they would help me get the Coaldale men out. This was in McAdoo. I told them to leave their men at home to take care of the family. I asked them to put on their kitchen clothes and bring mops and brooms with them and a couple of tin pans. We marched over the mountains fifteen miles, beating on the tin pans as if they were cymbals. At three o'clock in the morning we met the Crack Thirteen of the militia, patrolling the roads to Coaldale. The colonel of the regiment said "Halt! Move back!" (It was pitch-black dark.)

I said, "Colonel, the working men of America will not halt nor will they ever go back. The working man is going forward!"

"I'll charge bayonets," said he. . . .

They kept us there till daybreak and when they saw the army of women in kitchen aprons, with dishpans and mops, they laughed and let us pass. An army of strong mining women makes a wonderfully spectacular picture.

This was in 1900. By that date, the tradition of activist women in the mine fields was already deep and strong. Big Mary Septak had preceded Mother Jones. The little village of Lattimer had known both of these bold women and was to be the pivotal point at which the weakness of 1897 was transmuted into the eventual union victory of 1902.

Wednesday, August 18–Thursday, August 19, 1897

NEW YORK AND MCADOO

"DURING the past few days," the Hazleton *Daily Standard* reported on August 19, "letters came pouring in from all over the state encouraging the men, showing how widespread is the

righteousness of their cause and the extent of their sympathy."
Since Superintendent Lawall was unable to speak for "higher
authorities" at the meeting in his Hazleton offices on August
17, the strikers decided to send a committee of five to confer
with officials at the New York offices of the mining company.
Although the strikes had been begun by the Slavic mule drivers, some English-speaking miners were now in sympathy with
it. Several of their leaders were the best organizers. The assembly chose five men to go by train to New York: "Alex
McMullen and William Hopkins to represent the English-
speaking people, John Burska to represent the Hungarians
[Slovaks, Rusyns, Galicians], Pasco Deleco the Italians, and
Andrew Damian the Magyars," as the *Daily Standard* listed
them. "The committee represented every class of wage
earners."

The five men left on an early train for Manhattan, where
they met with Superintendent Lawall and C. H. Warren, assistant to the president of the Lehigh and Wilkes-Barre Coal
Company. The five miners may have felt uncomfortable in the
presence of the great buildings of New York and in the spacious offices of President Maxwell. The president himself, of
course, did not see them. The panelling on the walls, the
carpets, the potted plants, the quiet in which the secretaries
worked seemed a very long way from the pits in which the
company's money was made.

C. H. Warren presented the men with a letter addressed to
Alex McMullen:

Dear Sir:
. . . It is the desire of the Company to pay its employees the wages
paid by other companies for similar work in the Audenried
District. . . .
If they now desire to select and pay their own doctor, the company
will gladly have them do so. . . . If the employees return to work
promptly, investigation will be made not only of the question of
wages, but also in regards to the complaints concerning the personal
treatment received by employees. . . ."

The meeting was cordial. The five delegates left Manhattan
just before the streets filled with carriages and reached Hazleton on the 8:50 P.M. train.

The same day, John Fahy arrived on the 1:45 P.M. train from Pottsville. One of the most gifted organizers in the UMW, Fahy was now uncertain of his reception by the foreign miners, since he had thrown his full support behind the Campbell Act which levied a three-percent tax on alien labor. He needn't have worried. When he alighted from the train, he was given a cordial welcome.

John Fahy was thirty-three, steady, a man of peace. He was quite religious and had intense and candid eyes, the sort of man who inspired considerable trust. He was strikingly good-looking, with a delicate black moustache and large blue eyes. "The handsomest man in the union," one woman said. The men liked him and were cheered by his presence. The welcoming committee led him toward Michalchik's Hall in McAdoo, but so many men were eager to see him and hear him that they had to bring him instead to the Honey Brook baseball field.

Introduced under the hot blue sky, John Fahy scanned the motley crowd of over one thousand miners. His voice was high but strong, and he spoke slowly so that those who had learned but little English and depended on abbreviated translations could follow him. He had two goals in view. First, he intended to forestall violence. He was afraid that unruly men might precipitate a conflict they could not win, and that then for another ten years the region would go without a solid, practical organization. Secondly, he wanted the men to come to their own decision to form a union. If their own will was not behind it, no union could endure. So he stressed the need for a single union organization that could cut across company lines and negotiate for all the miners of the region at once. He argued that capital and labor needed each other: each needed a proper return. Ultimately, he argued, the miners had to have a large organization with a national base, in order to have power commensurate with that of the companies. He was not in favor of strikes, except where there was no other recourse. A strong union might make strikes, turmoil, and continual dissatisfaction unnecessary.

This appeal had a certain force, even though it left many of the workers, especially the foreign workers, restless. The day before, Lawall had sent back word that a ten-cent wage hike *might* be offered by the company. The men took that as a modest sign of victory, but such a raise would only bring them up to the level already provided by other companies in the region. It wasn't enough. Other miners who worked for other companies were supporting them precisely for that reason.

The young union organizer had to walk a thin line between discouraging tumult and speaking out against a successful strike, the first since the operators had broken the strike of 1887. He therefore asked for a sign of intention. He called for a vote on whether the miners wished to proceed with the organization of a UMW branch at McAdoo the next day, when their representatives would report on their findings in New York. A vote was taken and, amid much murmuring and voluble discussion, easily passed.

The next morning at nine, Alex McMullen reported on his committee's conversations in New York City and read the letter from the company. The *Daily Standard* reported the reaction: "The foreigners, especially, wouldn't entertain such a proposition as to return to work on the mere promise of having matters rectified. In fact, there were but few who felt otherwise." Almost unanimously, the men decided to continue the strike until they had something more definite from the company. They did not trust promises to make "inquiries."

Thus, on that long, hot Thursday, August 19, John Fahy plunged into the tedious business of organizing chapters of the UMW. He decided, because of language and natural feelings of solidarity, to organize chapters for each national group. The living patterns in the mining villages facilitated such organization.

Fahy also perceived that the interests of each of the ethnic groups was somewhat different. Fahy anticipated the dictum of John Mitchell, soon to become national president of the UMW: "There is not Irish coal, or Italian coal, or Slavish coal —only coal." But while he stressed unity and solidarity, Fahy could not avoid the fact that lay behind his lobbying for the Campbell Act: the American miners disliked the competition from the foreigners.* As much as possible, he stayed away

---

* Frank Julian Warne was later to summarize the situation in *The Slav Invasion of the Mine Fields* (Philadelphia, 1904): "When the competition of the Slav . . . became too strong, the English-speaking miners resorted

from the center of power. There was, perhaps, a certain diffidence or even weakness about him but it was intermixed with an intuitive wisdom about what would work. His own presence was soft, but practical and efficient. It laid him open to charges of being an opportunist.

Fahy went from group to group all through the afternoon until late at night. By the time he was ready for sleep, he had formed six branches, one for each of six nationalities, representing nearly eight hundred men in all. The next day, he had plans to meet with the Italians at Audenried and hoped to push the number over a thousand. After months of effort, this was the first and only good day he had had.

On August 20, a Friday, the organizing committee again met with Superintendent Lawall. The ten-cent raise went into effect. Lawall promised the men that the conduct of Gomer Jones would be looked into. The English-speaking miners favored conciliation, while the others vacillated. Individual men started drifting back to work and, even though somewhat restlessly, nearly all the others followed. For the foreign miners, the promised investigation into the conduct of Gomer Jones would be decisive. Tentatively, the strike was at an end.

---

to various methods of defense. Race prejudice, manifested in innumerable ways, was directed to keeping the Slavs out of the mines." The English-speaking miners tended to have a little more trust in the system than did the foreigners. The system, after all, protected their own higher-paying jobs, and they had experienced a tangible growth in prosperity during the preceding twenty years. In addition, they were "themselves largely responsible for the employment of the non-English-speaking foreigners. Instead of employing English laborers at the regular wage rate, the miner would employ a big Slav or Hun cheaply, increasing his own pay check quite an amount. His boasting of the 'snap' caused others to do the same." [*Pottsville Republican*, September 20, 1897.]

August 22, 1897

THE WEDDING

THE NIGHT before the wedding of Steve Jurich, Ben Sakmar went with his neighbor, Mike Cheslak, to the bachelor's party. Mike was forty, the father of five children, and a warden in Reverend Carl Hauser's Slovak Lutheran church of Freeland. Mike and his wife lived next door to the boardinghouse that Ben lived in. Across the street lived John Futa, seventeen, with his mother, a widow, and six boarders. Steve Jurich lived just down from Cheslak. All were at the bachelor's party in the basement of St. Joseph's church in Hazleton. The beer flowed freely. The men taunted young Steve about his impending servitude.

The strike was over. All felt relieved. Ben enjoyed their company. Their speech was quick and certain, for they spoke in Slovak; it was pleasant not to feel slow and stupid.

That night, they walked home in the darkness together, on the road from Hazleton to Harwood. The fireflies were thick. Pale moonlight made the white sandstones shine. The air was soft and cool, and the breeze smelled of heavy dew.

John Futa, seventeen, Steve Jurich, twenty-five, Andrew Jurechek, thirty-eight, and Jacob "Jack" Tomashantas, eighteen, walked ahead. Jurechek was the only married one of the four. He had one child; his wife was pregnant with another. Tomashantas was Lithuanian and lived with relatives in Harwood. He had learned Slovak far more quickly than he could learn English. He was swarthy in complexion, silent in manner.

Mike Cheslak had come to Harwood in 1882. He was almost a father to the others, nearly all of whom were twenty years younger. His own oldest child was nearly sixteen, almost as old as Ben. He was a short, thick man with a bushy black moustache, a calm man, hard and seasoned. He had worked eight years in America before he had saved enough to go back to Zámutov, County Zemplin, to bring over his wife and child. Since 1890, he and his wife had had four children in America.

The newspapers described the rickety houses of Harwood as "shanties," but to Mike Cheslak and the others they represented significant accomplishment.

Harwood was to become the departure point for the massacre that took place on September 10. Neither Cheslak, nor Eagler, nor Jurich could have known their own roles in it, nor realized that some of them would be alive for but two more Saturday nights. Harwood was home to them, two long narrow streets of company houses, surrounded by dense woods except where the earth had been pushed away for coal strippings and culm banks. A reporter saw their village with eyes very different from their own: "The mining village of Harwood," he wrote, ". . . is one of the most squalid looking places to be found in Pennsylvania. The place is owned by Calvin Pardee & Co., and as one enters the poverty-stricken village one is impressed by the appearance of the wretched hovels, called houses, in which the miners live." The reporter saw "a long street, without the pretense of sidewalks and in the center of which is a railroad track used in connection with the mines. . . . On either side are the black and grimy homes of the miners, many of them in such a state of unrepair that when it rains the water pours through the leaky roofs upon floors and beds. The only building in the place that makes any pretension to decency in appearance is the company store. . . ."

This unnamed correspondent, whose dispatch appeared in the Utica *Saturday Globe* (September 18, 1897), asked one of the miners, "What pay do you make?"

"Oh, me all right," he said, "me single, me not married. Make sometime, two dollar, sometime four dollar, a month."

"A week," the reporter corrected him.

"No, no, a month. Just two dollar, sometime four dollar, a month."

The reporter wrote that many men in Harwood were working only two days or four three-quarter days a month. "Constables from the town go among them in the mining region," he wrote, "and arrest them for merely trivial offenses. The constables need fees and so do some justices of the peace. Bosses in and around the mines have been in the habit of receiving a certain percentage of their wages for giving them work or allowing them to remain at work." Still, what the reporter could not know is that conditions in America were preferable to those in Slovakia. The housing was less solid, the peasants missed the farm produce they had shared in central Europe—but there the hunger was sometimes even worse, and here the laws were freer and the future held at least some hope.

Ben walked with Mike Cheslak, John Eagler, who was nineteen, and Andrew Meyer, almost seventeen. Meyer had worked under Eagler as a breaker boy. Andrew Meyer had never met his own father, who was in America, until Andrew was eleven years old. When Andrew at last came to live with his father in 1892, he of course knew no English and the other boys on the breaker mocked him and threw pieces of slate at his fingers. He didn't know how to defend himself. Eagler saw what was going on and put an end to it. Andrew, looking forward to his seventeenth birthday on September 15, had always loved Eagler for this. Eagler was one of the few Slovak breaker bosses.

The next morning, in their best Sunday clothes and Sunday shoes, the men sat listlessly through the wedding mass. Outside the birds chirped. Inside, the holy water sprinkler clinked against the brass bucket as the rings were blessed. Ben thought Steve's bride, Johanna, was beautiful. His heart ached with loneliness. The church smelled of freshly cut flowers. The choir sang. Women cried.

All but the youngest girls looked older than they were. Still, in their flowered patterns, lace, and colorful embroidery, the women seemed transformed. Gone for the day were their baggy black skirts, dark babushkas, and dirty bare feet. Sundays and weddings were like signs of resurrection.

Weddings were sometimes held on Sunday, the only day the men were not at work, but they usually lasted at least two or three days. The wife's family was responsible for ordering plenty of beer and many flasks of whiskey. The bridegroom bought the wife's wedding gown and was expected to contribute twenty-five or thirty dollars for the liquor. The women worked for days preparing *holubki* and *koláč*. The joining of man and wife was the most elaborate festival in a family's life. A touch of wildness and happiness were expected to break out.

Relatives might quarrel. Guests might drink too much and fight. Younger members of the family were sometimes assigned to see to it that one or other of the men didn't hit the bar too often. This assignment was usually futile. The Slavs caused much scandal among the Methodists and Baptists.

Strict zoning laws in some towns prohibited the presence of saloons. But saloons in other towns prospered and unlocked their doors on Sundays, only bowing to local custom so far as to keep the door closed to prevent the corruption of righteous passers-by. At weddings, however, alcohol flowed freely, and there was plenty to eat. Many stuffed themselves. The Slavs were usually quite inhibited about sexual matters; neither in dress nor in speech was much made of it. Yet at a wedding a certain amount of ribaldry broke forth. Sweaty, boisterous dances marked the celebration; otherwise emotionally repressed, the Slavs felt abandon in their dances. Sweat trickled down the backs of the dancers.

Usually, before the wedding, the older women sat the bride on a chair and slowly combed her hair out smooth before shaping it into a *konta*, a tight bun.* As they did so, they improvised songs about the hard life she would have; "She's not a girl anymore. She's a married woman now. She's a wife. She will have to keep the house. She will have to cook and scrub. Beautiful children will she have, one, another, and another. Oh, if her mother could see her baby now, a wife, a mother." The song was considered a success if it made the bride burst into tears. In this case, Johanna had prepared her hair herself. "You only want to make me cry," she told the disappointed women.

Mike Cheslak was prevailed upon to take out the maroon violin handed on to him by his father. John Futa played in the Hazleton Slavonic Band, and he and five of his friends came to the wedding in uniform, setting aside their gold-braided hats because of the heat. Futa played a gleaming silver trumpet. The beat of the drum was deep and strong during the polkas; the violin sang swiftly through the folk songs. "See a

* I have borrowed many details in the rest of this section from a short chapter which Thomas Bell did not include in *Out of This Furnace*, "Slovak Wedding Day," published in the Jednota Annual *Furdek*, 1977.

Slovak, hear a song," ran an old saying. The men at first danced reluctantly; often girls and older women danced with other females. The flesh of the arms of the older women drooped as they raised them for their partners, but their eyes flashed with remembered youthfulness. Every man danced once with the bride, stuffing a dollar bill in her bosom or handing it to one of the flower girls. John Eagler had the task of making sure that each man "paid up." He played the role of family clown, to tease them into it, dragging even the old and the lame to the bridal line.

During this *redova*, the bride was caught and whirled in a dance by every man present and virtually all the women, one after the other, without pause. The wedding cake was cut and each dancer as he or she finished was served a slice of cake and a drink. The best man was Andrew Jurechek, and he had the privilege of the last dance. Midway through their twirling, tradition commanded that Jurechek pretend to run off with the bride. The women shrieked. Then the groom was supposed to be alert and give chase. Steve Jurich ran through the crowd, caught his beloved by the arm and holding her hand high led her back into the center of the room. She was flushed, breathless, nearly exhausted, and now they belonged to each other forever.

John Eagler and Ben watched two of the older miners, brothers, begin a shoving match. One lived in McAdoo, the other in Harwood, and they met only at weddings or funerals. When Ben and John intervened, one brother was being pushed over backward in his chair. The other was shouting at him. Ben and John put their heads under the arms of the man on the ground, pulled him up, and turned him away from the other man. The sister-in-law, a large woman, marched through the crowd to take the other man roughly by the arm and lead him away. He went with her like a child, only throwing her arm off indignantly at a safe distance from the conflict.

In factory towns, when the six o'clock whistle blew, a new shift of guests would replace those who had left for work. At dusk, lamps were lit. Since Steve and Johanna were married on a Sunday, everybody stayed. Eating and drinking, dancing and singing went on all night and the next day, too. Since it was Sunday, Steve and Johanna tarried and did not leave until just before dark. Johanna thanked her mother for all her preparations and promised to come back to help clean up the next morning. "Are you crazy?" her mother asked. "Stay with Steve where you belong. Steve, if she shows up here tomorrow I slam the door in her face. She is yours now."

Steve and Johanna left the dancing with eighty-nine dollars in gifts—more than Steve might earn in a year, after paying his rent. The guests teased them as they parted. As they left, a ballad arose in the room behind them, about a great frost that froze a well, a white rose that grew under a window, a girl who cried, whose heart was breaking for no one would marry her because she was poor. "*Pod tym nasim obeneckom. . . .*"

Arriving at the room they would share for their first night, Steve lifted Johanna over the threshold. He kissed her and left her sitting on the bed. Then he went out back in the dusk and filled a pitcher with cool water from the pump (unlike Lattimer, Harwood had water). The handle squealed; the water gurgled and gushed. He liked the pleasant, restful sounds. He let the water cleanse his hands and threw fresh water on his face. He was anxious. He picked up the pitcher again and went back inside.

The bride and groom were given the right to be at home in one room of the family shanty for three or four hours. The young men whispered, laid their plans, and showed up not long after the couple had gone inside. They listened, laughed, and then suddenly whooped and hollered, throwing handfuls of rock and gravel in the air to fall like thunder on the roof. Then they ran away, laughing, some with arms around each other, back to the wedding celebration and the beer.

The day after a wedding, back in the mine, the men were surly, edgy, and slow. Work went badly.

The Last Days of August, 1897

THE STRIKE BEGINS AGAIN

ALTHOUGH the first phase of the strike of 1897 ended quietly by Monday, August 23, the first paychecks with deductions for the alien tax had been distributed on Saturday, August 21, to many grumbles and complaints. The explosion finally came on Wednesday, August 25, when late in the morning the young slate pickers at Coleraine marched off their jobs. One company official immediately tried to get hold of the superintendent, while another sent word for the men who worked outside on the strippings to take the place of the strikers so the breaker could remain in operation. While the men on the strippings were dropping their equipment and beginning to trudge in the brilliant sunshine toward the tall breaker, the foreman, a man named Smith, sent word that he had got the breaker boys to agree to go back on the job until Superintendent Roderick could come to hear their grievances.

The mood throughout the colliery was angry and, by a kind of spontaneous combustion, the reckless action of the breaker boys had ignited the other foreigners. Once in movement, the strippers took up the strike on their own and, instead of going to the breaker, marched in a body to the colliery offices, each man with a tool or a club in hand. In a romantic gesture, an unknown leader fixed a red kerchief to a tall pole and waved it aloft at their head. The mood was not romantic, however, but desperate, and those who refused to join the marchers were roughly handled. One Italian was beaten without mercy for refusing to go along. English driver boys were threatened if they didn't abandon their work. When the strikers got to speak to Superintendent Roderick, however, they were unable to articulate the source of their grievances. The superintendent was patient, recognized that they were among the least acculturated of the foreigners, and urged them to elect a committee to present their grievances fully the next morning. Meanwhile, he suggested kindly, they should finish their day's work. Docilely, they did so.

A sympathetic reporter from the *Daily Standard* put their case better than the poor strippers had: "The men are dissatisfied since receiving their pay on Saturday (August 21) when the alien tax was retained for the first time, and since the men could not intelligently state their object for striking, there is no doubt that it is due to the alien tax." At a meeting the night of August 25, he went on to report, the miners decided to call a general strike unless wages were raised to cover the tax. The strikers went around to awaken other men from their sleep to order them to be prepared to strike on the morrow.

A meeting with Superintendent Roderick on the next day, August 26, was unsatisfying. A number of men on their jobs, as well as many out of work, were talking strike. By the next day, the foreign miners at Coleraine assembled early in the morning and by seven composed themselves into "a strong and solid force" determined to halt all operations in the mine. Foreman Smith, Superintendent Roderick, and Officer Wersinger of the Coal and Iron Police tried to halt the advance of the Coleraine men, who were marching toward the breaker. The three officials were easily turned aside by the three to five hundred strikers. Inside, the slate pickers gave a loud cheer and poured out of the breaker to join the strike. From the breaker, the strikers headed for the colliery shops and swarmed past the protesting officials. They shut the shops, paused, and then marched toward Number Two slope. An Italian brakeman lowering two cars into the mines was ordered to halt. Perhaps not understanding, he continued to work. Menaced, he drew a knife. The crowd moved in on him on all sides, disarmed him, and beat him badly. Shouting and yelling, the men aimed next at the Evans colliery, a Van Wickle property about a mile distant. A few of the marchers shot pistols in the air. Several red kerchiefs bobbed on long poles. Nearly all the men were armed with clubs or iron bars. Successful at the Evans colliery, the men then marched toward Milnesville, hoping one by one to close all the Van Wickle works.

The mine managers tried feverishly to reach Mr. Van Wickle at his summer vacation spot on the New England coast. Finally they got through, and he talked with them for some time.

The Wilkes-Barre *Times* reported that "Three-hundred foreigners, very few English-speaking men" joined the daylong march. The Hazleton *Daily Standard* set the number of marchers at 500 and commented: "This is a strike in which the foreign element outnumber their English-speaking brethren three to one. For all this, however, the strike is a universal one among those paid by the day. . . ." The alien tax, of course, had been the catalyst, but the grievances were so many that one after the other they came tumbling out—the company stores, the company butchers, the company doctors, inhuman wages, lack of steady work. This time, the men were trying to arouse the miners of the whole region.

By 10:30 A.M., Friday, August 27, two weeks after the first outburst at Honey Brook, the citizens of Hazleton could see a cloud of dust rising in the still August air along the toll road. Soon the march that had begun in Coleraine and passed through Beaver Brook descended down Laurel Hill on to Broad Street in Hazleton, turned north on Cedar, and cut across to Wyoming Street on its way out of the city and on toward Milnesville. It was becoming a parade, a rally. Spirits were lighter now. One reporter described the marchers "yelling and shouting like baseball rooters when the score is tied in the thirteenth inning with two out and Kelly at bat." The men wore ordinary street clothes, although some had on their dusty black working clothes. The solid citizens came out to their storefronts and stood in their front doors. Some shared the excitement of the marchers. Some began to be afraid.

"The Hungarians and Italians are masters of the situation," wrote the Wilkes-Barre *Times* that evening, "and 2,000 men are idle pending the decision of the foreign element." In Milnesville that night, a large meeting of miners chaired by Patrick McHugh named Hugh Boyle, Fred Samier, Isaac Shaad, Bernard Gallagher, Andrew Coleman, John Bodman, Paul Gugliano, and Dominic Pompillo to present their demands to Superintendent Roderick in the morning: (1) to abolish the company store and company butcher and (2) to raise wages.

The Milnesville men said they would stand firm with the Coleraine men. Meanwhile, by 9:00 P.M., elements from the morning march got all the way out to Jeansville Number One breaker and compelled the men and boys to join the strike.

The next morning, Saturday, August 28, the company butcher making his rounds at Milnesville was greeted unceremoniously and driven out of town. Often the company butcher would drop off cuts of meat that families had not ordered, or deliver cuts in the wrong amounts or of the wrong types, and there was no way the miners could even be certain they were fairly charged. The butcher shop at Beaver Meadow had almost been ransacked by the marchers the day before, until the police prevented them. The Milnesville workers also placed obstructions on the train tracks so that the Pennsylvania coal engine arriving to pick up a string of loaded cars could not get to them.

At the moment that the butcher was making his getaway from Milnesville, Superintendent Roderick in Coleraine was being confronted by delegations from the Van Wickle collieries in Coleraine, Beaver Brook, and Milnesville. A sensible and kind man, he listened patiently and then tried to explain the Van Wickle policies. He suggested that the committee go with him to every other colliery in the area and compare wages. He said that if Mr. Van Wickle had to go any higher on wages, it would pay him to close down the collieries. He said he knew of no one who was ever fired for not trading in a company store. Then he added: "Of course, the employee who deals with the company store is sometimes given the preference in getting certain kinds of work, which does not seem unreasonable." Some of those present tried to tell him that miners who did not trade in the stores received their monthly statements with threatening X's in red ink on the line marked "store," but he smiled and discounted the threat.

The miners liked Roderick, but velvet glove or mailed fist, they always met with the same resistance. They left unhappy. Still, they reported back to him that a survey of all the other wage scales in the region would be conducted before their next meeting with him on August 30.

John Fahy had left the region the week before, but by August 27 had received no fewer than seven telegrams, one registered letter, and other communications requesting his presence at Coleraine, Beaver Meadow, Silver Brook, and other mining towns. The foreigners had at last begun to demand the formation of a union. The strikers at Honey Brook had watched ten days go by without any action whatever on the investigation of Gomer Jones. On August 28, alarmed by the news of a new strike, Assistant President Warren sent a telegram to Alex McMullen. He admitted that he had not acted on the grievances expressed in Manhattan but that he was coming and the men should trust his promises. But it was too late. The men no longer trusted him.

Sentiment in the region favored the miners. The businessmen of McAdoo, Bunker Hill, and Park View had several days earlier joined with the miners' grievance committee and had begun to prepare their own list of grievances "against the injudicious reign of Gomer Jones." If company stores were eliminated, independent businesses would prosper.

All day Sunday, August 29, miners in almost every town and hamlet were to be seen standing around in groups engaged in intense discussions. "Most of them," wrote the *Daily Standard*, "are willing to return to work and would probably do so were it not for the threats made by the foreigners." Superintendent Roderick told a reporter that no attempt would be made to resume operations on Monday, the thirtieth, but "if any English-speaking miners desired to return and would enter the pits, they would be afforded protection." A force of ten heavily armed watchmen was sent to guard the works at Coleraine and a similar force guarded Milnesville. "The English-speaking miners and those of the better and more law-abiding classes are anxious to return to work but are prevented and threatened by the others," said the Wilkes-Barre *Times*. "There was considerable drunkenness and quarrelling among the strikers at Milnesville yesterday (Sunday, August 29)."

Between one and two early on Monday, Hazleton police officers Dipple and Davis observed two men lurking near Superintendent Roderick's home on Cranberry Avenue; and two other men seemed to be standing watch down the street. As the officers approached, the men ran away in the night. The officers said they looked like Huns * and Italians. At the same hour the next night, the authorities used the cover of darkness to back a solitary Pennsy locomotive, heavily guarded by men with Winchesters, into the yards at Milnesville. The new engine pulled away the loaded cars that had been effectively blockaded on Saturday.

One striker at Coleraine pointed out to a reporter on Monday that the men might even accept company butchers who charged the same price as other merchants. After all, he said, the company wants us to equalize our wages with those paid by other companies, but does not make the company stores equalize their prices. If we meet competition, so should they.

On Tuesday, August 31, a large party of Coleraine strikers walked over to McAdoo to sit in on the meeting of the miners employed by the Lehigh and Wilkes-Barre Coal Company. A mass meeting was scheduled that night at McAdoo. Michalchik's Hall was once again overcrowded, and men lined the streets outside in the dusk. Assistant President Warren was due to arrive the next day and had requested a secret meeting with Alex McMullen and his committee. He wanted their total support in the coming negotiations.

The workers at Audenried joined the strike the next day, pending the word from Assistant President Warren. Over a thousand men gathered in the tiny town at 9:00 A.M., filling every street and alley. Assistant President Warren, superintendents Elmer Lawall and Gomer Jones, Chief Engineer Richards and the grievance committee met as at a court trial. John Bodan was there, with the crowbar Gomer Jones had used in assaulting him. It was impossible for reporters to get near the coal company office while the meeting was in process. By the time the tribunal broke for lunch, the crowd had swollen to two thousand.

Lunch lasted for two hours, and then the conference continued with a temporary adjournment at 8:00 P.M. Members of the committees who walked over to the crowd waiting in Michalchik's Hall had nothing to report. The mood of determination had hardened during the long and fruitless day.

* Local newspapers often used "Huns" instead of "Hunkies."

The Guns of Lattimer

Meanwhile, that very evening at the Central Hotel in Hazleton, the coal operators were holding a secret meeting. Reporters learned that 500 Winchesters had arrived in Hazleton and were now stored in the Coxe Company offices, and that 300 others were on their way to the A. Pardee and Company store. Although the Coal and Iron Police had been sent out to take up positions discreetly through the whole southern region over the last few days, the operators recognized the possibility that greater defensive measures might have to be taken. Sabotage, burnings, and other forms of destruction had been experienced in the past.

The operators were also disturbed by signs that the English-speaking miners were drifting ever closer to the foreigners in sympathy for the strike. The Hazleton *Evening Sentinel* quoted an Irishman: "Holy Mither! Is it meself that's quittin' fer the shallow-faced spaleens?"

Warren, Van Wickle, Coxe, Pardee, and Markle were going to have to make some important decisions in the next few days. First, one more card had to be played. Warren had another proposition to make at the next morning's session in Audenried. The month of August had ended inconclusively.

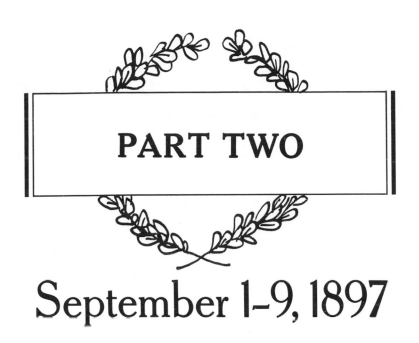

PART TWO

September 1–9, 1897

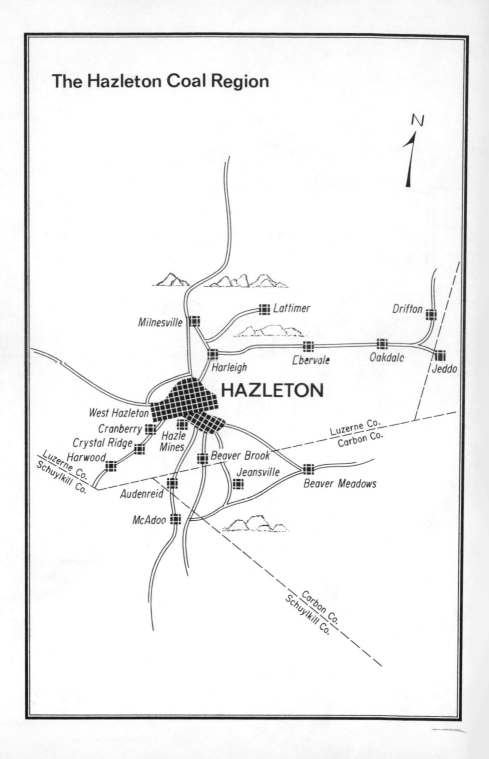

The Hazleton Coal Region

N

Milnesville
Lattimer
Drifton
Harleigh
Ebervale
Oakdale
Jeddo

HAZLETON

West Hazleton
Cranberry
Crystal Ridge
Hazle Mines
Harwood
Beaver Brook
Jeansville
Beaver Meadows
Audenreid
McAdoo

Luzerne Co.
Carbon Co.

Luzerne Co.
Schuylkill Co.

Carbon Co.
Schuylkill Co.

Wednesday, September 1, 1897

THE STRIKE VOTE

ON WEDNESDAY, September 1, only about a quarter of the miners who had jammed the streets and alleys of tiny Audenried the day before assembled outside the company offices. The rest walked to McAdoo, where they gathered in tiny buzzing knots. The men had come from outlying towns and closed down Dodson, Beaver Brook, Star, and Monarch along their way. Dressed in holiday clothes, their ranks swelled like an assembling army. Both Audenried and McAdoo had a festive air. The waiting strikers played horseshoes, cards, and fist-slapping hand games.

At 9:30 A.M., the grievance committee sat again. A few more witnesses were called in the case of Gomer Jones. Word was leaked that a report would be made to the men at McAdoo at 3:00 P.M.

Despite the heat of the day, Michalchik's Hall was packed to suffocation by two o'clock. A full complement of reporters was there, and the usual brace of interpreters to translate the proposition of the officials into the various languages. At the appointed hour, Mr. Warren appeared in the hall and spoke for the Lehigh and Wilkes-Barre Coal Company. The men heard his words in stunned silence. Stripping laborers who at present received less than a dollar a day would now be paid a dollar. Warren overcame his nervousness to read through the pay scales of neighboring companies, and said that Lehigh and Wilkes-

Barre could pay no more, but as the trade and price of coal improved, so would the wages accordingly. The company man tried to confine the discussion to technical details, as though he were presenting a financial report. On the question of the price charged to miners for coal, he said it cost the company $2.50 per ton to produce it, so at $2.50 the men were getting it at cost. Henceforth, all miners—not only some, as formerly—would be paid for props they brought for the mine. There was to be no compulsion about having a company doctor as the men had formerly thought.

Mr. Warren said he knew he was dealing with a fair crowd of men, but under no circumstances could the company he represented pay any more than neighboring companies or concerns. Then he came to the question requiring the greatest finesse. He promised fair and impartial treatment on the part of the bosses to all. The employees and the present superintendent—he did not mention the name Gomer Jones, only the office—would, in the course of time become more closely attached to each other and harmony would prevail. He tried to smile, as the interpreters stepped forward.

The men listened restlessly. The heat was unbearable; they were sweaty and uncomfortable. Fans were useless in air thick with body heat. A vote was deferred until evening. That night, knowing that other collieries had been raising their wages over the last few years while Lehigh and Wilkes-Barre had not, they were unhappy to a man. By a unanimous vote they decided to remain on strike until further concessions were made. "Among the foreign element," the Wilkes-Barre *Times* reporter wrote, "the feeling is very bitter."

On the other hand, up at Milnesville, Mr. Van Wickle was permitting Superintendent Roderick to raise the wages of the foreigners. At a meeting on the hill near the Mountain Scenery Hotel at 4:00 P.M., Roderick read a list of the new wage scales. First, a full day's work would be defined as ten hours. Second, the men would be paid for the hours they were at work, even if they were idled by a breakdown in the machinery. Previously, they had been docked for such delays. Third, although engineers, carpenters, firemen, and others in the higher skilled positions—the English-speaking workers—would not be affected, miners in the strippings would now be jumped to $1.50 per day; laborers first-class with a miner's certificate would receive $1.65; laborers second-class would jump from $1.35 to $1.52; laborers third-class from $1.15 to $1.36; laborers fourth-class (new men, for the first six months), $1.15; breaker boys and slate pickers, 80¢, 85¢, and 90¢; laborers in the strippings (as distinct from miners in the strippings), $1.10.

The men at Milnesville accepted these raises. But they suspected that the men at Coleraine would not accept them and extracted a promise from Superintendent Roderick that when the men from Coleraine marched to Milnesville to stop the works, the men at Milnesville would be given ample warning time to get out of harm's way. Superintendent Roderick went one step further. He promised to protect them.

The Milnesville men were right about Coleraine. The Coleraine men rejected the offer from Roderick. By nightfall, a full-fledged regionwide strike was formalized, with all of the Lehigh and Wilkes-Barre workers and the Coleraine workers of Van Wickle at its center. It seemed that their discontent might widen until the entire middle coalfield had been engulfed. Still, the foreign miners had never shown any real rebelliousness before, and some operators hoped that their discontent would come to nothing and dissolve.

Thursday, September 2, 1897

THE PEASANT UPRISING

EARLY on the morning of September 2, some fifteen hundred miners gathered in festive spirit at McAdoo and set off for Beaver Brook and Yorktown. The strikers carried red flags, clubs and iron bars, and "weapons of all descriptions," as the Wilkes-Barre *Times* put it. Alex McMullen and Thomas Duffy of the grievance committee were alarmed but could not contain the foreigners. "The peaceful miners and citizens along the route were terrorized." The newspaper went on: ". . . Thousands of ignorant foreigners have begun a reign of terror, having closed up all the collieries, wrecked the house of the Superintendent, and marched from one mine to another amid the wildest confusion, a howling mob without aim or leader. Riot and bloodshed is feared, property is expected to be destroyed, and it is very likely that the militia will be called out."

These words were written and published some thirty miles north of the troubles. What actually happened was that the fifteen hundred men who left McAdoo that morning picked up another fifteen hundred at Coleraine and elsewhere along the way and in somewhat rowdy fashion marched across the hills. The column was over a mile long; a cloud of dust along the road made them seem, from a distance, like a full division of an army. On their return, when they passed the house of Gomer Jones, about two thousand of them were still in the column. It was evening and, learning of their route, Jones and some armed friends slipped into the woods to watch. According to reports published later, the marchers stoned his house, breaking every window and door.

Now company officials in all the towns nearby began taking precautions, and the citizens of Hazleton and the outlying hamlets became genuinely alarmed. Andrew Bartosh [Bartoš], the breaker boss at Stockton Number Seven, spent the afternoons of September 1 and 2 at the top of the breaker watching for the column with binoculars. Mayor Altmiller of Hazleton issued a warning that the police and, if necessary, the citizens would prevent any marching through downtown Hazleton.

On the night of September 2, the marchers were tired but happy. Their clothes were covered with the fine dust of the roadways. Shoemakers were doing a brisk business. At least they, one paper was to comment, would benefit by the strike.

There was a meeting at McAdoo, and the most forceful speakers available were brought before the enthusiastic and cheering miners. The grievance committee to a man opposed the rising militance. Both Alex McMullen and Thomas Duffy warned the men against interfering with workmen at collieries where there were no apparent grievances. But control was slipping away from them. At 6:35 P.M., Duffy sent the following telegram to Elmer Lawall in Wilkes-Barre:

> If you can grant the advances that Van Wickle collieries have made we can meet you tomorrow at Audenried. If not, it would not be safe for us to meet you there. Answer quick.

At 8:00 P.M., Lawall dispatched an answer, which Duffy received while the meeting was in progress:

> Telegram arrived too late to confer with Mr. Warren. Will advise as soon as I hear from him.

Friday, September 3, 1897

THE FLOWER OF LOWER EUROPEAN CHIVALRY

EARLY enough for the sun still to be reflected off the morning dew, almost nine thousand men assembled at McAdoo. Sensing their power, the men were restive. The grievance committee was nervous: the naked human voice would hardly reach so vast a multitude. By 10:00 A.M., there had not yet been any word from Lawall.

But if unable to get word to the strikers, Lawall was at that very time talking to a reporter in Wilkes-Barre. "The English-speaking employees," he said, "are willing and anxious to return to work. But nothing can be done with the foreign element, which is in a majority."

The reporter asked: "Is it true that the strikers surrounded Superintendent Jones' house and smashed windows and doors?"

"No, they did not damage the house at all. They did surround it, however."

"If the strikers are bent on lawlessness, do you think the militia should be called out?"

"I am not in favor of this drastic course except as a last resort."

Then at 11:55, Lawall telegraphed Duffy:

Does the committee wish me to meet them and the men in a meeting at McAdoo, and when?

Duffy replied immediately:

If you cannot grant the advance that Mr. Van Wickle has made to his men, it will be unnecessary for us to meet you.

Lawall scribbled out an immediate rejoinder:

We can probably make same advances as Van Wickle has made if you allow us to have a similar store and butcher arrangement. Call me up on the telephone at 1:30 P.M.

Lawall seemed unaware that he had delayed too long. Even before these telegrams had been exchanged, the crowd at McAdoo had commenced marching. According to verbatim eyewitness accounts * of that September 3 gathering:

It was a spirited meeting full of Italian and Hungarian curses, threats and insinuations. . . . At 10:30 the expected message [from Lawall] had not arrived. . . . The committee reasoned, but to no avail, the miners were determined to give a demonstration. One burly Italian yelled at the top of his voice, "Whata da good of eighta da men to do'a the job? Too'a man'a! I'a kill a Lawall better alone, d' hell with him." And to demonstrate that he meant what he said he drew forth a good sized carving knife and flourished it in the air yelling "Vendetta!"

This burst of Italian eloquence tended to invigorate the crowd and whisperings as to whether the committee were in sympathy with the men caused the able body of eight to evaporate. The Italian continued the matter in hand, "We getta do move on, and closa up the district," he said.

This suggestion was hailed with a yell and the brandishing of . . . pokers, bats, fence pickets, and small saplings. The American flag was brought out, unfurled and saluted by the enthusiastic [shout] "America!"

The line of march was hastily laid out. Squads were detailed to round up deserters and to impress on the milder sympathizers that in unity there was strength. To arms! With a mighty cheer and a waving of clubs the column moved. Down the main street of McAdoo an army of one thousand marched, cheered on by the shouts of loyal women and children. The most affecting sight was at a house on the outskirts of McAdoo, where a Hun too tired to march sought seclusion in the cellar of his house. But the keen scent

* Quoted from Victor Greene, *The Slavic Community on Strike*, from the Wilkes-Barre *Times* (September 4).

of the round-up squad ferreted him out and he was assisted into line on the end of eight clubs applied to his person in none too gentle a manner. The scene was too affecting for his wife: she was assisted to her front yard and consoled by her sympathetic neighbors. There were many of these scenes along the line of march. The column moved on to Jeansville where a halt was called to give the "round-up squads" time to join ranks. Then with a cheer the army descended on No. 1 breaker. Down through strippings, over culm banks, through groves and over fields came the army of strikers like an avalanche.

Hark! the deep-toned whistle of the breaker announced the onslaught of the cavalcade and warned the working miners to defend themselves which they did by chasing out of the breaker and doing a hundred-yard dash over the adjacent hills. Hurrah! The breaker was won without a struggle, the enemy had fled. The Italians hooked a plank to the whistle leaving it blowing to announce the victory to the surrounding territory.

From the conquered breaker the army marched along the railroad track to Jeansville's main avenue. A halt was called and a discussion now arose as to whether it was best to march on to Hazleton.

Couriers were arriving with tales that the whole army of the United States and the militia of Pennsylvania were drawn up around Hazleton to protect the city from the approaching danger. This had little effect upon the body, but along the dusty highway, far away on the top of a distant hill was seen a speck. It was moving with the rapidity of lightning. Field glasses and all eyes were turned on it. There was a hush. 'Tis something important for no man would approach at such a killing pace if he had not news of the greatest importance. The Italian leader stood with bared head waiting.

The courier arrived. "Turn back!" he shouted. "Why?" asked the leader. "You know not the danger awaiting you," exclaimed the breathless arrival. "Tell us!" shouted a thousand throats, "Tell us!"

"Hark ye then! Not over two miles from here on the outskirts of the city of Hazleton now stand the police force." There was an awful suspense. Aye, the police headed by the gallant captain, stand four abreast . . . one wearing whiskers to defend the city.

The army trembled with fear. The whiskers were too much! The leader thought. He slowly raised his head and with a voice as steady as the earth on which he stood, exclaimed: "I gotta the right! I am a American citizen. I have my papers. They cannot stoppa us. Forward!" He pulled his naturalization papers from his pocket and waved them aloft.

The army revived. Enough! They were protected and with one throat the vast army yelled, "On to Hazleton!"

With a calm and determined step the miners marched on to Hazleton. It was a grand and glorious sight; fully three thousand five hundred strong. This noble array of lower European chivalry approached the beautiful city of Hazleton. There is a gradual descent from the mountain which enabled the citizens of the city of pits to observe the strength of the approaching foe.

Hazleton was in a fevered heat of excitement, the bolder of the inhabitants had gathered on the environs behind the resolute body of the police, four strong, whose stars glistened in the bright sun.

The captain of the police approached the strikers. They halted and he was heard to explain in resolute tones, "Why come ye here? Disperse ye agitators of the peace." The leader of the strikers with a voice equally as resolute as the captain's explained "Getta outa de way. We noa stoppa!"

The dismayed captain replied: "Disperse or I'll run ye in!"

"Ha, ha," laughed the leader of the strikers as he pulled papers from his pocket. "I am a Americano citizen. I a defia you. We a goa through your a city."

The captain seeing with what terrible power the leader of the strikers was armed suggested arbitration.

"Nita! Nita!" explained the leader. "We a go through the outskirts of the city to a Hazle Mine." The brave captain saw a chance to avoid conflict and suggested that he and his noble array of police accompany the strikers through the city so that they could not become lost in the various hiways and byways. The offer was accepted and the column again moved.

After the array had passed through the city it halted for the charge on the Hazle breaker. The ready telephone had got in its work, however, for as they broke from the city the deep-toned whistle announced the approach of danger and the breaker miners vacated within six seconds.

Victory! The strikers had again won the day. This was not all their laurels for soon after Cranberry and Hazle Brook followed the fate of No. 1 and Hazle breakers.

'Twas a grand stroke to march eleven miles and close up four breakers. Napoleon's greatest achievements were overshadowed. And as the setting sun cast its last ray over the distant mountain the grand army of striking Huns, Italians and Slavs marched to their homes to enjoy the calm and quiet peace after a day of war.

Saturday and Sunday, September 4 and 5, 1897

HOLIDAY WEEKEND

ON SATURDAY, the men of Silver Brook collected on the Phillipsburg baseball grounds and some two hundred of them joined a new chapter of the UMW. A grievance committee of eight—"Four Hungarians, two Italians, and two Americans" according to the *Daily Standard*—carried a list of grievances to the home of Superintendent Long. The men demanded: (1) an increase of fifteen cents per day for all employees; (2) the privilege of selecting and paying their own doctor; (3) pay for all the time they were kept at the colliery whether the machinery was out of order or not; (4) not to be compelled to deal with a company store or company butcher. Superintendent Long told them that unfortunately the president of the company, Dr. John Wentz, was away in Europe. He wasn't certain whether the vice president could make such a decision.

The men at Silver Brook then made plans to march to McAdoo for the Labor Day celebration, September 6. On the other hand, both Coleraine and Milnesville had their boiler fires and their water systems back in operation by Saturday. Roderick had once again proved both his skill with his men and his flexibility and got them back to work, on their terms. "Our men seem to be perfectly satisfied," Roderick told a reporter with evident pleasure. "There will positively be no compulsion to deal with the company store, nor will any intimidation be permitted by any of the subordinate officers of the company. The alien tax that was withheld last week will be repaid to the men next pay day." * One of Roderick's miners, B. W. Wilde, then summed up: "As to the company store and company butcher, the Superintendent has the right to continue the same, while at the same time the men have the privilege to deal where they desire."

At Lehigh and Wilkes-Barre, however, Elmer Lawall was

---

* It would be repaid because the Court had just ruled it unconstitutional.

not given such room to maneuver. The most his company would permit him was an offer to submit to arbitration. A ten-percent wage hike was a stiff jump for the owners to face. It is also likely that the backs of some owners were up. Many of the local newspapers declared the demands of the miners to be reasonable, pointed to their past record of quiet and docile work, and urged concessions for the sake of peace in the region—concessions, some of the editorials argued, that were long overdue. But looking at their balance sheets, some of the mine operators were in no mood to make a bad year worse, and they resented the thought of being coerced against their better judgment. They argued for a show of force against the strikers. The Huns, they said, were used to being dealt with by military force. "The Huns and the Ikes" as the phrase went, should see some metal.

The operators ordered the Coal and Iron Police * to show their Winchesters in the miners' hamlets. The gun that had been fired by one of the strikers on that first day seemed to the police reason enough to offer the Americans a little extra assurance and the foreigners a visible warning.

Meanwhile, so unconcerned was Sheriff James Martin about the strike that he had gone down to Atlantic City for his vacation. McAdoo and Audenried fell on the other side of the county line. They weren't his concern. Extending his long six-foot-four frame in the marvelous September sun, enjoying deep draughts of the salty ocean air, the sheriff had forgotten all about the troubles in the southern end of his jurisdiction. Sitting there in his broad-striped bathing suit, the sheriff was annoyed by a call to the desk to sign for a telegram. He unfolded it with annoyance and glanced at the name of his deputy, George Wall.

He swore violently.

The message was a request from Superintendent Lathrop of the Lehigh Valley Coal Company to return at once to Wilkes-Barre. The operators had decided to act, and a request from them was an order. Martin rubbed a hand on his beard and

* In 1897, although unpopular, the Coal and Iron Police were not yet a large or efficient force in Luzerne County. Their salaries were paid by the coal operators.

cursed again. He looked longingly out at the sands, the surf, the sky, and then sent back a telegram saying that he would come immediately. He enjoyed one last night in Atlantic City. On Sunday, September 5, he set out for Wilkes-Barre.

Sunday, September 5, 1897

BEN'S STORY

AS MORE and more men went on strike, Ben admitted to being afraid. He was a shy man, and he wanted to stay out of trouble. He had his eyes fixed on one goal only: to save enough money to go home. He was afraid that somehow he would violate some law he didn't know about and be thrown in jail or made to pay a fine. He had nightmares in which uniformed officers grabbed him violently by the arms and wrote something on official documents so that he could never hold a job. Then he was trapped in America, without any money or any means of earning any. Awakened from such nightmares, he had only one thing in all the world to rely upon: his physical strength, his ability to work.

He saw many feuds in the Slavic community. When they got drunk, some of the men got into violent fights. Sometimes, two men fought over the same woman; sometimes, over imagined insults. Now with the strike the tide of violence was rising. Men sometimes beat up other men in the name of the strike. Mike Cheslak told him about a miner's shanty being dynamited over in Beaver Brook.

In Harwood on Friday, some of the men began throwing stones at a rolling train. Ben was ashamed to remember, because he had thrown a stone, too. He felt that someone had seen him and that he would be punished. He had seen the hatred in the eyes of the constables who came through Harwood on days when there were funerals or weddings. One reason that he and John Eagler had acted as policemen at the Jurich wedding was to keep the constables out. In Europe, he had learned to hate the law.

Ben was afraid of the strike. There was no place to hide.

Ben, Steve Jurich, and his bride, Johanna, walked home from church. He liked to be with them. Johanna was tall and blond, with features like his sister. Her presence made him feel how much he missed being with a woman. Her body, her smile, her glances exuded a strange power that made him excited and happy. The love between Steve and Johanna warmed him. It made him feel closer to others but lonelier, too.

"Will you join the strike?" he asked Steve in Slovak.

"Of course. We must all join."

"You aren't afraid?"

Steve may have been talking bravely because of Johanna. She took his arm and pulled herself closer as he talked.

"What can they do to us?" Steve spat. "We work two, three days a week. In a strike, we will not work for two, three weeks. Then we work every day. We must go on strike."

Ben was silent. He didn't want to say he wished that there were no strike, that no one would bother him, that he could just concentrate on going from day to day.

"Now is good weather to strike," Steve laughed. "Now we can pick berries, make jelly, preserve tomatoes." He took a deep breath of air. Steve placed his hand over Johanna's arm, then raised his hand to her chin. "We have more time together." Johanna laughed and blushed.

In the presence of Steve, Ben felt timid. Steve was the one who should be afraid, with a new wife to support. Then he thought about the dollars Steve had collected at the wedding. Perhaps for a few weeks Steve and Johanna would not need a payday.

They were coming down the hill from Hazleton, passing Cranberry, when Steve pointed out a small white stucco cottage to Johanna. Behind the house was a well-formed grape arbor and two plum trees. Tall hollyhocks and sunflowers stood like sentinels inside the hedges.

"There," Steve whispered to Johanna. "Someday, I will build a house like that for you."

The days of early September were unusually splendid. It had

not rained for weeks and the dust in the roads was fine and deep. The air cracked with heat. The sky almost sang, it was so deep a blue. The dusty sumac and honeysuckle filled the air with smells; even the ragweed in the far fields danced in fragrant yellow bobbings.

Ben enjoyed being above the ground. Someday, he wanted a job outside the mines. He wished he were an American. His slowness in learning English discouraged him. He was ashamed how slow his progress was. His tongue and teeth were entirely untrained for English sounds. The languages of eastern Europe seemed so easy. In all the different languages, he could recognize sounds and similar words and the rhythm of the sentences. English was a language beyond his capacities. He felt doomed to a kind of half-life in America. If only he had been to school here or come as a little boy.

"Did you hear the story about O'Rourke?" Steve asked him. Both their thoughts had turned to America and money.

"No," Ben said, his heart distracted by vague and wordless yearnings.

"O'Rourke came to Hackensack," Steve began, putting on his storyteller's voice, knowing that he could impress Johanna with his knowledge of the world. "O'Rourke came to Hackensack and put up signs. Big white posters on the wall. 'Wanted: 300 Strong Men, Brave Men, Good Workers, To Become Rich in the Klondike. Fabulous Wealth. Mine Gold in Klondike.' O'Rourke held open meetings in the park. Three meetings. He spoke like an angel, describing conditions in which only the bravest could expect to succeed. He, O'Rourke, had already taken 1,000 men to the Klondike, and all had become rich. All had left him. He needed a new supply of men who wanted to be rich. Who were tired of working for others. Streets in Hackensack aren't paved with gold, he said, but in the Klondike . . . ah, in the Klondike! Gold lies almost on the surface of the earth. You touch the waiting earth with a pick, and there it lies. On this voyage, however, O'Rourke was sorry to say, there is a limit of 150 men. He would study all applications, and he would pick only the 150 fittest. He would tell them what to bring with them, and how to prepare. Then he would go to New York and bring the boat that would start them on their voyage to unimaginable wealth. A thousand men had already followed him. A thousand had become rich." Steve was enjoying his own tale and played O'Rourke with gusto.

"When did this happen?" Ben asked him.

"In June, I think. John Nemeth told me about it. Ask him." Steve was impatient to continue. "O'Rourke collected the applications. The next day he appeared again in the park and called out the names of 150 men. To each of them, he gave a piece of paper. From each of them, he collected six dollars. Six dollars is all it will take, he said, to pay the captain of the boat. He is now ready to sail. He is waiting for me right across the river, O'Rourke pointed to New York. At five o'clock in the morning, meet me at the Hackensack pier. Kiss your loved ones good-bye. Tell them you will not see them again until you are rich. The lucky men who received the white slips were congratulated by the unlucky ones, whose faces were long with envy. That night, there were many parties in Hackensack," Steve said, and glancing at Johanna, he added, "and the married men made happy love."

Johanna turned her face away and Steve, pleased, continued.

"Next morning at five o'clock, before the sun came up, the men began to appear. They carried their bundles of clothes. Some of the women were weeping. At five o'clock, there was no boat. As the sun came up, still no boat. The men grew restless and scanned the water. Only in the full light of daylight did they realize that there was no boat. That O'Rourke had disappeared with all their money. Nine hundred dollars."

Ben whistled.

"Oh, the poor men," Johanna said.

"The dirty son—" Ben exclaimed. But he felt a secret admiration, too. O'Rourke knew where there was gold, all right. He marvelled that some men could think to do such things and pretend so well for three full days. He wondered how many times, in how many places, O'Rourke had done such things.

"Think," Steve said with some excitement, "Think how many days you have to work to earn nine hundred dollars."

"Three years," Ben said.

Steve said: "Know what? Know what I heard? You know my cousin, Jurechek?" He asked more for Johanna's benefit than for Ben's. Johanna was from Audenried and didn't know the Harwood men. "When Jurechek was working down in Pottsville, he found a bag of gold along a stream outside the mine. He told the police, but no one claimed it, so he kept it. They say he left Pottsville because of the money. They say he has it hidden in his yard."

"A bag of gold?" Ben asked.

"A whole bag of gold."

"Why does he keep working?

"He is saving it. He wants to build a house. He has told no one."

"Do you really think it's true?" Johanna asked. She knew no one who had a bag of gold.

"They say it's true," Steve insisted.

For some reason, Ben suddenly remembered the three fat rabbits his mother used to keep outside the kitchen door, white, pink-eyed, lazy, mouths in motion. They received lush green blades of grass, chunks of bread, vegetables left from the kitchen table, and everything else by which the love of his mother could fatten them. It would be nice, he thought, to have a bag of gold.

Monday, September 6, 1897: Labor Day

THE LAW IS LAID DOWN FOR THE SHERIFF

ON LABOR DAY, September 6, Sheriff Martin did not call upon the local police chief in Wilkes-Barre, nor upon the mayor. He went directly into a meeting with superintendents Lathrop, Lawall, and Stearns (of the Cross Creek Coal Company). The coal companies had reached a joint decision. They had determined not to yield to the workers' demands. They were willing to pay for an armed force of deputies to supplement the Coal and Iron Police. They ordered Sheriff Martin to go down to Hazleton and call out a posse.

At the very hour when Sheriff Martin was meeting with the operators, thousands of miners were holding peaceful Labor Day marches throughout the coal region. More than three thousand miners assembled at Bunker Hill, bringing as many American flags as they could muster. The Slavonic Band and other bands came in uniform. Drums and brass echoed through the rolling hills. John Futa played his gleaming silver trumpet and sweltered in his bright, braided uniform. The parade wound through McAdoo, Audenried, Yorktown, and Beaver Brook and then back to Bunker Hill. The marchers covered ten miles in all. At Bunker Hill, John Fahy and other leaders addressed the throng. The men were quiet and orderly, their ranks punctuated by the colorful bands and drum corps, and a forest of American flags.

Meanwhile, however, Superintendent Lawall was talking simultaneously to Sheriff Martin, to the Wilkes-Barre *Times,* and to the grievance committee in McAdoo; and each was getting a different story. Possibly Lawall was only carrying out orders and at the same time trying, behind the scenes, to reach a peaceful settlement. It is also possible that Lawall was merely trying to build a record for his company of seeking negotiations— even as it was secretly putting up money for a posse. The reporter for the Wilkes-Barre *Times* was Lawall's conduit: "Whatever may be said concerning the strike in the Hazleton region, it cannot be justly claimed that Superintendent Elmer H. Lawall of the Lehigh & Wilkes-Barre Coal Company, is not making every effort to bring the strike to an end. He is certainly giving the strikers every opportunity of having the trouble arbitrated in a manner that will insure their being treated fairly and if the strike is not soon settled it will be, so far as the case can be impartially judged, because the strikers will not meet the officials half-way." The *Times* then reprinted the exchange of telegrams passed to it by Lawall, after he had dispatched Sheriff Martin to Hazleton to organize the posse.

WILKES-BARRE, PA. SEPT. 6, 1897.
What do you think of arbitrating all differences? E. H. LAWALL, Gen. Supt.

MC ADOO, PA. SEPT. 6, 1897.
It is useless for the committee to meet you unless you grant the same advances that Mr. Van Wickle has made. THOMAS DUFFY, Secretary.

WILKES-BARRE, PA. SEPT. 6, 1897.
If Van Wickle's terms are fair don't you think arbitrators would decide so? If arbitrators decide so there would be no alternative. You select an arbitrator, we select one, and let those two select a third. The arbitrators to be disinterested persons. Is not this a fair proposition? E. H. LAWALL, Gen. Supt.

MC ADOO, PA. SEPT. 6, 1897.
We refuse to arbitrate. If you cannot give the A. S. Van Wickle advance, committee will no longer exist. Answer at once. THOMAS DUFFY, Secretary.

WILKES-BARRE, PA. SEPT. 6, 1897.
Will refer to Mr. Warren your ultimatum with regard to arbitration and will advise as soon as I hear from him. E. H. LAWALL, Gen. Supt.

While the Wilkes-Barre *Times* seemed to side with the operators, the Hazleton *Daily Standard* consistently saw justice on the side of the laborers.

There is no good reason why the Lehigh & Wilkes-Barre officials or even the Lehigh Valley Coal Company officials should not pay the same rate of wages as A. S. Van Wickle; they are in a position to do it and ought to. Obstinacy on their part is not creditable. If there is to be an average rate of wages let all the operators join the combination and pay it. The obstinacy of either one company or the other is simply injurious to the community, and for the benefit of all, we suggest that the operators at least meet the men half-way, and the trouble will soon be a thing of the past.

While the miners were enjoying the parades and holiday celebrations—both Sunday and Monday proved to be peaceful days throughout the region—and while the operators were establishing a new course of action leading toward a showdown, Sheriff Martin had his guard up. He took George S. Ferris, his lawyer, with him on the train ride up to Hazleton. The sheriff was annoyed about losing his holiday at the beach for what seemed like damn-fool reasons. The two men diagnosed the various pressures on them and sorted out their options. The sheriff smelled a trap and so did Ferris.

On their arrival in Hazleton, Martin and Ferris went directly into a conference with Mr. Zerby, assistant superintendent of the Lehigh Valley Coal Company. They did not go to Mayor Altmiller, or to the Hazleton chief of police, or to any of the local justices. This neglect suggests either deviousness or uncertainty. For one thing, if a posse had to be called, there was no clear provision in law about how it should be paid for. The county might be obliged to pay, but if not, the sheriff might have to meet the posse's expenses out of his own pocket. So one of Martin's first objectives was to get clear about the operator's commitment to pay salaries and costs. Ferris said he would handle that end of things so that the sheriff could know as little about it as possible. The two men's objective was to assess with great care just what the coal operators wanted and to be certain that there was no misunderstanding among the different levels of officials in New York, Wilkes-Barre, and Hazleton. In their conversation with Zerby and then with Ario Pardee Platt, the manager of the Pardee company store—who had been named for his uncle, Ario Pardee—they got the message loud and clear: the owners wanted the strike broken and operations resumed. How the sheriff accomplished this was up to him. They had put him in office and they would hold him responsible.

Martin and Ferris went over the legal background. The riot act of 1860 allowed the sheriff to declare a state of disorder, constituted by a riot or a threat of riot that injured life or property. The text of the riot act would be given to the newspapers. The sheriff would proclaim a state of disorder, permitting him to organize a *posse comitatus*. There were scores of men in Hazleton who owed their living, directly or indirectly, to the coal interests; emotions about the strike were running at a high pitch; so the recruitment of able and enthusiastic men for the posse would not be difficult. In fact, by drawing on the most respectable citizens of the city, the posse might carry a large segment of public opinion with it. The operators recommended three assistants for Martin, including Thomas Hall as chief deputy. Hall ran the blasting company in Hazleton and thus had direct interests in mining operations. The owners had already seen to it that multiple-shot Winchesters were gathered under Mr. Platt's direction at two warehouses, at G. B. Markle and Company and at A. Pardee and Company.

Before they had left Wilkes-Barre, Martin and Ferris had drafted a sample proclamation. They released it to the Wilkes-Barre *Times* before the sheriff had even set foot in the strike area. And somehow, despite the fact that it was a holiday, the sheriff and his lawyer also got the proclamation to a printer, ready for posting on trees and buildings.

Ferris was satisfied with the legalities so far. But the next step was crucial. He and Martin met with Sheriff John Scott of Schuylkill County and Sheriff Milton Setzer of Carbon County and persuaded them to issue similar proclamations.

Ferris worried that the center of the strike lay in McAdoo, over the county line. The owners could have shifted the burden to Sheriff Scott if they had wished. But their own interests and power lay almost solely in Luzerne County. They had control over politics in Luzerne County but not in Schuylkill. Sheriff Martin was their man. Ferris didn't want his client to become their fall guy. He warned Martin to be careful.

Someone had already begun to notify a hundred influential men in the area; by early evening, eighty-seven of them had gathered on Broad Street at the Hazleton Machinery Supply Store. Many were professional men. All earned their living directly or indirectly from coal. All but one bore English, Irish, or German surnames. The Lehigh Traction Company had supplied a special trolley car for swift movement and the railroad company also held a train in readiness.

Sheriff Martin looked over the eighty-seven faces in the machine shop on Broad Street. Cream of the cream, he thought; churchgoers to boot. Ferris felt that the company of such men would surely protect Martin. Martin in a ritual way asked them if they were citizens and swore them in as deputies.

The new rifles, still wet with packing oil, were handed out, as were heavy-shelled bullets and buckshot. The heavy shells were three inches long and could blast through metal. The buckshot shredded bone as well as tissue. The sheriff warned the men, most of whom were unfamiliar with such weapons, that at some point their lives might be in danger; only in that case would they have to use the weapons. A certain amount of joking followed.

The owners seemed to have recognized very early the key to later developments. The two breakers at Lattimer Mines lay north of Hazleton, away from the active strike zone to the south. If Lattimer was closed, the whole Pardee operation was closed. If on the other hand Lattimer Mines stayed open, the operators had a base from which to begin the reopening of other mines. Calvin Pardee, the owner immediately involved, may have drawn the line at Lattimer Mines.

Among the operators, the Pardees were particularly tough. They prided themselves on having built Hazleton almost from nothing and having dramatically improved the economic standing of thousands of families in the region. They believed that for over fifty years they had had the good of the region in mind. Unlike the Markles and Van Wickles, however, they were no longer much on the immediate scene. Throughout the turbulence, Calvin Pardee was to remain at his home in Germantown, just outside Philadelphia. Philadelphia moneymen, like the Philadelphia newspapers, seemed unanimously opposed to laborers and foreigners. The only representatives of the family who were to be around—the young Calvin Pardee, Jr., and Ario Pardee Platt—became active members of the posse.

According to the riot law of 1860, there needed to be conditions of riot, and indeed specific and flagrant acts of riot, to justify the summoning of a posse. At the time that his proclamation was given to the newspapers on Labor Day, Sheriff Martin had neither visited the scene at first hand nor conferred with other officers of the law. His only information about the situation had come through the coal operators. Besides, on Sunday and Monday, the very days he had traveled from Atlantic City to Hazleton, what was going on in the region was not a riot but the celebration of a holiday.

James Martin had an easy confidence in his ability to pull things off. He was aware that people liked him, and he had a feeling he could talk the miners out of their disruptions. He could feel his adrenalin pumping as he pictured himself single-handedly persuading workers to be good fellows and call off their marching.

That night before retiring he read once more the proclamation that would be posted all over the region beginning the next day, after Sheriff Scott and Sheriff Setzer had joined him in announcing it. He relished the cautious language Ferris had insisted on writing into it:

It having come to my knowledge that a certain condition of turbulence and disorder exists in the neighborhood of the city of Hazleton in the county of Luzerne, by reason of which acts of disorder are said to have been committed, and men forcibly prevented from pursuing their daily avocations, and the peace of the com munity seriously disturbed:

Now, therefore, notice is hereby given to all good citizens to refrain from tumultuous and unlawful assembly and from all acts of disorder or violence, and from all acts interfering with the liberty of other citizens, or tending to a breach of the peace.

Notice is further given that all such acts of disorder and lawlessness will be summarily repressed and punished in accordance with the laws of the land.

James Martin
High Sheriff of Luzerne County

He especially liked the phrase: "James Martin, High Sheriff."

Monday, September 6, 1897, Evening

BEN'S STORY: THE UMW COMES TO HARWOOD

CROSSING Pennsylvania from the west along the new Interstate 80 just north of Hazleton, the contemporary traveler sees lovely hills shrouded in various degrees of mist. At dusk early in September, the farthest ranges look palest and the closer ones, shouldering each other into the background, look darker and clearer. Turning south on Interstate 81, the traveler seems to be cutting deeper into the mountains and finally begins the steep ascent toward Hazleton, like a medieval city built on the top of a great hill. This stunning hill rises sheerly from the luxuriant farm country to the west. The panorama of different-colored fields, clumps of trees, and lazy columns of smoke eases the soul, restful amid spaciousness and majesty. Whoever owns Hazleton presides over an especially beautiful and ample corner of the world. From the brow of the hill, which the interstate highway cuts, the driver of an automobile today then passes through the outermost growth of West Hazleton. Eastward from that brow in 1897, one would have seen a gently sloping dip of trees and fields, and on the farther upward side, just below the steeples and towers of Hazleton, a few cottages and houses. To the south, a deep valley cuts off Hazleton, so that the city in its high splendor presided over the south as the quiet woods presided over the west. The new four lanes of Interstate 81 cut off the west tip of Harwood where today, to one's right, one can see three abandoned, dilapidated company houses. Traffic moves too fast for one to catch, to the left, more than a glimpse of the modern patch that has replaced the Harwood of eighty years ago.

Only with difficulty today does a driver, leaving the interstate highway, find the entrance into Harwood. The oldest part of the still poor mining town has been "modernized" more than once, but the old structures are discernible beneath the aluminum siding, the remodelling, and the improvements. The company store is now a two-family dwelling. Old Street is still as narrow as it was, although no railroad track now cuts through the center of the street. The breaker that once rose to the west was torn down. The modern residents, mostly descendants of the older residents, are likely to be sitting out on the porches, or fussing over the thick gardens behind their houses. The picnic grounds below Old Street are still discernible, but thick underbrush has grown over the bare spots left by the strip-mining of a generation ago and the mining pits of the preceding two generations. Culm banks from as far back as eighty years ago are not wholly covered by foliage.

Old Street in Harwood lies over the side of a hill, hidden from the newer Main Street. To get to Hazleton from Harwood, oldtimers would have walked up a black, hard-packed road to the stripping above town, then down over the hill on the other side into a valley, and then up the steep slope to West Hazleton. The distance from Harwood to the city on the hill— its forest of spires and towers against the sky making it seem like a fortress—is two miles. Across the valley, it looks much closer, almost as though one could throw a stone and reach it.

Descending from Harwood, one sees to the right, off the main route, an even poorer town, Crystal Ridge. In 1897, the main road from Harwood by-passed Crystal Ridge, which is today surrounded by culm banks and slag heaps. Rusty rails follow the valley from Harwood to Crystal Ridge, however; there was a back route between the two villages.

After the turnoff to Crystal Ridge, the direct road passed Cranberry, today a village of ten crosshatched streets, four streets deep. The narrow road then ascends very steeply into West Hazleton. On a hot day, with the sun beating on one's head and back from the south, the climb is a hard one. From above, marchers from Harwood can be clearly seen, today as eighty years ago, as they toil upward on the steep hill. The old Hazle Mine used to lie on the side of the hill. The trolley line of that time ended near the mine. From the trolley, the shortest route to the Cranberry road was up over the ash and slag of a culm bank.

On the night of September 6, 1897, after the Labor Day parades and picnics in Harwood, the men of the village gathered at the schoolhouse. John Eagler, although one of the youngest men, sat at the table in front. John Futa and Steve Jurich clowned at the tiny school desks. Most of the men had had only three or four years of schooling. In Slovakia, more years than that were seldom permitted and the Magyar laws demanding that further schooling be conducted in Magyar were fiercely resisted. Nearly a hundred persons had been put in jail in Eastern Slovakia for using the Slovak language in public functions. It had been a long time since many of the men in the room had sat in a classroom.

Ben Sakmar felt both excitement and dread. The Harwood colliery was still in operation. A few of the men from Harwood had taken part in one or another march over at McAdoo, but most had not. They were still being cautious—keeping their eye above all else upon their livelihood.

There was at least one of Sheriff Martin's proclamations posted in the village, near the company store and mining company office at the eastern edge of Old Street. Most of the men could not read it, and like other notices from the outside world, it seemed of no concern to them.

Cautious as the men had been, the decision taken at the meeting of September 6 was to go on strike the next morning. Then they agreed to reassemble at the school house at 3:00 P.M. next afternoon to hear John Fahy and have him sign up the Harwood men for a new chapter of the UMW.

Ben thought long about surrendering thirty cents to pay union dues. He believed he should go along with the others, but he wished they had decided there was no need for the union. Thirty cents represented a third of a day's work, and many weeks this summer he had earned only three dollars. He was far behind in his target for savings for the year. He had allowed himself almost nothing and still had saved only one hundred dollars.

During the long meeting, Mike Cheslak had let him have the Hazleton newspaper someone had brought to the meeting. Ben tried to form the English words with his lips. To read in Slovak was a struggle for someone with only four years of schooling, but at least he knew the sounds and could, if slowly, get the full meaning. His greatest comfort lay in reading from the prayer book he had inherited from his father. It was thumbed and already brown at the edges, but rich in sounds and phrases he knew by heart. The sight of the full page of English newsprint depressed him.

And the next day at 3:00 P.M., his heart pulsed with envy as he watched the handsome young John Fahy speak with poise in smooth English words. He did recognize a few words like "strike" and a few proper names like "Pardee" and "Sheriff Martin." St. Martin was a patron saint of a famous Slovak city, so Ben wondered idly if Martin were a Slovak name. He admired John Eagler tremendously, for the tall blond youth stepped in each time Fahy completed a few sentences to render the words into Slovak. It seemed to Ben that there was almost a glow around the two young men, who seemed to be so much in charge and to know so clearly what they were doing.

Fahy warned the men crowded in the small schoolhouse not to carry weapons, not in any way to arouse the authorities. Fahy stressed their right to conduct themselves peacefully. They had rights, he said, to peaceful assembly, and even to peaceful marches. But they must not be violent or even seem to be violent. He explained that the sheriff could arrest anyone who was violent; as long as they were peaceful they had a right to march in public places. But the most important thing for him was not to march; it was to build a strong union. Then their officers could talk to the owners as equals, and could negotiate with all the owners at once. Then there would be equity in all the mining companies. Fahy praised the capitalist system and said that there was room in it for both capital and labor. Each must work together in fairness; both capital and labor needed each other.

The men felt some resentment toward the owners and particularly toward the police, but they understood the need for order and they agreed with the wisdom of Fahy's words. Fahy told them that he already had enrolled eight thousand miners in the region in the UMW and that they were no longer alone. Afterward, the vote was unanimous for forming a union. Fahy had Eagler, Joseph Michalko, and Andro Sivar take down the names of each man who came forward to pay his dues.

When Ben Sakmar approached the table to give his name and to part with his thirty cents, he felt as self-conscious as he did when he walked forward in church to receive Holy Communion. He was ashamed of being no more than a peasant and a lowly miner's assistant, third-class, and hoped that he didn't seem too clumsy. John Eagler was busy with his new duties but thanked Ben for joining.

Once enrolled, all the members voted in the first four officers of their chapter. When Fahy left them to rush off to another meeting, many shook his hand, avoiding his clear blue eyes, mumbling in Slovak or broken English. The feeling of satisfaction among the men was intermingled with anxiety about the future. All of them were living on the margin of survival, and when they went outside they could see with their own eyes the stick fences and flimsy wooden shacks in which they lived, and the fine dust blowing along Old Street. The breaker stood silent.

Tuesday, September 7, 1897

THE STRIKE RESUMES IN EARNEST

AT 7:40 A.M. in Pottsville, a posse of fifty men led by Sheriff Alexander Scott and deputies Smith and Bedell settled back in their seats for the short train trip up to McAdoo. Sheriff Scott had begun the process of recruiting a posse at 10:00 P.M. the evening before. Every hardware store in town was cleaned out of revolvers, each man in the posse being supplied one. Each deputy was also given train fare and the promise of two dollars for every day's work.

The day before, after meeting with sheriffs Martin and Setzer, Sheriff Scott had issued a guarded proclamation fulfilling his obligation to "admonish and warn all persons to avoid and keep aloof from any unlawful assemblage and refrain from any and all acts of violence." He did not declare a state of disorder. Sheriff Milton Setzer of Carbon County merely repeated Sheriff Martin's proclamation verbatim. While Sheriff Scott and his men were journeying to join him in McAdoo, Sheriff Martin told the reporter of the Pottsville *Republican* "that it is his intention to prevent interference with the workingmen employed at any of the mines in Luzerne County. . . ."

In McAdoo, Sheriff Scott told his deputies to wait at the train depot while he and Deputy Smith, accompanied by Coal and Iron Police officer Sam Synn, walked over to meet the other sheriffs. Three thousand miners from every section for miles around had begun to assemble here, according to the *Republican*, carrying provisions of cooked chicken. Although he saw none, the reporter heard rumors that the miners had revolvers and that they intended to march the full thirty-five miles to Wilkes-Barre.

John Fahy tried to dissuade the men from marching but he failed. When the line of march at last reached the point where all the armed deputies were standing, the sheriffs issued a command to halt, Sheriff Scott reading the proclamation ordering the strikers to disperse. Fahy, from the side of the column now, explained the legal power of the sheriffs, and awed by the forest of Winchesters, the men submitted. The Pottsville *Republican* concluded: "In view of the fact that the strikers have no intelligent leaders, it is not known what their next step will be. The authorities will not leave the scene until they are assured all danger of an outbreak is over."

By the end of the morning, Sheriff Scott and his men were on the train back to Pottsville. The sheriff complained to a reporter about being called out in such unpleasant heat. He was also out one hundred dollars, he said, since he had to pay the costs. In Hazleton, Sheriff Martin spent the afternoon at the bicycle races. The collieries in Jeansville, Beaver Brook, and the Coxe collieries were all working.

For the rest of the day there were only a few scattered incidents. A contingent of marchers approached Ebervale, and a committee went to meet Superintendent John G. Scott, who happened to be the brother of Sheriff Scott, to demand that he draw the fires in the boiler house. Instead of drawing the fires, the superintendent drew his revolver. Three members of the committee also pulled out pistols. In the standoff, both sides retreated. A few moments later, a hail of stones bombarded the superintendent's office. No one was hurt, but windows were broken. At 3:00 P.M., whistles blew in Hazleton to summon the deputies to Ebervale, but by the time some of them arrived, like a volunteer fire company, the strikers had gone.

A quite separate crowd of strikers also marched through Lattimer Mines that Tuesday. Deputy sheriffs were waiting for them with Winchesters ready. The marchers shouted, waved sticks and clubs, and hurried through the main street. The colliery continued operations. The appearance of the strikers during the school day frightened many of the women at Lattimer Mines. It was the first time that the village had seen strikers. One can only surmise what Big Mary Septak thought when she saw the strikers come and looked at the line of Winchesters.

That night, there was another "monster meeting" at Michalchik's Hall in McAdoo. Women and children were milling around. The men felt bold and strong. It was resolved to continue to strike, to resume marching the next day, and to assert that the presence of the armed deputies was not necessary, because the strikers "have not up to this time, nor do they intend to commit, any overt act." The men were determined to keep up the excitement and to gain new recruits. Not surprisingly, the news that so many collieries were working again "was not received with much favor." After the meeting the strikers went peacefully to their homes.

Wednesday, September 8, 1897

SHERIFF MARTIN'S SUCCESS

FOR THE FIRST TIME, many English-speaking miners joined the foreigners assembled for the day's march. The crowds came from all directions over the hills, into McAdoo, refreshed by the long rest of the day before. Nearly every man carried a club. Women and children followed on their heels, applauding them as they lined up. The leader said "Forward march" and a cheer went up. First they went to Jeansville, stopped the colliery, and peacefully persuaded all the workers there to join them. At Coleraine, they ordered the men to throw down their tools, thus swelling their ranks to fifteen hundred. Here one group split off for Hazleton and Cranberry, while the main body then closed down the colliery of Evans and Company.

The night before Sheriff Martin had gone home to Wilkes-Barre as usual. He arrived back in Hazleton in the morning to find his deputies rushing back and forth over the region as one colliery after another telephoned to announce the arrival of incoming marchers. Like many of the other deputies, George Treible was on the squat and heavy side; moving around under the hot September sun was more than he was used to. This was the second full day the posse had been on call, but already the men were weary of the dust, the sweat, the hurry. Light oil from their rifle barrels stained their fingers, and some wished they had time for target practice so they'd know better how to handle the weapons assigned to them.

Just after 1:00 P.M., a breathless miner reached Hazleton with the news that the strikers were coming down the Beaver Brook turnpike. Rumors had swept the city all morning so Police Chief Fuller quickly led a force of constables toward the south end of Broad Street. To his chagrin, he saw Sheriff Martin and Officer Trescott of the Coal and Iron Police already on the spot. On that side of the city line, the sheriff had jurisdiction.

During the time it took for the long column of hot and sweaty miners, surrounded by a great wreath of yellow dust, to come into earshot, Sheriff Martin twisted his moustache patiently. Then he strode forward with uplifted hand to make the men stop. The sheriff read from his proclamation. Most of those who could hear his deep, commanding voice could not understand English. Many were uncertain who he was. He wore no uniform. They could see that he wore a pistol and that his companion carried a Winchester rifle. The sheriff shouted that parading through the city was prohibited. They should go home.

Some of the men walked off into the woods. The main body cut across country toward Cranberry. The sheriff and Officer Trescott walked along behind the straggling column to keep watch. He had long since shrewdly ordered the main body of deputies to Cranberry.

As the men skirted the southern valley below Hazleton, the sheriff nudged Officer Trescott and the two of them hurried to gain the head of the line. He saw the line of deputies with ready Winchesters up ahead. About fifty yards from the Cranberry breaker, the sheriff raised his hand for the strikers to halt and again told them to disperse. The men in the line grumbled, then slowly turned and retreated along the railroad track back toward McAdoo. The sheriff watched them disappear into the distance. Twice in one day he had, virtually alone, dispersed four hundred strikers.

"The situation at Cranberry looked serious for a time," he could read when he got back to Wilkes-Barre for the night, "but the armed deputies used good judgment and thus prevented what might have resulted in bloodshed."

At 3:00 P.M., Gomer Jones anxiously telephoned Sheriff Scott in Pottsville; the main body of strikers had appeared in Audenried and had physically prevented the firemen at colliery Number Four from keeping up the fires under the boilers. The fires had gone out and the power was off. Superintendent Jones insisted angrily that Sheriff Scott come with his posse immediately. Sheriff Scott refused to bring a posse unless some arrangement were made to pay for it. He'd be damned if he'd pay it out of his own pocket again. He pointed out that the Lehigh and Wilkes-Barre Company was calling for help and ought to pay for it. On top of the money, he was irritated because he and his men had lost a whole night's sleep the day before over what turned out to be less than an emergency.

The strikers were taking heart. As many as ten, perhaps fifteen, thousand of them were now out, even though some of the collieries they managed to close were able to open the next day, since so many men were desperate for work. September 8 had been the best day so far. Indeed, the strikers were certain that but for the deputies all around, they would win. Sheriff Martin had not been well known in the region until now, but he was getting to be a most unpopular figure. The Schuylkill *Republican* ran an article headed "SHERIFF MARTIN'S UNPOPULARITY" and subheaded: "His Antipathy for the Foreign Element is No Secret." The story read: "Whether deserved or not, Sheriff Martin of Luzerne County, it is alleged, entertains a unconquerable hatred for the foreign element. It is said he made no secret of his feelings toward these men. . . ." The story spoke of many reports in circulation at the time, and cited one occasion on which the sheriff reportedly stated that "a little cold lead" is the only way to halt these strikers. These stories probably originated among Sheriff Scott's men, who met Sheriff Martin in McAdoo on September 7.

In actual practice, Sheriff Martin seemed to have taken a moderate and cautious approach to the strikers. Whenever possible, he approached alone and kept his deputies in the background. He did not bully; he did not let his men get rough. In fact, he felt called on to defend his moderation in a report to Frank Pardee. "While the strikers simply confine themselves to talking to the men quietly and persuading them to quit," he wrote, "it is none of my business and I have no right to interfere."

At night, a telegram addressed to Thomas Duffy in McAdoo from Superintendent Elmer H. Lawall in Hazleton brought good news: the company had agreed to another across-the-board 10¢ per day raise for the stripping laborers, bringing the total to $1.10 a day. Mr. Warren had also agreed to settle the other differences directly with the committee. Mr. Lawall would meet with Duffy and his committee at 11:00 A.M. on September 9. At McAdoo there was jubilation. Lehigh and Wilkes-Barre had now come up to the level of the other collieries. Added to the 10¢ raise granted a week earlier, this concession marked the second small victory in two weeks.

Thursday, September 9, 1897

THE OPERATORS STIFFEN

CHEERED by the telegram from Lehigh and Wilkes-Barre and the prospect of meeting later that morning, the strikers in McAdoo cancelled the marches planned for Thursday. Thousands lined up outside the train depot, waiting for the appearance of Lawall. The sun moved slowly in the cloudless sky toward its midmorning height. The children, barefoot, flashed their bronzed legs as they ran about in various games; some looked almost black from the sun. Barefoot women spoke a Babel of languages.

Meanwhile, however, at the Coxe and Company colliery in

Beaver Meadow, some of the men had declared a strike and were just forming a circle around the colliery when Sheriff Martin and his deputies turned up on a trolley car. The deputies in Beaver Meadow were in a sour mood. Then Sheriff Setzer arrived with his deputies and joined Sheriff Martin's men in trying to drive the strikers from the breaker. When they couldn't get the men to disperse quickly enough, Sheriff Martin ordered some of his men to fire a volley over the strikers' heads. The explosion of gunfire echoed and reechoed through the breaker. No one was hurt. The men dispersed. For the strikers, this was their first, unanticipated experience of gunfire.

For Sheriff Martin's men, it was the first firing of their guns. The shots seemed to shock the shooters as much as the strikers. The men were moving back slowly. Was this a new policy? Did Sheriff Martin have orders to raise the level of resistance? Or was he merely trying to release some of the tensions among his men? Most of the deputies were men in their forties and fifties. Many had desk jobs and were unaccustomed to the physical exertions of the last two days. They were sick of getting up so early. They had begun to loathe the strikers for causing them discomfort and frustration. Under the daily searing sun, the strike seemed endless, like trying to plug a sieve with ten fingers. As soon as a posse turned up in one place, trouble broke out at another. Even with lemonade from home, and sandwiches, and the easy ride in the trolley, they grew weary of sitting, sweating, and wiping the dust from their beards and moustaches. "Tantalizing, dictatorial, domineering, unnecessary, brutal language was used toward the strikers," reported the Pottsville *Republican*.

And when the eleven o'clock train pulled into McAdoo, with much whooshing and squealing of wheels, Lawall was not on it. A man came running from the telegraph office, with a telegram, explaining that Lawall had been unavoidably delayed and that he could not definitely state when he would meet the committee.

The more cynical among the strikers believed that the companies had deliberately tricked them to gain a day of peace. A few others speculated that Lawall was himself having trouble with the owners. At least one of the owners did seem to have taken matters into his own hands. Calvin Pardee, Jr., joined the deputies under Sheriff Martin; his father remained behind, watchful, in Philadelphia. Soundings may have been made with state authorities whether people who believed in law and order would stand behind the sheriff, in case trouble broke out.

On the evening of September 9, an Italian miner walked from Lattimer Mines around the south end of Hazleton and across to Harwood, a distance of almost six miles. The men at Harwood were holding another meeting of their own that night. Their new officers, John Michalko, John Eagler, and Andrej Sivar were presiding. They heard out the stranger, who said his fellows at Lattimer Mines wanted to join the strike. If someone would march over and give them help, they would join the strikers. Like Harwood, Lattimer was also a Pardee colliery; between them, 2,257 men worked for Pardee. The first major act of the new UMW local at Harwood might be to go answer the request of their brothers from Lattimer. No concessions could be expected from the Pardee company unless both Lattimer and Harwood were shut down.

Most of the men in Harwood did not know Sheriff Martin by sight. They had not yet encountered the deputies. They knew that if they carried the American flag, and if they were nonviolent, they had the rights of all citizens in America, even if more than half of them were still foreign subjects. They were instructed that night to bring no clubs or weapons of any kind. They were told that they had the right to peaceful assembly, so long as they marched without disruption. John Eagler sent word to Alex McMullen at McAdoo, requesting assistance. They planned to assemble in the morning, and to decide then whether to send a small delegation or to march en masse.

John Eagler, Steve Jurich, John Futa, and the other young men were excited that evening. They might be taking part in their first major action, like the hundreds of others that had taken place at every mine in the region during the nearly four weeks that had passed since the first strike at Audenried.

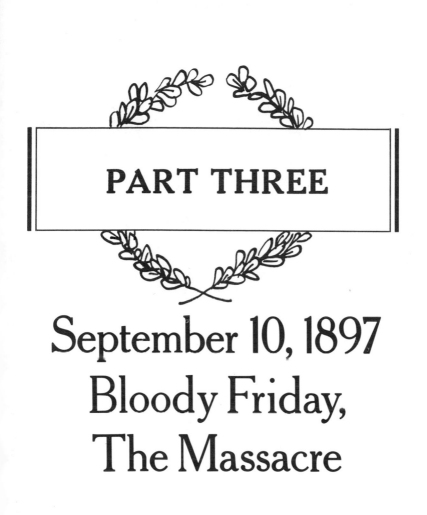

PART THREE

September 10, 1897
Bloody Friday,
The Massacre

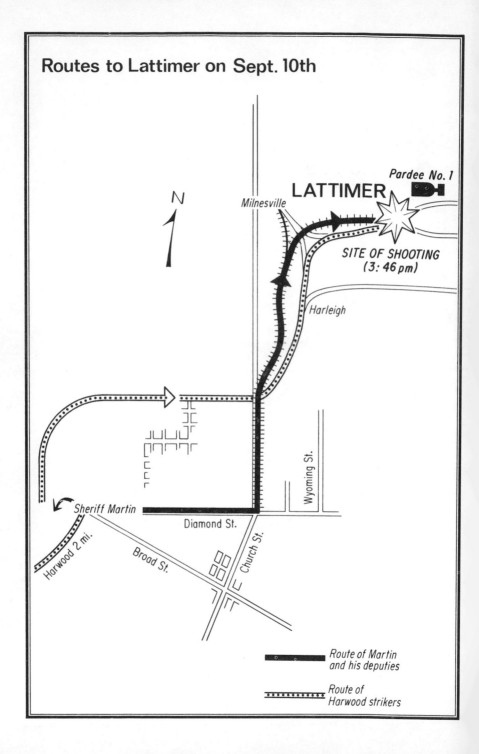

Routes to Lattimer on Sept. 10th

Pardee No. 1

LATTIMER

Milnesville

SITE OF SHOOTING
(3: 46 pm)

N

Harleigh

Wyoming St.

Sheriff Martin

Harwood 2 mi.

Diamond St.

Broad St.

Church St.

Route of Martin
and his deputies

Route of
Harwood strikers

Bloody Friday

INITIATIVE IN HARWOOD

ON FRIDAY MORNING, the sun rose brilliant. A gang of the breaker boys from Harwood planned to go swimming. By the time the men began to assemble for the march to Lattimer Mines, some had already been out over the hills in Butler Valley to pick berries. At nine o'clock, John Hlavaty, a Slovak from Lattimer, came to the home of Thomas Racek in Harwood and said again that the men at Lattimer planned to walk out that afternoon if the men from Harwood would come to call them out. Racek took Hlavaty to Jacob Sivar's house, and they called the men together. There was still discussion as to whether a large crowd should go to Lattimer or whether they should just send a committee. Some said everyone should go, or else the company might blacklist the men on the committee. This idea was generally approved.

The men recalled John Fahy's instructions of the night before about the sheriff and his armed men. Fahy had warned them not even to take marching sticks, like the garden fence poles that walkers in these parts usually carried. He instructed them about the rights of free assembly, but also about the sheriff's use of the riot act. Yesterday, he told them, the sheriff's men had fired warning shots and were reported to be more and more hostile; great caution was necessary. Fahy did not plan to accompany the marchers to Lattimer. He said he would be posting signs in nearby Milnesville; he would come over to Lattimer later. He never took part in marches.

John Eagler, who was to lead the march, was excited. He had sent a message to Alex McMullen inviting the McAdoo men to come along. McMullen said no. Echoing Fahy, he warned Eagler again not to march without an American flag. So Eagler told the men to hold off until he could find a flag to carry. With three companions, Andro Sivar, Joseph Michalko, and August Kosko, he hiked over to Humboldt.

Those who waited behind decided that the youngest boys would not be permitted to march. It would be twelve miles or more, round trip, under a broiling sun. Only boys over fifteen would be allowed to accompany the men; these were sent inside to put on shoes and decent dress. Some of the men may have fortified themselves with a little whiskey; in any case, the sheriff was later to allege so. Meanwhile, unknown to the marchers, someone from Harwood—possibly an employee at the company store—telephoned Sheriff Martin about the plan of march, its route, and destination.

In the days just before the march, visible signs of conflict frightened some of the American women of Harwood, who nervously embroidered on them at the trial. Thus, for example, Mrs. Catherine Weisenborn heard one foreigner threaten another: "If you don't come, we'll kill you." She also testified she heard some strikers threaten people like her: "We'll show the *white people* what we'll do when we come back!" Mrs. Eliza Grace, whose husband hid in the brush, remembered that the marchers "tramped through my fruit garden, and broke my beanpoles in two to make clubs." Mrs. Rose Gillespie sent her four boys into the brush to hide, and Mrs. Catherine Brennan hid her fifteen-year-old boy. The foreigners, she said, "were armed with clubs, hammers, and stones. One man fired a shot in the air. Others fired into the brush, where many of the men were hiding." Mrs. Michael Gallagher said that she, personally, had stones thrown at her by the strikers, and Mrs. Charles Miller said her husband had gone to West Hazleton when he heard the strikers were coming.

By the time John Eagler got back, the men had had time for an early lunch. A cheer went up when they saw Eagler and

Sivar return with not one, but two, flags. Stragglers poured out of the houses. Steve Jurich kissed his pretty bride, and the others teased them both. The older men waved good-bye to their families. At almost every doorway and out in the street women and children waved and shouted as the men moved into position. Eagler and Joseph Michalko walked down the line, telling individuals to discard their walking sticks and suggesting that they start out four abreast. There were between 250 and 300 men. They started from two separate locations and met at the picnic grounds. Joseph Michalko and Steve Jurich walked out in front with the American flags snapping in the breeze. A crowd of breaker boys fell in behind the flags, but their elders sent them unhappily away. As this unarmed band got themselves organized to answer the request of their Italian brothers at the Lattimer mines, many were taking part in the first civic act of their lives. Most had not been in the previous marches; Eagler hadn't; Cheslak hadn't. Most had never laid eyes on Sheriff Martin; none, perhaps, had seen the guns of the deputies. It was just after one when the command "Forward march!" was shouted by Michalko.

As they walked along, they picked up new recruits. They did not aim to create a big crowd, and they did not plan to have a large rally. Frequently, they called out to friends lined up to watch them on their route. The breaker boy Andrew Meyer, five days short of his seventeenth birthday, saw John Eagler in the line as the parade passed through Crystal Ridge. Meyer's father had helped to lay the foundation of the city hospital in Hazleton when Andrew was only eight years old and still in Slovakia. Now the boy joined the line and, as often happened when a newcomer joined, a small cheer went up. The men were relaxed and festive. For the past year, most had worked only one day out of every two, and the activities of the strike—giving promise of some small but basic changes in their lives—seemed far preferable to being out of work.

The night before, the strikers had formulated three grievances and taken them to the superintendent at Harwood. They demanded a pay raise of 10¢ a day, a reduction in the price of powder from $2.75 a keg to $1.50, and an end to the company store and the company doctor. They particularly resented the prices at the company store: a dozen eggs that cost 13¢ at an independent store cost 23¢ from the company; butter at 8¢ a pound elsewhere cost 26¢; and the powder they needed for their work came from the manufacturer at 90¢ to $1.00 a keg. On the average, excess charges to miners in the Hazleton region worked out to $217.50 per capita per annum.

Their ranks swollen by recruits from Crystal Ridge and Cranberry, four hundred men were now raising a cloud of dust on their way toward Hazleton, jackets over their arms, their handkerchiefs often in use to wipe their necks and brows. No effort was made on this day, as there had been on others, to close down other breakers as they passed. They passed the Cranberry breaker, calling to their friends, shouting threats to scab workers. The marchers were unarmed and determined to be peaceful, in order to avoid trouble with the sheriff.

The strikers felt patriotic under the flag. They also felt protected. Marching down into the valley and up the opposite hill, the thin yellow dust rising in the still air behind them, many felt a surge of purpose and accomplishment. John Eagler, at nineteen, although walking at their head, was not really in charge; neither was Michalko. Older leaders like Anthony Novotny, Mike Cheslak, Andrej Sivar, and others quite naturally talked things through and decisions emerged among them by common consent. Each had been carefully reared not to be boastful, assertive, or proud. No one should be in the position of attracting criticism. The traditions of serfdom and peasant life operated like censors upon anyone who might stand out too far above the group. Oppression from above had been internalized. The community cut would-be leaders down to size.

Harwood lay two miles southwest of Hazleton. The plan was to proceed by the road at the bottom of Buck Mountain and on up through the city of Hazleton. This would be the shortest route to Lattimer Mines on the far northeast side of town. Even so, the march would be about six miles.

It was almost two when the marchers in the front line caught sight of armed men hurrying toward them in West Hazleton.

Bloody Friday

BEN'S CONFUSIONS

BEN SAKMAR had been very impressed at the meeting at the Harwood schoolhouse Thursday night. He envied John Eagler tremendously.

He still had misgivings, though, about anything out of the ordinary that could mean the end of his job. A stable job meant everything to him; he had to have it or die. He joined the march but felt uncomfortable and even guilty every step of the way. He had opened an account with John Nemeth in Hazleton and was happy to deal with someone whose language he understood. His mother would be surprised to find him trusting a Magyar. It would be hard to explain to her what life was really like in America. He could see her face plainly as he marched: the red wart on her nose, the shining gray eyes. He had often admired her wedding picture and knew, if he had met her then, that he would have fallen in love with her himself. Men still said in Brutovce that she had been the most beautiful woman in any village on the mountain. Now she was heavy and old—not really old, like Baba, but no longer beautiful.

Men were lucky to stay handsome and strong, while women aged swiftly. Ben had special sympathy with women. Women always liked him. He thought that was because he had become responsible at such an early age for caring for the family. The sun hurt his eyes as they turned up the hill toward Hazleton; the muscles behind his knees hurt on the steep climb. He could see as clearly as the hollyhock standing in the sun every detail of the wooden and stucco cottage built into the side of the plunging hill in Brutovce. When it rained, great gulleys of brown water flowed down the road beside their home. Even the rocks piled up there every autumn were tumbled away by the rush of waters in the spring as the heavy snows melted off the fir-covered mountains and the crop-grass pastures.

His uncle Emil had a larger house than Ben and his

mother's, higher up, built around an open courtyard, with strong floorboards and heavy rafters, like a cottage fit for a gróf. His uncle's lands were the most productive on the mountain. Emil had made early successes breeding cows, sheep, and goats and was respected as head of the most prosperous branch of the family. At one side of Emil's courtyard were stables for three horses and a kennel for the dogs. Across the way was a storeroom and a workroom. Emil's children slept in a warm, comfortable garret above the heat from the kitchen. When Ben thought of risks he must now take in America, powerful memories of Brutovce overwhelmed him.

Ben was thinking he had been right to join the union. It was the only way. Even in Slovakia, sentiment was gathering for social and political upheaval. As long as peasants didn't band together, forward movement was stopped. In Slovakia, there was little hope for the future. The troops of the empire kept a firm hand, and the organization of Magyar landholders could never be defied. The Slovaks were doomed to remain huddled in their homes and villages. They were not strong enough to throw invaders out. Not for nine centuries had they been free; the peasants still sang songs about the freedom of that time nine centuries ago. It was now a crime to teach Slovak in the schools, and persons were arrested for using Slovak in public places. The peasants were expected to produce revenue for the local gróf, who had received the lush territories for services to the crown.

Ben had parted with the thirty cents required for membership and hoped against hope that Fahy was not cheating them. The dues represented a week's postponement of his return to see his loved ones. He had never walked all the way to Lattimer Mines. He was curious to see whether the Italians lived as poorly as the Slovaks, Poles, and Lithuanians in Harwood.

Ben stayed well back in the crowd. He saw Andrew Meyer join the group, and for a while ran up ahead to walk with him and Eagler, Jurich, Futa, and his other friends. Sweat trickled down his brow; he wiped it off. After a while, he fell back into the center of the crowd. He felt like being alone. He felt a kind of dread, as though he were doing wrong.

Oddly, he was dreaming of Maureen when the group began

to halt outside of West Hazleton. The heat and the exertion and the rhythm of the men marching in the dust pushed erotic images into his thoughts. He felt safer in the middle of the march. Some day he would marry and have a wife to embrace. Sometimes at night his arms ached for someone to hold. He bumped into the man in front of him, and someone stepped hard upon his heel.

Bloody Friday

CONFRONTATION AT MCKENNA'S CORNER

FROM THE SIDE of the column of marchers on the steep hill up to West Hazleton, the clatter of an armed force descending the culm bank at the end of the trolley line spread momentary anxiety. Sheriff Martin and his deputies, rifles in hand, were hurrying to beat the column to the top of the hill at the entrance to the city. As they passed through the ranks of marchers, the deputies were unaccountably rough. Overnight, the coal operators had let the sheriff know that mobilized bands of marchers must be stopped. Today, the sheriff and his men were men with a new mission.

The first trouble on September 10 had been predicted at Drifton, ten miles farther north than Lattimer, and it was there that Sheriff Martin had joined his deputies. He swore in some new deputies early, although everything was quiet, and took his weary men back to Hazleton about noon. The trolley car used every day by the deputies had been nicknamed the White Squadron and, although the cars were open in summer, the men inside sweated profusely and the leather seats showed wet marks at virtually every touch. The deputies hurried to water pumps when at last they disembarked for lunch at the lumberyard in Hazleton's south side. Some had errands in the city. Some were heard to boast as they came out of a hardware store that today they were "going to shoot some strikers."

Just after one o'clock, Sheriff Martin got a telephone message about the march from Harwood to Lattimer. He resolved there and then to intercept and to disperse it. He ordered his men back into the trolleys "on the double." A few minutes later, William E. Joyce, editor of the *Sentinel*, the sole paper to cover the afternoon's events, learned both the sheriff's destination and the marchers' intended route and ordered reporter W. A. Evans, a friend of several of the deputies, to hurry to McKenna's Corner at once. Joyce also ordered Thomas McHale, the typesetter, and James Codden, the proofreader, to set up relays between Evans and the office. The *Sentinel* would hold its afternoon deadline as long as possible. Disaster was in the air. As events unfolded, Joyce himself alternated between the field and the office.

In the lead trolley, Sheriff Martin warned his deputies once again to remain cool and to avoid trouble, if possible. He made it clear that they would stop the strikers and that a show of escalated force was in order. The trolley squealed to a stop at the end of the line behind a culm break. Only when the sheriff and his men had climbed, grunting, to the top of the dusty, slippery culm bank did they get a view of the long column of four hundred men, four abreast, toiling up the road toward West Hazleton. With a whoop, the sheriff and his men hurried down the shifting, sliding slate, slipping and catching themselves with their hands, choking in the dust. Some then hurried alongside the road to gain McKenna's Corner at the entrance to West Hazleton before the strikers did. Others pushed and shoved their way through the docile ranks of marchers, letting them know that today the deputies meant business. Some deputies pushed with their rifle butts, others spun marchers out of their way by grabbing their sleeves. Sheriff Martin was among those who broke through the ranks of the marchers. He grabbed the sleeve of Martin Kislewicz [variants: Kascavage, Grenkavicz, etc.] so tightly that the latter begged to be released. "You seem to be a good fellow," the sheriff smiled. "You had better get away from here as there is going to be big trouble today." With that, the sheriff shoved him aside.

Joseph Mechky (Mečky) was told that those who wouldn't get out of the way would be shot down like dogs. Anthony Gayno felt a sharp yank that spun him around and tore his sleeve and he became so frightened that he ran home. Thomas Lynch of West Hazleton had been watching the orderly procession of marchers, four or six abreast, as they came up the steep hill from Cranberry and turned up Wayne Street. As the marchers approached, Sheriff Martin told Lynch and some of the other spectators that they had better get out of the way as there was liable to be trouble if the strikers did not disperse. Such speech was not like Sheriff Martin. Both he and Mayor Altmiller on different days had single-handedly, by words alone, persuaded other marchers, more boisterous and numerous, to turn aside and return to their homes. On this occasion, Deputy Manley followed up the sheriff's stern words by striking Lynch for not moving fast enough, and shoving another bystander, Herman Pottunger, off to the side. Other deputies pushed back bystanders or took preparatory aim at the line of marchers. "I could get a bead on that fellow," Lynch heard one say through his sights.

The West Hazleton Chief of Police, Edward Jones, reached McKenna's Corner in time to observe these events. What he saw did not please him. In another part of the crowd, someone apparently said something to John Cook, a short and feisty officer of the Coal and Iron Police. Years later, William Joyce was to recall Cook's response: "What a wallop he had in his fists. His tormentor was laid low with a broken jaw. This was about the first real encounter between the police [sic] and marchers and marked the beginning of an intensity permeating the atmosphere and exciting apprehension in all circles of society."

The sheriff's men had thrown a line across the corner of Wayne Street and Broad Street in front of McKenna's Hotel and the United Charities Building. Along the line, a small forest of Winchesters shone in the sun. Some of the marchers were confused by seeing men in business suits carrying guns. It made no sense to them. They studied then the hostile faces behind the guns.

September 10, 1897 Bloody Friday, The Massacre   *117*

Bloody Friday

THE DEPUTIES

DEPUTY Ario Pardee Platt boasted of ancestors who had fought in the Revolutionary War, in the War of 1812, and in the Civil War. (During 1861–65, little Hazleton had supplied almost two thousand men to the Union cause.) Platt was the chief bookkeeper of the Pardee company, and the general manager of its company stores in Hazleton, Harwood, and Lattimer Mines. It made his blood boil to see all these foreigners carrying the flag his ancestors had championed. Platt was looking for action, he had wanted action all along and was not happy with the overcareful way the sheriff had been handling things.

Thomas Hall, another deputy, was a leader in the Coal and Iron Police. He was a man who had organized the posse for the sheriff and who directed it in the sheriff's absence. Before the strike had even begun, as far back as August 12, the owners of the mine companies had called a meeting in Hazleton to discuss their dissatisfaction with the performance of the Coal and Iron Police. Even without a strike looming up before them, they were complaining that they were paying for one hundred policemen, paying well, too, and not getting the protection they needed. The police were spending too much time at Hungarian weddings, they said, and not enough time protecting property. They were paying for protection and they intended to have it. The tenor of the meeting was then leaked to the newspapers. So now, only one month later, Thomas Hall was not of a mind to occasion any further dissatisfaction from his employers. It would be his task to teach Sheriff Martin the way things were done in the lower end of the county and to keep the pressure on him to do them. His own neck was at stake.

Deputy Alonzo Dodson was a miner who lived in Hazleton. He was heard to say, "We ought to get so much a head for shooting down these strikers. I would do it for a cent a head to make money at it."

Deputies George and James Ferry—the latter known to everyone as Pinky—were also heard to say at McKenna's Corner that they would blow the strikers' brains out. Perhaps it was the power of suggestion that was working on the consciousness of the deputies, for one of them, Harry Diehl, even threatened to blow out the brains of Herman Pottunger, if he did not get off the road. Pottunger himself heard Deputy Wesley Hall say of the marchers: "I'd like to get a pop at them."

Deputy Roger McShea, a schoolteacher, was the only Catholic among the deputies. He was married to a Protestant girl who had become a Catholic in order to marry him. He was later to become a paymaster at A. Pardee and Company, and one of his several children was to become the Roman Catholic bishop of Allentown.

Deputy J. W. Bornheiser struck up a conversation with Christopher Brehen, a miner from Cranberry who happened to be in West Hazleton when the marchers arrived. "Every one of these strikers ought to be shot," Bornheiser observed.

"They have as good a right to strike as anybody," the miner replied, "and I would not stop them."

"You're a coward," Bornheiser said, "or else you would get a gun and go out with us to shoot them."

"If you want to shoot them, all right," Brehen said with enough contempt to make Bornheiser look at him twice.

George Treible, a heavy man, had been huffing for some time after getting up the hill. His clothes were soaked with sweat, and his spirits were sour. He tended to be a little self-regarding in any case and carrying arms was not his line of work.

Also among the deputies were Robert Tinner, the superintendent of the central Pennsylvania Telephone and Supply Company, Willard Young, a lumber merchant and contractor, and Samuel B. Price, who held the contract to build a new breaker in Harwood, work on which was being held up by the strike. All in all about forty deputies had accompanied Sheriff Martin to West Hazleton. Nearly all these men owed their livelihood, or a portion of it, to the mining companies. Other deputies were waiting for the marchers at Lattimer.

Bloody Friday

TWO O'CLOCK: FIRST BLOOD

SHERIFF MARTIN'S fondest hope seems clearly to have been to put an end to the march right at West Hazleton. But he was in something of a spot. He knew he didn't have jurisdiction inside the city, at least not without consultation, and the marchers had already reached McKenna's Corner. He was being pressured to "teach the strikers a lesson" that would get them off the roads. His own inclination still seemed to be to keep matters peaceable and under his control.

The sheriff walked directly toward the two men carrying flags, Andro Sivar and Joseph Michalko. He had his pistol in one hand. He took the nearest man, John Yurchekowicz, by the coat, brandishing the revolver in his face, and announced vigorously: "I'm the sheriff of Luzerne County, and you cannot go to Lattimer."

Steve Juszko pushed past Yurchekowicz, saying defiantly, "Me no stop. Me go to Lattimer."

The sheriff again said: "If you go to Lattimer, you must kill me first."

John Eagler, who had been fifty paces back in the line when it stopped, walked forward and now spoke up in a reedy voice: "We ain't goin to. We are going to Lattimer. We harm no one. We are within the law."

Before the words were fully out of Eagler's mouth, Anthony Kislewicz [variants: Kascavage, etc.] bent over for a flat rock (he later said) to strike a match for his pipe during the halt. One of the deputies brought the butt of his rifle down viciously on Kislewicz's arm. Then Deputy Hall moved toward Steve Juszko, who had stepped forward, and swung through the air twice with his rifle butt, crunching across the two arms the boy raised to protect himself and hitting his head. Blood flowed. Both arms hung limp.

The sheriff pointed his pistol right and left as though holding off a legion.

Ario Pardee Platt, fired up by the bloodshed, ripped the flag from Joseph Michalko's hands, broke the stick across his knee, and stood there shredding the flag with contempt. He dropped the torn rags in the dust.

John Eagler, watching Deputy Cook raise his gun, stopped to pick up a stone. The sheriff waved his pistol and Eagler dropped the stone. Other deputies mixed it up briskly with the marchers.

Deputy Cook fired a shot into the air and the hillside reverberated. The marchers did not move. They were baffled.

John Eagler stepped forward to obtain the name of the deputy he had seen hit Juszko. Sheriff Martin held Eagler with a gesture and pulled a paper from his pocket. The sheriff had seen disorder and now had his opportunity. "This is my proclamation and you can't go any farther. It's against the law."

Then Chief of Police Jones walked forward shouting to John Eagler and the sheriff, and Sheriff Martin put his paper back in his pocket. Jones told the sheriff the strikers had a right to march peacefully, and he, the sheriff, knew it. To Novotny the chief said he had confidence in the way the marchers were conducting themselves; he would let them march around the edges of West Hazleton but not go through the city. He was willing to show them how they could go, so as to continue on to Lattimer in peace.

While the principals of this drama stood in the road, most of the marchers milled around nearby. Some, frightened, left for home and did not go on to Lattimer. An old man, John Laudmesser, who lived in West Hazleton, told some of the strikers they should listen to the sheriff and go home. The strikers told him: "Sheriff no good."

The deputies were furious at the interruption. Alonzo Dodson held Steve Juszko against a fence with the muzzle of his gun. A bystander offered sympathy to Juszko, whose head was streaming blood. Pinky Ferry, at Dodson's side, told the sympathizer: "If you don't shut up, I'll blow your head off." Still another said, "I'll get even with the dirty bastards when we get to Lattimer." Louis Kiczki was seized by the coat, spun around, and his shirt torn. He watched several marchers run off into the woods and was tempted to join them.

While the deputies stood to one side of the corner with their two wounded "prisoners," the marchers milled around on the other.

Novotny told Eagler what Chief Jones had said. The strike leaders conferred. Mayor Altmiller of Hazleton and Chief Jones confirmed their right to march but had forbidden them to march through the cities. Chief Jones was suggesting a march up North Broad Street to Washington Avenue,* then eastward to Alter and 20th streets, past Fisher Hill to Harleigh, and so to Lattimer. They decided to continue and began lining up their band. On the spot they gained some new recruits to fill the places of deserters.

Murderous joking, meanwhile, seems to have gripped the deputies. They had talked all morning about shooting and killing. Herman Pottunger heard a deputy say quietly to a friend: "I bet I drop six of them when I get over there." August Katski and Martin Lochar stood near the trolley car as the departing deputies were boarding. Two deputies went after them and hit them, but one said: "Let them go until we get to Lattimer and then we'll shoot them." It may have been a form of macabre humor, intended only to frighten.

William A. Evans, the reporter, arrived just after the confrontation, while the men were still standing on opposite sides of the road. He saw one of the strikers picking up a stone as Ario Pardee Platt tore the flag. No stone was actually thrown.†

Doctor John Koons of Hazleton was called by the chief of police to treat the two wounded men in the jail. One of the men—Juszko—had to be examined by force. His scalp wounds required nine stitches. Juszko appears to have been listed the next day as among the wounded in the hospital. Six months later, he was still unable to use his arms.

Chief Jones did, as he offered, point the way for the marchers to cut through West Hazleton, adding another mile or so to the trip. It was after 2:30 when the marchers returned to their

* Later, 15th Street.
† Evans' first field dispatch on this event is full of errors. In particular, he tells of a skirmish at Cuyle's strippings on September 6 as though it had happened along the line of march on September 10. He had to write his story hurriedly and probably misunderstood the deputies' account.

original plan. Now only one American flag waved in the sun, but the men were feeling vindicated and safe under the law. Mike Krupa from Crystal Ridge had joined them in West Hazleton with several of his friends, and the marchers made Krupa and his friends throw away their walking sticks. George Yamshak also joined them and was told to throw away the small stick he was carrying. The marchers had learned that their best protection was lack of arms.

W. A. Evans scribbled out his garbled story on the confrontation which he arrived too late to witness. He rode on the trolley with the deputies, and handed the short text to Tom McHale, his runner, who descended gladly from the trolley at Wyoming Street, not wishing to be a witness to the tragedy he felt was coming. As he hurried up the street, he told a reporter from the Hazleton *Standard*: "There will be trouble. If those strikers attempt to get into Lattimer, there is sure to be a clash and some shooting will be done."

Bloody Friday

MASSACRE

LATER, the editorialists were not to overlook the symbolism of the day and the hour. It was almost three o'clock and the detachment of deputies assigned to wait at Lattimer was restless. A mile away, at Harleigh, Sheriff Martin and the deputies who had seen action at West Hazleton sat in the trolley and waited. Some removed plug hats to wipe away the sweat under their hatbands. Others fingered their Winchesters. A few of them were later to claim that they believed then that the miners had guns in their pockets; some even may have believed it. In any case, a dispatch in the Wilkes-Barre *Times* datelined 3:30 P.M. summed up the general mood:

The news that two strikers had been assaulted has aroused considerable feeling among the other men and bloodshed is feared. A large body of striking miners are marching on Lattimer in defiance of the sheriff's orders, and a body of deputies has gone to meet them. Serious trouble is anticipated when they meet.

For the deputies sitting on that trolley in front of Farley's Hotel in Harleigh, the waiting was almost over. In a cloud of dust, the marchers were beginning to appear around the bend, the lone American flag still at their head. The deputies watched the strikers pause while eight men or so from the first two lines huddled. The other marchers broke ranks to drink water from a pump. The question for the huddled leaders, posed by John Eagler, was whether to march first to breaker Number One in Lattimer Mines or to breaker Number Three. Finally the strikers started walking again. John Laudmesser, the hotel-keeper, counted the marchers as they passed, there were 424.

Mrs. Ellen Witchie was in another trolley on the way to Lattimer and was frightened by the careless way the deputies held their guns, which was endangering her.

In the past, strikers had often changed plans in unexpected ways, and the sheriff was taking no chances. He ordered the trolley to stay right alongside the marchers. For almost a mile, deputies and strikers went along eyeing one another. A few insults may have been exchanged. At the last fork in the road, when it was plain that the strikers could be taking no other road except into Lattimer, the sheriff ordered the trolley to speed up and race ahead to the village.

John Welsh, the school director from Hazleton Township, happened to be on a trolley car headed for Milnesville when the car turned around and came back to the turn for Lattimer. Some deputies who had been waiting to see what the strikers would do now climbed into the car Welsh was in.

Welsh knew Deputy Edward Turnbach, who was puffing and seemed exhausted. "I suppose, Ed Turnbach," Welsh said, "that's the hardest day you ever worked."

Turnbach replied: "Yes. I do not know what the sheriff means by fooling us around all day like this without giving orders to fire."

Andrew F. Adams, a travelling agent for the Washington Baking Powder Company, was on the same trolley when it

Hazleton, turn of the century; homes of the quality folk.

Regional transportation, from Hazleton to surrounding mines and hamlets, used by the deputies on the day of the massacre.

Miners' housing, rented from the company.

Even in the most beautiful of natural surroundings the world might look rather grim.

The Harwood breaker.

The marchers on their way to Lattimor Mines, secure in the protection of their new found flag.

Sheriff Martin's posse, soon to be
acquitted (above and facing page).

A newspaper sketch of Sheriff
Martin.

Members of the Third Brigade, Pennsylvania National Guard, under the command of General John Peter Shindel Gobin.

Lattimer Mines, the site of the
shooting; the huge tree at left was
dubbed "The Massacre Tree."

The funeral hearse; burying the
dead went on for days.

John Eagler

Andrew Sivar

John Perkonas,
unknown man, and
Andrew Eshmont.

The widow and family of Mike Cheslak.

Matthew Cazja (left), among the wounded, and his brother Adalbert, killed.

was commandeered by several deputies. "The talk," Adams later told the Pottsville *Republican,* "was all about shooting and each man seemed eager, especially Hess." Hess was an important lieutenant.

In Lattimer there was by now considerable commotion. The colliery whistle sounded a warning. Those deputies and private police who had already been waiting in Lattimer had made their preparations. One of them told Mrs. Craig, "Go inside, as there may be some shooting today." Trolley cars shuttled in from Milnesville, Drifton, and points north. Doors slammed. Some mothers hurried to the school to bring their children home. Fear of the foreigners had been intense ever since the Tuesday before, when a band of noisy strikers had marched through the village.

On his arrival by trolley, Sheriff Martin took command of the assembling deputies. His force, bolstered by some of the new deputies from Drifton, now numbered almost one hundred and fifty. Some of them stood guard at the breakers and the superintendent's office. He divided the others into three companies, under Samuel Price, A. E. Hess, and Thomas Hall. He called the men down off the trolley bank and stationed them across the single road leading into Lattimer, just before it forked into Main Street and Quality Row, with the schoolhouse lane above. Dissatisfied, he then ordered all of them off the road to take up positions in an enfilading crescent on the lower, north side of the road. In this way, they would be able to cover the entire length of the march as it filed in front of them. The Craig house on the end of Main Street was surrounded by a white picket fence. Inside, Mrs. Craig fretted nervously. Outside, across the street, stood a tall gumberry tree, later to become known as "the massacre tree." Almost in its shade, Sheriff Martin stood near the house with the white fence and looked up the empty road toward Harleigh. As he did so, A. E. Hess was showing his men one last time how to fire their guns.

From where the sheriff stood, the road swept gently upward over the brow of a distant hill. Not far from where it came over the hill, the trolley track crossed over it and continued to parallel it on the south but on a raised embankment. The marchers would come over the hill and then be caught between the embankment and the line of Winchesters. In addition, the road then gradually curved closer and closer to the deputies down toward the house where the sheriff was now standing. Thus, if the marchers kept coming, their first rank would be no farther than fifteen yards from the line of deputies, and those in the last ranks would be no farther than thirty or forty yards. The sheriff was satisfied and strode up the line a little, nearer to the center of his deputies.

Mrs. Kate Case was in the third house, upstairs, looking out the window. She watched the deputies take up their positions and wait. It was almost 3:30.

At last the marchers came over the hill. Next door to the Craig house, John Airy watched from his home as the unarmed marchers walked in rank toward him. As at West Hazleton, so at Lattimer the marchers felt secure under the law. In the first two rows were Steve Jurich, carrying the flag, John Eagler, John Pustag, Michael Malody, Mike Cheslak, wearing an odd pointed cap, Andro Novotny, and George Jancso. All were from the two counties of Sariš and Zemplin in Slovakia.

After dismissing their students when anxious mothers came to gather their youngsters, Charles Guscott and Grace Coyle, the teachers, stood at the doorway of the schoolhouse, and watched the slow-motion drama unfold. They stood about one hundred yards from the gumberry tree. About sixty of the ninety men in the deputies line, they later recalled, had their rifles raised in firing position as the strikers, led by the flag, began to file past them.

Sheriff Martin told Hess and Price to keep an eye on him. He said he would find out the marchers' intentions. "If they say they are not going to do anything I may let them go on and we will go along with them." When the flag had come about two-thirds of the way past the far flank, Sheriff Martin strode forward as he had now done on four previous occasions to see if he could handle the situation alone. He had his revolver drawn. He held up one hand. The men kept coming as he advanced and he had his hand almost in their faces when he announced in official manner: "You must stop marching and disperse." Those a few ranks back could not hear him at all, and the others behind them could not see him. "This is contrary to the law and you are creating a disturbance. You must go back. I won't let you go to the colliery."

The front ranks stumbled, trying to halt. Someone from behind called out in English, "Go ahead!" The marchers behind kept coming. The front row was pushed forward.

Angered, the sheriff reached first for the flag. But Steve Jurich pulled it erect. Then the sheriff reached into the second row and grabbed Michael Malody by the coat, thinking that he was the one who had said, "Go ahead!" The sheriff didn't know which man was the leader. Frightened, Malody insisted he hadn't said a word. Andro Novotny, who was next to Malody, intervened in his defense. The sheriff then grabbed Novotny with one hand and pulled his revolver up, aiming it at Novotny's chest. By now, the sheriff had pulled four or more men to the deputies' side of the road. The other marchers continued on. Eagler was among those pushed partially forward down the road. Those near the sheriff—including, now, men from the rear like John Terri and Martin Shefronik (Šefronik) were afraid and puzzled.

"Where are you going?" the sheriff asked, pulling on Novotny and beginning to panic. The front of the column was getting farther and farther past him. Novotny said in English, "Let me alone!" He swept his arms up and pushed the barrel of the sheriff's revolver away from his own chest.

George Jancso reached in and pulled the sheriff's other hand free from Novotny. The sheriff then grabbed Jancso's coat and pointed his pistol at Jancso's forehead; Jancso and Eagler heard the pistol snap—Sheriff Martin also felt it snap—but it did not fire.

In that instant, the sheriff's second in command, Samuel Price, left the line of deputies and stepped forward to come to the surrounded sheriff's assistance. Other deputies frantically called him back, since he was now in the line of fire. He stepped back.

Mrs. Kate Case from her third-floor window heard someone shout "Fire." She thought the deputies were firing over the marchers' heads. Then she saw some marchers fall. She screamed.

Novotny heard the sheriff command "Fire," and Jancso heard him shout "Give two or three shots!" Some witnesses thought that in the struggle the sheriff had fallen briefly to his knees; others said he remained standing. His body was directly between the deputies and Jancso when a shot rang out, then three or four in unison. The sheriff raised both arms as though to stop the action. But a full volley rang out again and again.

Watching from the schoolhouse, Charles Guscott saw the first puff of smoke come from the fourth or fifth man from the farthest end of the deputies' line, Hess's men. It seemed to those closer that the whole line erupted with fire.

Steve Jurich had held the flag and was the first to fall. "O Joj! Joj! Joj!" he cried in the ancient Slovak cry to God. "Enough! Enough!" Bullets shattered his head and he died as he bled.

John Eagler saw Cheslak drop, his peculiar peaked hat falling from his head, so he, too, dropped to the ground. Eagler saw trickles of blood flowing in the dust toward him from Cheslak's head. He realized then that the deputies were not using blanks.

John Terri threw himself on the ground. Another striker fell on him, dead. Terri saw Cheslak beside him and tried to speak to him. Cheslak's eyes were open but he did not speak. Then Terri got up and ran.

Andro Sivar, in the fourth row, turned his back at the first shot. When the man beside him caught a bullet in the back, Sivar fell with him. Michael Kuchar, nineteen, was about ten yards from the sheriff and could neither hear nor see what was happening in front; at the loud shouting, he threw himself down. George Jancso tore himself from the hands of the sheriff and ran to throw himself in a ditch as flat and close to mother earth as he could press himself.

Martin Shefronik stood close to Jurich, and saw blood spurt out the back of Jurich's head and also from his mouth. As he dropped, Jurich was completely drenched with blood. Shefronik ran toward the schoolhouse, until he was thrown forward by the impact of a bullet in his shoulder. John Putski of Harwood also ran toward the schoolhouse until a bullet in his right arm and another in his leg spun him to the ground. Andrew Jurechek ran toward the schoolhouse and almost reached safety before a bullet struck his back and exploded through his stomach.

Watching from the schoolhouse, teachers Charles Guscott and Grace Coyle had looked on in horror as dust and acrid gunsmoke filled the air. "They're firing blanks," Miss Coyle said. "No, see them dropping," Guscott said. The firing went on for two or three minutes. Some deputies turned, wheeled, and followed running men, shooting some down at a distance of 300 yards. Many men ran toward the schoolhouse; one was hit, spinning, just before he reached the terrified teachers. Other shots crashed into the schoolhouse sending showers of splinters. Running toward the teachers, Clement Platek clutched his side; he too was crying: "O *Joj! Joj! Joj!*" The teachers saw, in addition to those mentioned: the brains of one man splattered forward; still another hapless man shot through the neck so that his head was almost severed. Grace Coyle ran forward to help Andrew Jurechek, who was clutching at the entrails slipping from his stomach and who cried out to her: "No! Me want to see wife. Before die." He died before her eyes. His wife was heavy with child.

Mathias Czaja had been standing ten or twelve feet from the sheriff. He had seen the sheriff pull his revolver and point it at the man with the flag. He had heard him say, "If you go any farther, I will shoot you." He had been frightened. He did not hear the order to fire. His back was blown open by a bullet.

Michael Srokach (Srokač) saw eight deputies run forward thirty yards or so to gain better shots. From the public road, the miners fled backward toward the trolley line and up over its bank, either up the hill west toward Harleigh or east toward the schoolhouse.

One man fled as far as a telephone pole on the trolley line when he was hit. He pulled himself up, holding to the pole. As other shots poured into him, his body buckled two or three times. He slid to the earth.

William Raught and another deputy, according to several witnesses, broke from the line of deputies in order to pursue the fleeing strikers. In order to get a line of fire, Raught and the other man climbed up on the trolley tracks, still firing. Srokach heard some deputies answer pleas from the wounded with the shout: "We'll give you hell, not water, hunkies!" Others heard: "Shoot the sons of bitches!"

The smoke from the first volley was thick. Dust was raised by men running. For a while it was difficult to see. From his home, John Airy saw deputies take careful aim and pick men off as they were running to get in the shelter of the hillside. "They shot man after man in the back," he reported. "The slaughter was awful." He estimated that the deputies fired "at least 150" shots. "They kept firing for some time. Men fell on the ground and screamed in agony and tried to drag themselves from the murderous guns. At last it was all over."

Cries of pain, groans, and shrieks remained. Andro Sivar got up from a circle of dead and wounded. Andrew Meyer—seventeen-year-old breaker boy—pleaded for help for his shattered knees. John Slobodnik, wounded in the back of the head just above the neck cried out for water. Slobodnik and John Banko, also shot in the head, were carried by friends to Farley's Hotel in Harleigh, looking for medical attention of some kind. John Eagler ran, bent over, for 150 yards before he turned. He saw one of the men from Crystal Ridge bleeding from his arm and back. The man asked him: "Butty, loosen me suspenders and collar, they hurt me much." Eagler pulled down the man's shirt and saw a big hole in the back of his neck spouting thick blood. He pushed a handkerchief in the hole. Then he bent to help Frank Tages. He pulled off his own coat, put it around his friend, led him to a trolley car for a ride to the hospital. Sick and afraid, Eagler saw some of the deputies begin to offer water to the wounded. Then he started on the long walk back to Harwood. In shock, he could not comprehend what had just happened.

Cornelius Burke was eleven years old and lived in Lattimer II, the next settlement up from Lattimer. During recess from school, he was overcome by curiosity about the commotion in town and ran down to Lattimer to see the excitement. He was part way up Main Street when he heard the terrific crack of rifles. When he got up to the site, he recalls, " . . . Oh, my God, the poor fellows were lying across the trolley tracks on the hillside, some had died and some were dying. Some were crying out for water." Connie picked up a little can and carried water to one of the dying miners. "It was a terrible sight and so much confusion existed. Everyone was running in all directions. They searched the men who were shot and found they carried no weapons."

One of the deputies, George Treible, was wounded by a bullet that creased both his arms. The Wilkes-Barre *Times* reported that he believed he was shot by one of his own men, who had wheeled to fire after the dispersing strikers. Bullets flew, Treible said, in every direction. Some of the deputies at the right end of the crescent (farthest from Lattimer), who seem to have fired most of the shots, were shooting back toward Lattimer at the strikers fleeing toward the schoolhouse. "The deputies," said the paper, "were not under control. The odor of smoke inflamed them."

The fury of some was not yet spent. Some of the deputies walked among the fallen, kicking them and cursing them. A. E. Hess told one bystander who was crying shame, "Shut up or you will get the same dose." John Terri, who had fallen beside Cheslak, went through the smoke of battle to find water for his wounded uncle and cousin. Asked for water, a deputy named Clark said, "Give them hell," grabbed Terri, kicked him, and held him prisoner for an hour. Joseph Costello, a Hazleton butcher, saw Hess kick a prostrate victim (who was in fact Andrew Meyer) and denounced Hess for the butchery. Hess told him, too, to shut up. Grace Coyle, the schoolteacher, upbraided Hess for his manner among the fallen, with his cigar in his mouth. Hess did not defend himself.

John Welsh saw Sheriff Martin after the shooting and asked him how he was.

"I am not well," Sheriff Martin said.

The sheriff was pale and shaken. He turned his revolver over to a detective. Many of his deputies had fled and some went into hiding. Some of the others were lifting the wounded into conveyances. But John Airy witnessed the most saddening scene of all: "The trolley car in which the sheriff and his deputies came was right in front of my house and the officers got in it. They were laughing and telling each other how many men they killed." Another bystander also heard them: "Yes, and one of them said he took down a dozen 'Hunks,' and knew what he was shooting at every time. He was boasting of what a fine shooter he was. They sat there for some time, joking and laughing about it, and then they rode back to the city."

Bloody Friday

ON THE FIELD OF BATTLE

ESTIMATES on how long the shooting lasted ranged from twenty seconds to five minutes. Some of the strikers ran all the way to the schoolhouse and the firing continued even after they had reached there. One striker sitting against the schoolhouse after his hard run had his hat pierced by a shot. To empty a sixteen-shooter in rapid fire would have required at least a minute.

Many of the Winchesters held sixteen shots. Some deputies did not fire at all, but some emptied their magazines. The shells of the bullets were three inches long and sheathed in steel; most tore right through human bodies and continued in flight. At least eight men died on the spot and nearly sixty had wounds, many of them multiple wounds from which at least another eleven would die. At least one hundred twenty bullets found human flesh. Adam Smishkay (Smiške) had six gun wounds in the face and a gash on the side of his head; Steve Jurich had three bullet wounds an inch apart in his forehead. Blood from his wounds flowed away on the rocks in a culvert.

In the field, deputies and marchers both went to the assistance of the wounded. Deputy Price asked Mrs. Craig and some of the other women of Lattimer to bring sheets to tear up for bandages. The wounded were begging for water, and men and women were bringing them cups and pans of it. Big Mary

The Guns of Lattimer

Septak was very likely among them. Some of the men, including many of the deputies, tore pieces from their own jackets
and shirts to staunch the wounds. Even persons accustomed
to mine disasters could not bear to look at some of the torn
bodies, splattered brains, and dangling intestines. The 44.40
bullets with pointed heads tore everything in their path as they
spun through human bodies and exited. The flat-headed types
tore gaping holes. The buckshot used in some of the rifles
shredded flesh.

Within minutes of the shooting, telephone calls to Hazleton
alerted the city to the disaster. Soon the road from Hazleton
was clogged. A reporter who rushed out to the battlefield
described what he found:

"At Farley's Hotel there were two men lying on the porch. They
were shot in the head and legs and one of them had three bullets
in him. Groans and appeals for doctors or death were heart rend-
ing. All along the road, the wounded men who were able to leave
the fields scattered themselves and sought the shade of the trees
for protection. . . . The marchers couldn't talk intelligibly and
only with the greatest difficulty could information be gleaned. . . .
Along the bank of the trolley road men lay in every position . . .
some were dead, others were dying. Bodies were face down and
would lay along the line. Three others were but a short distance
away. On the other side of the road as many more bodies lay. The
schoolhouse was transformed into a temporary hospital. Two
wounded men shot through both legs were already loaded into the
colliery ambulance. Alongside the hillside wounded men were found
in the woods, on the green, on the roadside, and in the fields.
Many others who had been carried to a distance could not be found
by the reporter."

Reverend Karl Hauser was on his way to Hazleton from his
parish in Freeland when he heard the news. The carts and
carriages already in motion toward Lattimer made his heart
sink. He boarded the first trolley of wounded when he saw it
round the corner at Diamond Avenue and Wyoming Street in
downtown Hazleton. He saw the rifles stacked inside and hesitated. A sullen deputy looked at him. "Will I be shot?" the
minister asked. Deputy Clark motioned for him to board:
"Don't worry, Reverend, they're empty." Reverend Hauser

discovered the pale inert body of one of his vestrymen, Mike Cheslak, and thought immediately of Cheslak's wife and the five children.

Martin Shefronik, clutching his wounded shoulder, boarded a trolley back to the hospital. Andro and Jacob Sivar lifted the body of John Slobodnik onto another trolley, at Farley's Hotel. When they opened his coat, blood gushed out. They prayed that he would live. He was still holding on to life when the trolley reached Hazle Hall, switched off to the Broad Street track, and went to the end of the line near Poplar Street to the hospital.

It took an hour to clear the ground of the dead and wounded. The sun was just about setting when the last car left with its load of injured. Nothing but blood, footmarks, and an assemblage of dumbfounded men and women remained at Lattimer.

BEN'S WALK HOME

AT FIRST, Ben Sakmar had run. Then, tripping on someone's leg, he realized it would be better to hug the ground. In the dreadful silence after the long volley he picked himself up. His instinct was to run back to Harwood—back across the ocean to his mother and sister.

Ben Sakmar was in a daze. The shooting seemed to him impossible. It made a mockery of America. He couldn't believe it had happened. He remembered falling back in the ranks after West Hazleton. He had been afraid of the guns. Most of the men had seemed to feel that nothing could happen to them. Mr. McMullen, Mr. Fahy, and the leaders of the strike had told them the law. The police chief of West Hazleton had assured them it was so. Yet the acrid smell of gunpowder and the clouds of dust that shrouded the scene of battle showed that they had been misled. The groans and screams of the wounded were pitiable. The memory of the beaten face of his own father filled him with nausea.

Ben helped one fallen companion who had been hit in the heel. He saw Andro Meyer writhing in pain from a leg whose torn pants were dark with blood. He saw another man clutching his wounds, while blood streamed through his fingers. In a stupor, Ben wandered back to search for Cheslak, Jurich, and Futa. When he looked on the still bodies, so pale and without life, he could hardly believe that an hour before, taking a drink at Farley's Hotel pump, they had been alive. He helped three men lift Cheslak's inert body, bullet holes in the forehead, onto a wagon. Sticky blood covered Ben's hands and clothes. He saw Jurich in the culvert beside the road, streams of blood flowing among the rusty rocks. He wondered who would tell his bride, and in his ears he heard the mourning of Harwood.

Ben hardly even saw the deputies. Wagons, drays, and ambulances began to appear. Men on horseback arrived from the city. The trolley cars were loaded with dead and wounded. Over fifty bodies lay about. It seemed like hundreds. What would he do? Who would be his friends? Who would protect him?

Perhaps they had violated some law he did not know. He couldn't comprehend.

The long walk back to Harwood—the most painful ten miles of his life—was like a nightmare. On the road, he passed women from Harwood walking barefoot, carrying their shoes, tears in their eyes and looks of great fear on their faces, as they streamed toward the hospitals. As he passed they begged for news and word of their loved ones. He couldn't answer. He shook them off and in a sullen stupor sought his room, his bed, and a few moments of oblivion. It was almost dark when he arrived. Some men, particularly those who had not gone, spoke of vengeance. He felt faint and collapsed into his bed, throwing his heavy feet high in the air on a roll of blankets to draw blood back to his head, and forgot everything he had seen.

THE FUNERAL HOME

THE SOUND of plodding horses and creaking carriage wheels filled the evening air. Thousands of citizens from Hazleton and the surrounding communities lined the sidewalks. Doctors, ministers, orderlies, and reporters rushed from place to place. The wails of mourning women rent the air. Around the hospital, crowds struggled against the city police to get inside. Thousands of people were in the streets.

The Lehigh Traction Company put extra cars on the Lattimer line. Mr. Markle, the dispatcher, coolly sent out couriers to every neighboring doctor and minister. In just over an hour, every dead and wounded man had been lifted onto a conveyance. Horses were maddened by the confusion, and difficult to control. Blood covered some of the victims from head to foot. The United States Express Company's large delivery wagon, Sager's dray wagon, busses from the livery stables, common dirty drays, wagons, carriages, everything available was on the road. Trolleys carrying the dead crossed Broad Street and continued down South Wyoming Street to the morgue, or to two of the city's undertakers, Boyle's or Bonin's. Those carrying the wounded squealed around the turn on Broad Street and made their way to Hazleton Hospital. Alerted, the hospital staff had sent home many patients to make room for the wounded. By 5:30 P.M., emergency operations began. They continued for twenty-six hours.

Inside the hospital, bedding was blood-soaked, and floors were slippery with blood. The 44.40 caliber shells made ragged wounds. The victims were deformed, ugly, and pathetic. A man with holes in his head two-fingers wide was able to talk to a reporter, who could not forget the victim's glassy eyes.

At the morgue, a reporter saw a "Hungarian" woman with a baby at her breast bend over a dead man and look away with relief. She repeated the sequence again. At the last body, she uttered a frightful shriek and fell upon the inert body, clutching him with one hand and the baby with another.

Margaret Bonin was nine years old, shy but curious, and

was out in the street playing just before dinner time. She saw cars and wagons filled with bodies. She thought she saw blood dripping into the road. Men and women walking near the wagons were crying. Suddenly, she guessed the carts were heading for her father's funeral home. She ran back to the house and at the door met her mother, to whom she tried frantically to explain that something must have happened, and that people were coming with wagons of bodies. Her mother pulled the girl's head against her skirt and shepherded her inside.

A loud pounding at the door drew her father. Stroking his large, round beard worriedly, Hilary Bonin walked to the door and kept it ajar as he spoke to those outside. Then he threw the door open wide. Stretchers bearing bodies were marched through the doorway and with heavy feet went down the steps to the basement where her father worked.

Little Margaret watched the first body as the men lifted it past her. A large man filled her vision, his belly rising above the stretcher. His arms dangled over the edges. One arm touched her. It felt alive. Terrified, she remembered the touch all her life. She later asked her father the man's name. It was Sebastian Brotkowski. IIe had a gaping hole in the back of his head. Body after body went past her down into the cellar.

There was no time that night for the Friday fish dinner. Margaret's father made his own coffins. She heard him say he didn't think he would have enough coffins. Little Margaret spent a long evening feeling sorry for the dead men downstairs, who (she thought) had no one to turn to in this country. Their relatives in Europe wouldn't even know that they were dead. In later life, every year she went to St. Stanislaus Cemetery on Memorial Day to place flowers on the victims' graves.

At Boyle's funeral parlor up the street, Mr. Boyle would later testify that nine of the eleven bodies he prepared for death had been shot in the back. One had three bullet holes, each an inch apart in his forehead; the back of the skull was missing.

Hilary Bonin, Margaret's father, also noted that most of the wounds were in the back.

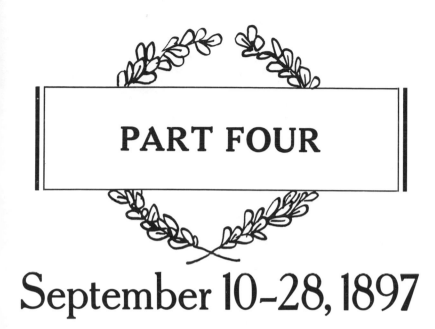

PART FOUR

September 10–28, 1897

SHERIFF MARTIN'S CONFUSION

AT THREE O'CLOCK on the afternoon of September 10, 1897, Sheriff James Martin had been at the apogee of his career. Coolly, he had directed the trolley on which he and his men followed just behind the men marching four abreast up the dusty road toward Lattimer. Forty-five minutes later his whole life had been changed. He was aware that he might now be put on trial for murder.

He had said to his men that if the marchers caused no trouble he might accompany them through Lattimer. But first he would try to urge them to turn back. The marchers had already had good reason to know the mood of the deputies.

Several of Sheriff Martin's men were Coal and Iron policemen, strangers to him whose loyalties lay in Hazleton. One Pardee was president of the Hazleton National Bank and another was vice-president, and with them on the bank's board of directors sat J. F. Roderick, A. M. Eby, A. S. Van Wickle—coal operators who represented the money and power of Hazleton. The men in his posse worked for them. From the beginning the sheriff had been wary of being caught in a trap in which he would end up the mine operators' sacrificial lamb. Thus when he ordered the marchers not to move farther into Lattimer, he knew that much was at stake for him in their compliance. A reporter in Hazleton wrote: "Lattimer was one of the collieries that had not yet been stopped by the strikers and it needs no stretch of the imagination to perceive what a strain must have rested on the sheriff and also on the men whom he beckoned to return home." When the latter refused to be impressed, when those in the rear pressed forward past their leaders with a shout of defiance, the violence of his own response was perhaps more than the sheriff had really intended. Moreover, he was not in uniform, and so was left without even the power to intimidate lent him by the outward trappings of authority. At the moment the marchers grappled with him, Sheriff Martin lost control of his own men—and of the rest of his life.

William E. Joyce, the editor of the Hazleton *Sentinel*, who lost his job for running "MASSACRE" in his headline for the day, reached the site of the killings fifteen or twenty minutes after the shooting and witnessed the change that had suddenly overcome the sheriff. As Joyce made his way along the Lattimer road on horseback, pitiably wounded men grasped the horse's bridle and appealed to him for God's sake to save them. Joyce had to guide his horse from the road to avoid trampling wounded and dying men. He saw the sheriff and dismounted. Sheriff Martin could give him no coherent statement. Years later, Joyce again met Martin on Broadway, New York City, "when he appeared to be still in a daze showing that he never fully recovered from the shock as indeed, few, if any, of the other men identified with the affair did."

For years, the sheriff remembered standing amid writhing, bloody men and hearing the screams and shouts, smelling the acrid smoke and seeing the swimming confusion of firing, running, and falling. It was a miracle that he himself had not been cut down.

The first witnesses to recall seeing Sheriff Martin after the shooting found him silent and subdued. He was pale, but unmarked and not at all dishevelled. He handed over his malfunctioning pistol to Detective McKeever.

The sheriff returned to Hazleton on one of the first trolleys with some of the wounded, and when he got there, some of the Hazletonians begged him to remain in the district because they feared there would be a terrible uprising that night. Indeed, some American families in Lattimer were already evacuating the village to seek safety with nearby relatives. But the sheriff headed straight for the 5:00 P.M. train for Wilkes-Barre, lonely and distraught. Just before boarding the train he told a reporter for the Hazleton *Plain Speaker* that more than anyone, he regretted the bloodshed and stated "in emphatic terms that he did not give the order to fire."

During that long hour on the train, alone with his thoughts, the sheriff began to pull himself together. In the station at Wilkes-Barre, he said to a reporter who caught him as he got off the train: "I halted the marching column and read the proclamation. They refused to pay attention. . . . I hated to give the command to shoot, and was awfully sorry that I was compelled to do so, but I was there to do my duty."

The Pottsville *Republican* recorded the sheriff's entire first statement in Wilkes-Barre. He was emotional about the strikers:

They acted very viciously, reviling and kicking me, knocking me down and tramping upon me. I called upon my deputies to aid me, and they did so, but they were unable to accomplish much. I realized that something had to be done at once or I would be killed. I called to the deputies to discharge their firearms into the air over the heads of the strikers as it might probably frighten them. It was done at once, but it had no effect whatever on the infuriated foreigners, who used me so much the rougher and became fiercer and fiercer, more like wild beasts than human beings. . . . I then called upon the deputies to defend themselves and shoot if they must to protect their lives or to protect the property that they had been sent to guard from being demolished. The next second there were a few scattered shots fired into the infuriated foreigners and a moment later the entire force of deputies discharged a solid volley into the crowd. I hated to give the command to shoot and it was with awful sorrow that I was compelled to do so, but I was there to do my duty and I did it as best I knew how. . . .

Lawyer Ferris had come down to the train station to prevent his client from making just such an admission, and he seized the sheriff's arm, pulling him across the street into the Hotel Redington where he had already rented a room for this contingency. While a flock of reporters waited in the lobby downstairs, Ferris was instructing the sheriff about what he was to say and do. He warned his client that sentiment against him was high in Wilkes-Barre and that he might be charged with murder. At about seven o'clock in the evening, the two men called the reporters up to the room and gave them what was to become the sheriff's official version of his story. He had regained his poise and told his story with sincerity and feeling.

The men started on their journey [he said to the press] and I went to Hazleton and summoned the deputies and told them to take their Winchesters with them. There were about seventy-five of them altogether. We boarded trolley cars and started for Lattimer. When within a short distance of that place we saw the column advancing toward the mine and we stopped the car and got out into the road. When the strikers reached us I ordered them to halt and they did so. For the third time I told them that I had warned them to disperse and that if they did not obey my warning there would be trouble. A few of the men came from the head of the crowd and all shouted at once that they did not care for me or my deputies and that they intended to go to Lattimer and stop the mine. While I was arguing with the men I saw them talking secretly and knew that some sort of trouble was brewing. The first thing I knew some big Italian * [sic] came from the crowd, one of the men who had been shouting at me, and grabbed me by the throat. He called me a vile name and said that I had no right to interfere in their business. The fellow pulled my head under his arms and struck me on the shoulders, and when I got a chance to look up I saw that I was surrounded by several fierce looking men. I shouted to the men that they should arrest the person who had attacked me, but in the confusion the deputies evidently did not hear what I said.

Then I heard a shot and it was soon followed by another. This seemed a signal for a combined volley on the part of the deputies and before I could extricate myself from the crowd that had surrounded me there was one rifle crack after another. I do not know how many shots were fired, but there was an awful din and I imagine that at least 150 bullets were sent on their deadly mission. The whole thing did not last over a minute. After receiving a few punches from the fellow or fellows who held me they released me soon after the firing commenced, and when I was away from the crowd I saw the strikers scampering away in all directions. The scene was an awful one. About us lay the dead and the dying. There were men who had already become corpses and others from whose wounds the blood was flowing upon the road. Some lay motionless and others screamed and moaned with pain.

I at once ordered the deputies to take the wounded to the cars and convey them to the Hazleton Hospital, which was done as speedily as possible. The news of the affair had reached Hazleton and the settlements along the route and the people were wild with

* There were virtually no Italians among the marchers. Later stories featured "a big Hungarian."

144   *The Guns of Lattimer* excitement. After the wounded had been attended to the dead were taken care of and sent to their late homes.

The order to fire never came from my lips. When the deputies saw that I was attacked I suppose they thought it was their duty to protect me. One of the men fired, then another, and then the firing became general. I suppose they thought the strikers were about to attack them also and followed the example of the first man who fired.

I of course deplore the incident. Although my life has constantly been in danger in that region I have remained there day after day and have directed the operations of the deputies. Yesterday was the fifth time I was attacked by strikers and at no time did I call upon the deputies to avenge the injury done me. I knew I had the law and the deputies on my side, but I refrained from committing any act of violence intending to hold such an extremity in reserve until the strikers had passed all law. From the way they had been acting, I feared that something desperate would have to be done, but it came sooner than I expected.

I will go down tomorrow morning. I do not know what the feeling is towards me on the part of the strikers, and whether or not they intend avenging the death of their fellow strikers, but it is my duty to go there and face the music. I may find it necessary before morning to advise the Governor to call out the troops, but if I do not do that I will summon fifty or a hundred deputies from here, as I find them on the street, and will order them to go with me. With this force I will do what I can and if I find myself unable to cope with the situation I will then advise the Governor to furnish aid. The deputies were drafted from citizens in the Hazleton region and they are all good men

When the reporters filed out, Sheriff Martin and Ferris remained at the hotel and began making telephone calls. It was crucial, Ferris said, that they proceed carefully now, without mistakes. They would call the governor and ask that he call up the National Guard. If the governor agreed, the sheriff could simply bow out. The coal companies would no longer have to pay the deputies. The strike would be broken.

Meanwhile, before he could go home to Plains to get some sleep, the sheriff needed to establish immediate assurances of moral support, bail money, and guarantees of an adequate legal defense in the trial that would surely come. "Don't worry, Jim," Ferris said to him, "no jury in Pennsylvania is going to convict an officer of the law trying to do his duty while in danger of his life." The sheriff wanted to believe him.

September 10, 1897

THE PUBLIC MEETING IN HAZLETON

MOMENTS after correspondent Evans's frantic phone call from the company office in Lattimer, just minutes after the disaster, telegraph and telephone began to carry word of the massacre to New York, Philadelphia, and the world. Just as speedily, word spread through the streets of Hazleton. Sheets, blankets, hot water, and extra helping hands were needed at the hospital. It seemed that all Hazleton was swept into action. Fears spread that the whole region would be inflamed and that thousands of marchers might descend on the city. Talk spread of possible dynamitings and thefts of arms.

Six doctors with heavy aprons were at work all evening—and would stay at their grisly task until late the next day—in the emergency room of the Hazleton hospital.

Outside, by eight o'clock, those citizens who could not help in any direct way met in a series of public meetings. The largest gathered on the old baseball field on Donegal Hill, where over two thousand persons expressed "their indignation at the action of the deputies in committing wholesale murder without any cause whatever." The Reverend Spaulding, a Protestant pastor, implored everyone "to be loyal to the stars and stripes and remain coolheaded." He said the guilty would be punished for "downing our fallen comrades," and issued a commandment: "Don't break the laws, and the company stores and company butchers will be done away with." Frank Tulcas and John Deac, each speaking in a different eastern European tongue, urged action on behalf of the victim's families. Conrad Rosenstock said in German that the wage earners of the region are treated worse than the slaves of 1860. Unanimous consent was then given to four resolutions:

> WHEREAS, a sad calamity has befallen this community and an unwarranted and uncalled for attack has been made upon peaceful persons seeking redress,

Resolved, that we, as a body condemn and deplore such actions, which were perpetrated on the public highway without justification or excuse,

Resolved, that in anticipation of the Governor sending the State militia, we protest against such action, because their presence is not necessary to preserve the peace of this community,

Resolved, that we demand the prosecution of the Sheriff and his deputies for the crimes committed this tenth day of September,

Resolved, that we extend our moral and financial support to the friends and relatives of those dead and wounded, and that we express our deep sorrow for the widows and orphans.

Then members of the audience began to shout "Fahy! Fahy!" and the union leader got up and spoke calmly of how the calamity demonstrated the need for organization. He urged everyone to be quiet and peaceable—and to organize. Americans and foreigners mingled freely in the hot September air.

Both in Harwood and at the hospital, the priests of the Polish and Slovak parishes were rushing about trying to assist the injured and to console the survivors of the dead. Outside the hospital, a contingent of women kept up a steady weeping and wailing.

The sentiment in Hazleton was bitterly against calling the National Guard, and the deputies must have begun to feel frightened by the force of the public's hostility to them. Many of them went into hiding that night, and some were not to be seen in the area for weeks.

September 10, 1897

JOHN NEMETH'S RIDE

OF ALL the citizens in Hazleton, John Nemeth at the shipping line and foreign exchange office was probably in the best position to grasp what had happened. He knew the quiet belief of the Markles, the Pardees, and the Fells in Anglo-Saxon superiority, and in the idea that the foreigners were of a lower order of intelligence and feeling. He understood the pressures on Sheriff Martin.

When word of the massacre first came, Nemeth ran out into the street to learn everything he could. He went to the newspapers, the hospital, the undertakers. Then he returned to his offices and put through a call to Philadelphia, informing Consul-General Theodorovich of the Austro-Hungarian imperial government that at least eleven Austro-Hungarian subjects had been killed and that perhaps thirty others lay wounded and in danger of death. Nemeth remembered that when eleven Italians had been killed in a frenzy by the most respected citizens of New Orleans in 1891, the Italian government had nearly gone to war with the United States. So he wanted to alert Theodorovich to the serious duties that might devolve upon him. Speed was essential, he said; the consul general might wish to arrive at the scene before matters got worse. Hanging up, Nemeth made a reservation at the nearest hotel. Then he took up his cap, sought a horse, and rode off in the gathering dusk for Harwood.

The road from Harwood was dotted with women dressed in black and urchins barefoot beside them, with hesitant men and young boys whose faces were frozen in impassivity. Nemeth knew that John Eagler and Joseph Michalko had been elected leaders of the local, and he intended to seek them out. He wanted to assemble eye witnesses immediately. Along the single dingy main street of Harwood, he met Reverend Karl Hauser from the Slovak Lutheran church, who was accompanying the body of Mike Cheslak in a wagon. At the Cheslak home, the new widow began to moan and scream in Slovak fashion, while her five children stood dumbstruck. There was a bullet hole between the dead man's eyes, from which fluids drained. Someone began bringing ice to pack around the body. Cheslak's wife was left to wash away the caked blood and staunch his still seeping wounds. The children were at last shepherded away by neighbors: Ella, fifteen, Mary (the first born in America), five, Anna, four, Veronica, two, and John, eight months.

All over Harwood Nemeth met scenes of poignant grief, not

only in the households to which the dead and seriously wounded had returned. No one knew exactly how many others had fallen, or which ones had merely lingered to assist the fallen. Many of the women of Harwood began to walk to Hazleton to seek the missing. Rumors spread that the deputies intended to pursue and to slay those who had escaped.

The shock of seeing Mike Cheslak's torn body deeply affected Nemeth. He had known of the impending march since the night before, but had expected it to pass as uneventfully as the dozens of other marches during the preceding weeks. No one, he knew, would get the foreigners' side of the story. Even well-intentioned officials and reporters would be halted by the language barrier. He felt it was his duty to collect accurate testimony and to begin alone, if necessary, to swear out a warrant against the sheriff and his men for murder.

He tried to get the story from everyone he could. He explained to reluctant witnesses that the Austro-Hungarian government would need their testimony and would probably seek compensation on their behalf. Some, like John Eagler, talked easily. Others refused, speechless and afraid. They feared for their future employment and their lives.

Survivors of the massacre struggled back into Harwood all night long. When he had gained a clear picture of what had happened, the weary Nemeth mounted his horse and galloped out of Harwood and down the hill toward Cranberry. The city of Hazleton was silhouetted on the farther hill against the moonlit sky.

It was midnight when a reporter spotted Nemeth riding back toward Hazleton. His horse raised a cloud of whitish dust along the road into West Hazleton. The young reporter from the Wilkes-Barre *Times* had missed much of the early story but was making up for it by watchfulness that night.

The reporter halted Nemeth as the latter rode slowly along Broad Street. Nemeth told him that "the families of the men killed are mourning and that no greater calamity could have been visited upon them, not even a terrible mine accident. The feeling in the town is intense." Nemeth explained that he had telegraphed the Austrian consul, and expected him to arrive in Hazleton by morning or no later than four in the afternoon.

He told the reporter that the killing was outrageous and that he intended to take steps to insure a full investigation. "The killing of the Hungarians is a matter of some moment to the United States Government," Nemeth was eager to have the reporter say in print, "which may have to indemnify the families of the deceased as was done in the New Orleans riots some years ago where Italians were killed by Americans."

Nemeth, excited by his journey but sick at heart, then rode off to his home.

Midnight, September 10, 1897

GOMER JONES'S HOUSE

THE SAME REPORTER from the Wilkes-Barre *Times* was soon rewarded for his vigil with yet another story. Coming in from the other road, to the southeast, he heard the clatter of a very fast horse. As the rider entered the city, the reporter stepped out and called to him but the horse sped by. The reporter ran down the street, following sight and sound. Eventually, he caught up. The rider's name was Russel. He had ridden in from Audenried, looking for police headquarters. On Wyoming Street he found Lieutenant Ferry and confided to him that a mob was advancing toward Hazleton from Audenried. The night seemed so quiet that the lieutenant was skeptical. And indeed no mob was to arrive at Hazleton.

But Russel had not been entirely wrong. A mob had marched on Audenried but had advanced no farther. It was rumored that five thousand men in the McAdoo area restlessly sought weapons and five hundred shots were fired into the air, with two persons being accidentally wounded, and several homes and buildings broken into. Gomer Jones, who had for weeks refused pleas to leave the district, had word from informers that a group of men was intent on breaking into his house to steal the 200 rifles he kept there. Jones with seven associates hurriedly managed to get the guns out of his house by a back way. In the woods, from a vantage point from which they could see without being seen, Jones and his men sat with Winchesters gleaming in the darkness beneath the branches. They watched several dozen dark forms approach the house, shout, throw stones, and then rush the doors.

Jones was later to claim that the strikers stole $200 worth of silverware from his house and smashed the furniture. He also said that his men wanted to shoot, but he would not allow them to. Two hundred dollars, the amount Jones assessed as the value of his silverware, represented two-thirds of the average annual wage of a miner's assistant in 1897 in Luzerne County. Like some of the deputies, Jones, too, went into hiding for several days.

September 10–11, 1897

THE NATIONAL GUARD IS COMING!

AT THE VERY TIME the huge gathering in Hazleton had resolved to ask the governor not to send the National Guard, the coal operators held a private conference in the Van Wickles's drawing room, for the opposite purpose.

In Wilkes-Barre, meanwhile, at 10:30 P.M., Sheriff Martin and Ferris had arranged to meet Colonel G. Bow Dougherty, Commander of the Ninth Regiment of the Pennsylvania National Guard at the Lehigh Valley Coal Company offices in the Coal Exchange Building. By 11:00 the three men had agreed to ask the governor for troops. From the Capitol in Harrisburg the state's attorney general said the governor would consider their request and call them back with his answer at midnight. When the governor called back, he asked to speak to Colonel Dougherty and ordered him to have the Ninth Regiment in Hazleton by daybreak if possible.

Five years earlier, in 1892, the Ninth Regiment had been

called out all the way across the state to quell riots at Homestead, near Pittsburgh. Thus they had a routine worked out: higher officers were to call those on the next lower rank; using telephones, bicycles, and horses, these officers sent the message to outlying companies in neighboring communities. Now, with only a few hours till daybreak, the colonel had to hurry. He sent his adjutant, Lieutenant Sharpe, to notify field and staff officers; Colonel Miner, who had a bicycle, agreed to contact officers in North Wilkes-Barre. Colonel Dougherty then took over the classy Westmoreland Club and asked friends of his gathered there to help him make telephone calls. He requested trolleys to be at prearranged embarkation places by 2:00 A.M., and requested that the Lehigh Valley Railroad have a train of nine passenger cars and one baggage car ready by 5:00 A.M.

The governor, too, had been busy and had sent telegrams to the commanding officers of the National Guard to alert their subordinate units and to come personally to Harrisburg at once. At an all-night meeting in the governor's office, strategy was outlined and supply lines activated, and in the wee hours, the weary officers departed Harrisburg by train to take up their command at Hazleton.

At 12:15 A.M., just as a correspondent of the Pottsville *Miners' Journal* telephoned from Hazleton that "Everything has been quiet and peaceful here tonight" and that "the troops will have nothing to do when they come," the courthouse bell in Wilkes-Barre had begun ringing out nine sharp peals, four times repeated. For three hours, this prearranged signal rang out every fifteen minutes. All across the city, members of the National Guard awoke, dressed themselves, and hurried to assembly points.

Twenty miles away, in Scranton, Lieutenant Colonel Charles C. Mattes was asleep at his home when, at 1:05 A.M., he was aroused by a vigorous ringing of the doorbell. Sleepily and in irritation, he found a messenger boy with copies of the orders addressed to Colonel H. A. Cousen, his commander in the Thirteenth Regiment of the Pennsylvania National Guard. The first announced that a riot had occurred at Hazleton and the second read as follows:

Move your command to Hazleton at the earliest possible moment and reach there by daylight if possible. Railroads have been notified to assist you. . . .

At 3:00 A.M., before the special bells had reached their full three-hour cycle in Wilkes-Barre, the Second Battalion from Plymouth, consisting of 42 men and 3 officers, in heavy marching gear and with two days' rations, was already assembled at the armory. Major McKee had been telephoned by Colonel Dougherty at 12:30 A.M., and had his men in rank within two and a half hours. By 4:30 A.M., company after company had lined up at the armory, and the march to the railway began. At 5 A.M., the men began boarding the train. At 5:20 A.M., Company C of Pittston reported by trolley. Colonel Dougherty waited anxiously for Company H of Pittston, which finally arrived, and at 5:40 A.M., the train jerked to a start. Three hundred twelve armed men were on board, with 12,000 rounds of ammunition. Lieutenant Jenkins of Company E stayed behind to organize stragglers and would report to Hazleton by 3:00 P.M. with 94 more men. By Monday, 442 out of the regiment's full strength of 476 would be on duty.

Colonel Dougherty assigned the best sharpshooters of the regiment to ride on the cowcatcher, footboard, and tank of the locomotive, in case any person might commit an overt act against the train. The governor's man, Colonel Asher Miner (later to be a hero of World War I), took command of the sharpshooters. His men shivered in the damp air of the predawn hours, chilled by the rushing air. A beautiful moon lit up the silent countryside as the train roared southward through the valleys. At 7:45 A.M., the train puffed into Hazleton. Following strict orders, the men disembarked quickly and in absolute silence, throwing out a skirmish line and clearing the field below the Church Street Station.

Surveying the scene with pleasure, Colonel Dougherty estimated that the crowd of citizens already gathered at the station numbered three thousand. He pulled out his watch. For the Homestead riot, his men had required six hours and twenty minutes from the first order to the first call at the armory. This time, they had made it in four hours and thirty minutes.

September 10–28, 1897   *153*

They were actually in place on the field of assignment, sixty-five miles from their home armory via the railroad route they had been assigned, within seven hours and forty-five minutes of the governor's order, without any advance warning. Colonel Dougherty was very satisfied indeed.

Meanwhile, General John Peter Shindel Gobin, commander of the Third Brigade (and later lieutenant governor), had travelled from his home in Philadelphia to Harrisburg to be briefed by the governor. As he and his staff arranged for tents, food, ammunition, and medical supplies to be shipped immediately from state storehouses in Harrisburg, Gobin received reports about the movements of the six regiments of his brigade. A large, hook-nosed man, Gobin was an experienced officer who had led the guard at Homestead in 1892. Governor Hastings had himself won fame as the hero of the Johnstown flood of 1889, and there too he had brought the resources of the National Guard into quick and active play. By 4:00 A.M. Gobin was seated on a train to Hazleton.

Gobin and Hastings both knew that the foreign strikers presented an especially ticklish problem; their psychology as well as their language was different and very difficult to comprehend. As Gobin was to put it to a reporter for the Pottsville *Republican*: "These foreigners are born and bred under the lash; they are raised amidst hardships that only the strongest survive, consequently they are dull to fear and indifferent to death; there is trouble ahead till these foreign laborers understand what American government means; they are used to law officers attired in gaudy uniforms, and our local constabulary are neither feared or respected by them; yes, the trouble is coming; it may not get here this year or next, but when some intrepid Hungarian officer gets over here one of these days, some man of war experience, brains and scheming, we are going to catch it." *

Gobin wanted his six regiments of infantry placed in a strategic line from Lattimer on the north flank to Audenried

---

* In his official report to the U.S. War Department, Captain Alexis R. Paxton wrote: "Most of the strikers knew very little of our language, laws and system of government, and a majority of them were of a low order in origin and intelligence."

on the south, with strong reinforcements at the center, in Hazleton, ready to move out in any direction. He wanted Captain Fred Ott's Governor's Troop, the first-class cavalry unit, to show itself in every village of the area, so no one would doubt the state's intention. He ordered Captain Ott to cover upward of twenty miles a day. He would want his other officers to familiarize themselves with the roads of the vicinity. The hills, rocky terrain, and scrub growth would limit both cavalry and infantry mainly to the roads, and they might need to move swiftly. By midday, he ought to have nearly twenty-five hundred men to establish his defense line. Tents, foodstuffs, thousands of rounds of ammunition, Gatling guns, and assorted other paraphernalia of war were already being loaded onto trains at the state arsenal. The First Brigade in Philadelphia had been alerted to stand by in case of necessity. General Gobin had utmost confidence in the National Guard system.*

When his train arrived in Hazleton at 7:30 A.M., General Gobin went directly to the Lehigh Valley Company offices to make them his first headquarters. He expected to see—and he did—linesmen installing new telephone lines out to the sites selected for his encampments and to Harrisburg. He wasn't quite prepared for the peacefulness of the scene at Hazleton, or for the hostility toward the deputies he now observed, even among the English-speaking.

He had to deal immediately with the warrant sworn out for the arrest of the deputies and the sheriff. He refused to honor it, citing the precedent of Homestead: a sheriff, he said, is the

---

* "The National Guard of Pennsylvania is officered by a class of men representing the highest social and intellectual class, men of standing in the state," Captain Alexis R. Paxton was to report to Washington, "and to them is due the high state of efficiency attained in organization, drill and discipline, while the rank and file, composed of the better element from town and country, make discipline a comparatively easy matter." A profile of the ninety-seven commanders of the guard during the period 1870–1905 shows that nearly all were Anglo-Saxon Protestant, often members of old established families, staunch Republicans, active in politics, and leaders in the business life of their communities. Of thirteen who indicated their religion, only one was Catholic; most of the others were Episcopalian and Presbyterian; eleven were Masons. Many had close connections to the newspapers in their home districts.

chief executive officer in the county; there will be time later for a trial. His first consideration now must be the restoration of order. To his surprise, a reading of the mood of the city suggested to him that the arrest of the deputies might lead to a lynching.

A reporter asked the general what he would do if local detectives arrested the deputies. "I would send a squadron of cavalry after them," he replied icily, "and drive them to hell until I recovered every one of them."

All through the day, new units arrived, most of the men sleepy from the long exciting night. Orders had to be given. Camps had to be established. Senior officers had to mark out campsites. Junior officers had to supervise work details. The Lehigh Valley Coal Company provided each company "a dainty supply of grub" on its arrival: a barrel of milk, lunch crackers, several cans of condensed milk, six hams, candies, coffee, and cake.

The general wished to intimidate the enemy as quickly as possible. He asked Mayor Altmiller to close all the liquor stores. And he asked to meet with the clergymen of the city about the upcoming funerals.

On the bright sunny day of September 11, an almost holidaylike peacefulness prevailed. There were no skirmishes or violent incidents—not one. Not a single soldier was to be threatened or wounded. The correspondent travelling with the Eighth Regiment from Pottsville sent this dispatch from Audenried: ". . . nothing has occurred, and the 'Hunks' and the 'Dagos' are quite as peaceable as lambs. Your correspondent hasn't heard the unintelligible chatter of any of the strikers since his arrival." And from Delano station: "A crowd of Hungarian women engaged in a crying match and these were the first crystal globules we had seen descending since Pottsville. At McAdoo and Beaver Brook, girls flocked to the station, joked and chattered with the soldiers and were in anything but a crying mood. The English-speaking peoples at these places are overjoyed at the coming of the soldiers."

Even the foreigners, other correspondents noted, viewed the bright uniforms of the soldiers with awe, curiosity, and friendly respect. People's hostility toward the deputies did not spill over upon the National Guard. The only complaints came from a few Hazletonians who complained of the guard's excessive drinking and flirtation with Hazleton girls. (Within twenty-four hours, two men were to be drummed out of the guard for being intoxicated on the public streets.)

By nightfall on Sunday, September 12, a day that turned cold and cloudy, making life in the tents uncomfortable for the soldiers, more than twenty-five hundred troops had been assembled in five different campsites. These campsites had been set up in a cross: south at Audenried; on a site west of Hazleton; inside Hazleton; at a position east of Hazleton; and on the north at Lattimer. On September 14, General Gobin sent the Fourth Regiment to Drifton, thus extending the northeastern flank out beyond Lattimer. For the most part, the encampment turned out to be first a lark—and then a bore.

Saturday, September 11, 1897

ARRESTS AND COUNTERARRESTS

GENERAL GOBIN was rather uncertain. He was worried about the upcoming funerals, and he warned his junior officers to have their men conspicuous but not obtrusive throughout the rituals and processions. He wanted no incidents, but on the other hand a firm show of force.

By midafternoon, with the help of attorney John Garman, John Nemeth succeeded in having warrants sworn out for the arrest of the sheriff and 102 deputies. Constables Airey and Gallagher of Hazleton were ordered to serve a warrant on A. E. Hess, who had probably made himself the most hated of all the deputies. At about three o'clock, the constables found Hess on the corner of Broad and Wyoming streets. Just as Constable Airey finished reading the warrant, Hess bolted and climbed aboard a moving trolley headed for the encampment at Hazle Park. Airey and Gallagher were forced to wait for the next trolley. At the gates of the bivouac, soldiers with bayonets forbade them entrance. When they explained their mission, they were shown no sympathy. Hess had recently been an officer in the guard.

John Nemeth understood from what had happened to Airey and Gallagher that Gobin meant to resist the warrants. Now he feared there would be a cover-up. He sat down to write up his notes on the testimony he had collected in anticipation of the arrival of the secretary to the Austrian consul.

Although some of the deputies, like Hess, quite openly walked the streets, many of them had already fled town. J. Potter Clarke, Calvin Pardee, Jr., and S. B. Price had registered under false names at the Traymore Hotel in Atlantic City and were to stay there incognito until September 16. Many citizens tried to clear their names of rumors that they might have been among the deputies. Daniel Brickof, Fred Steinheiser, and Edward Treible ran paid ads in the Hazleton paper to clear their names: "Not a deputy. A rumor, and one that does me a great injustice. . . ."

Dr. Theodore Theodorovich finally arrived, wearing a tall hat and gloves. A young man of energy and intelligence, he had broken off his honeymoon and hurried to catch an early train, believing that the Austro-Hungarian government would demand a full and prompt report in order to open an action against the United States. His ambassador in Washington had been requested to contact the U.S. secretary of state and to demand federal supervision. But he understood that the issue would have to be settled locally before the federal government would get involved, and so his own conduct of the affair here in Hazleton would be critical.

Theodorovich, in addition to being intelligent, was inordinately proud. As he stopped at the Hazleton Western Union office to cable to his government, his young bride was with him. When he finished cabling, he noticed that a small diplomatic pouch was missing and instantly he accused a Hazleton correspondent who had been standing near him of taking it. Fearing that the loss might mean the end of his career, he grew excited, told the journalist that his denials were lies, and challenged the man to a duel.

The reporter kept his wits. "Take the lady back to the hotel, then come back," he suggested.

By the time the young diplomat had got back to the hotel, his bride had succeeded in calming him. Then to his mortification, it turned out that he had carelessly left the pouch on the lobby writing desk and that various persons, trying to identify its owner, had looked through the pouch's contents. It swiftly became known around town what his business was. The duel was forgotten.

Theodorovich quickly redeemed himself, however, by getting Kislewicz and Juszko out of jail on the grounds that no proper hearing had been held. He saw to it that Juszko was admitted to the hospital, the thirty-ninth of the wounded, and was himself given a grim tour of the wounded and dying at the hospital. Sheets and bedding were still bloody. Nor had the floors near the emergency rooms and the operating room yet been thoroughly cleaned of the day-old gore.

After dark, a meeting was held in the Alter Street school-house. Charles Kennedy presided and Joe Costello acted as secretary. Speeches in English, Slovak, and Italian denounced the sheriff and the deputies. Arthur Evans addressed the crowd in Hungarian. James E. Roderick made a speech and contributed one hundred dollars to the newly forming Prosecuting and Charity Committee. He was a superintendent at Van Winkle's colliery in Milnesville and had formerly been a state mining inspector.

"A great calamity which will go down in history as the greatest crime of the Christian era has befallen this peaceful community," the meeting resolved, "and the rights of people to assemble for a redress of grievance has been attacked in an unwarranted manner." Those assembled then by voice vote: (1) condemned the shooting as inexcusable; (2) asserted that the community was in a state of peace and did not need the state militia; (3) called upon James Martin to resign; (4) called upon the Markle Company to demand the resignation of its employee, A. E. Hess, "as a disturber of the peace and promoter of riot"; and (5) called for the prosecution of the sheriff and deputies "for disgracing American citizenship."

Later that evening on the green at the end of South Wyoming Street, a larger rally was held within earshot of the nearby camp of the National Guard. Reverend Staš of Freeland presided and urged in Slovak that the men hold themselves in check, keep their tempers, and follow the law in all respects. "We were not born in this country, but we can be as good citizens as any," an interpreter summarized. P. F. Loughran explained that the purpose of the meeting was to organize a Prosecution and Charity Committee. Matthew Long, a young and popular union activist, was elected president by acclamation. (The Reverend Richard Aust was later made president, with Matt Long willingly acting as secretary.) In a booming voice Long called for a committee of action, for which John Nemeth, Father Aust, Reverend Karl Hauser, Reverend John Staš, and Edmund Lambrech were elected. Five separate clergymen addressed the throng, each in a different native language. John Nemeth was asked to say a few words: "Above all things, keep quiet, say nothing to anyone to provoke their anger, use no bad or denunciatory language; go home and stay there; go to work or stay away as you deem it wise. Follow these rules and you will win your cause."

Meanwhile, all day long soldiers had been guarding the Hess home. Constables Duser and Airey once more attempted to serve Hess his warrant and were turned back by the guard. Later they spotted a platoon of soldiers marching down the center of the street, with Hess protected in their center.

Duser knew that the law was on his side. He stopped the platoon in the street and asked testily: "Which one of you is the Officer of the Day?"

"Yes, sir," snapped a young man.

Duser explained his mission.

The officer cut him short: "I refuse, sir, to recognize your warrant."

Duser exploded. "I will take Hess dead or alive. I have done some shooting myself and you boys don't frighten me."

"Surround these men!" the young officer commanded. His twenty men took both constables and all the spectators into custody and marched them all back to camp. There were loud and boisterous complaints. At the camp, all were released except Duser, who was locked up in the guardhouse. Meanwhile, the rest of the platoon marched Hess to his home. The guard outside was reinforced.

It took until four the next afternoon for attorneys Matt Long and Frank Needham to persuade General Gobin to release Duser. Duser was still fuming about being arrested while a man wanted for murder went free under the protection of armed troopers.

Sunday, September 12, 1897

THE FIRST FUNERALS

TINY ELLA CHESLAK had wept from the moment the body of her husband had arrived back in Harwood by wagon Friday night. She and her eldest daughter, Ella, were partially in shock. In their world, women without men could scarcely survive. Even with Michael's work, they were not far from starving. For young Ella, who had been apart from him for twelve years, her father had become a giant in her imagination.

Reverend Karl Hauser suggested to the widow that the funeral service be conducted at home, to avoid her attempting the long trip to the church in Freeland. So on the front porch of the company house in which he had lived, Mike Cheslak's pine coffin was draped in white. While the service was being read in the clear morning air, miners from the entire South Side continued to gather. The members of the Hazleton Slovak Band came in uniform, some of them holding their gold-laced caps, all of them wearing long strips of black crepe. Ella wept profusely and from time to time cried out. Her oldest daughter stood erect and stunned. The littlest ones looked about at the crowd.

Ten men from the houses nearby were dead or dying. Next door, John Futa, eighteen, lay in a coffin banked with flowers.

His silver trumpet, which he had played in the National Slovak Society band, lay on the coffin amid the flowers. In the silence, Futa's young mother climbed upon a chair and shouted into the narrow street, where the tracks of the coal line to the breaker were covered by hundreds of mourners: "My boy is dead. My boy. My only support. When he worked, he earned seventy-five cents a day. My good boy. He took care of his poor mother well, his widowed mother. Now my boy is dead. He was killed by dogs—a sheriff who was a dog, men who were dogs." She could not stop. Slavic women were often more hotheaded than their men. "They killed your people. Now the soldiers have come to kill all of us. We must not let them! We must fight. We must avenge their deaths." Her words were embarrassing, disturbing. Someone helped her down from the chair.

Across the street, in another company house, six men made ready to lift the body of Steve Jurich. Down the street, others were already carrying Andrew Jurechek. The members of the St. Joseph's National Slovak Society, wearing white, blue, and red sashes across the right shoulder (the colors of the Slovak flag), and the Italian St. Peter and Paul's Society members, wearing blue and gold uniforms and carrying silver cavalry sabers, began to form in ranks. Behind them formed the Polish Socrasa Fondata wearing gray uniforms and carrying traditional sabers, and a fourth group, in green and silver. At a signal, the brass band at the head of Old Street began to play the mournful death march, drums rolling slowly. Then came the five hundred men of the four burial societies. Then the draped wagons with the four bodies, the pallbearers, families, and friends. The first hearse was followed by two hundred mourners on foot and thirty carriages. Each of the hearses that came after also trailed a retinue of walkers and carriages, improvised from coal and delivery wagons. Behind these came a seemingly endless line of miners from the entire South Side. The cortege climbed up from Harwood, past the strippings on the brow of Holler's Hill, and down into the valley past Crystal Ridge— along the same route the victims had been following so lightly and happily two days earlier. As the long procession began to ascend past Cranberry, hundreds of residents stood atop the culm banks. All could hear the rolling dirge and the creak of the wagons. Many men from Cranberry fell in behind the others. By the time the long line toiled up the steep hill toward West Hazleton, it numbered three thousand. When the band reached West Hazleton, the last ranks were just leaving Cranberry, over a mile away.

Slowly, the great procession marched from West Hazleton down the slope toward St. Joseph's Slovak Church on the far hill of Hazleton. The sermon in the tiny church was fiery. Clergymen of several faiths attended. Father Richard Aust, worn and exhausted but hot with controlled passion, exhorted those who could hear him in the stifling, flower-drenched air inside, and those listening outside through the open windows, that they should trust in God's wisdom, and that beyond human justice was God's justice.

Some who heard him understood Father Aust to be saying that God himself would punish the guilty deputies. From this, a legend grew up about a curse under which the deputies would henceforth live, and in later years little children listened to macabre tales of how each of the deputies, one by one, were dying painful or unusual deaths. Even as an old man, John Moye of Lattimer, although he was born after the massacre, was to recall such stories vividly.

Standing on the porch of the Valley Hotel, General Gobin stroked his beard as he watched the five hundred men of the burial societies flashing their sabers. He was angry. He had assumed that the members of the procession would be unarmed, and didn't like the sabers at all. This was precisely the sort of display he didn't want. He waved for Captain Shultz and told him to instruct the Polanders not to carry any arms during the larger funeral scheduled for the next day. He sent orders for the clergymen to meet with him before then.

As the procession passed, "a prominent Hungarian"—probably John Nemeth—explained to newspapermen that the foreigners respected military uniforms. The immigrants, he said, may not have recognized men wearing ordinary clothes, some of whom they knew from familiar occupations, as genuine representatives of the law. Military uniforms, sashes, medals—such things represented the majesty of the state. Lavish military ornaments suggested a civilized and aesthetic military presence, exercising its power symbolically rather than through brute efficiency. He pointed out how much more respectfully the people were responding to the National Guard than they had to the deputies.

Meanwhile, in the mines at Audenried and at other places, the shutting down of the boilers had lowered the steam pressure underground; some mines were more than half-flooded. At Jeddo, John Markle himself went out to face a band of marching miners. The guard was not at this time patrolling as far north as Jeddo and Eckley, so the coal operator had to face the strikers alone, as Sheriff Martin had. Markle was able to turn the marchers away with words. He explained that he had already met with a grievance committee and had promised that he would give them an answer within ten days. Until then, he didn't want his men disturbed in their work. The marchers, who were from Eckley, broke up and returned home.

On Sunday, Jurich and Jurechek, who were cousins, were buried in a single wide grave. Futa was also lowered into a grave of his own. The three of them and Mike Cheslak were buried at St. Joseph's Catholic Cemetery in unmarked graves. It was learned at the funerals that on the day of the massacre, Jurechek had been subpoenaed to appear on a minor charge in Wilkes-Barre. Work was so scarce all that year that he had no money to pay the fare. He had marched to Lattimer instead.

That afternoon, members of the Knights of St. George, a Polish society organized to provide benefits for the widows and orphans of its members, began sawing two-by-fours and nailing together a solid platform in front of the altar of St. Stanislaus Polish Catholic Church in Hazleton. Women in long black skirts decorated the church with flowers. Out at St. Stanislaus Cemetery, workmen blasted a large circular grave, nine by twenty-one feet, out of rock. All over the Lehigh Valley, printed "In Memoriam" cards were handed out, requesting help for the families of the victims. Not all the men to be buried on Monday were Polish, but most of them were; some were Austro-Hungarian citizens from the Tatra Mountains, where Slovakia and southern Poland overlap.

Sunday, September 12, 1897

BEN AND MAUREEN

STILL DAZED from his escape two days before, Ben Sakmar trudged along in the funeral procession with the others. He recalled the warnings of his Uncle Emil about the cruelty of America. He kept trying to believe that they were actually dead, Steve Jurich, Mike Cheslak, Andrew Jurechek, John Futa. All his best friends, except John Eagler, were dead. The words of the mass seemed empty. The words of the priests seemed empty. He felt a surge of strength at the size and might of the communities gathered at the funerals, but he seemed to be walking in a dream.

As he turned away from the cemetery and began walking aimlessly back toward Harwood with no one to speak to, he heard her voice. She had been looking through the crowds for him.

"Ben!" she called out. "Ben!"

He joined her in the doorway where she waited.

"I had to talk with you. Oh, I'm so sad. So sad." Her eyes were red. Tears had been on her face. He grasped her two white arms. "I want to go with you," she said. She nodded toward the street.

Ben began to shake. She pulled close to him and he lowered his head. Her hands clung to his back. So many people were weeping that their own emotion was hidden in the general sorrow.

Ben had not seen Maureen since the Fourth of July. He now realized that he had missed her every day. Steve and Johanna's wedding had been a message about her. The beating her brother and his friends had given him had been a deflating rejection. Was that past? Could he trust her? He survived by being a realist. He told himself not to count on her emotions on an occasion like this.

But he needed her. The faces of grief in the crowds reflected his own grief. It did not seem wrong to take comfort from her embrace. Then, abruptly, she pulled away and dabbed her eyes.

"Come with me," he said. He took her arm.

He pulled her into a doorway. It was John Nemeth's shipping house. "Will you see me?" he asked. "I come McAdoo?"

She seemed to hesitate. He saw how young she was. "Yes," she said. "Come." He saw the resolve in her eyes.

"I come," he said. "I talk your father."

"Yes," she said. "Come. I'll tell my father you're coming."

"You tell?"

"Yes."

He didn't know whether to embrace her. It seemed better to walk. Her eyes were open to him, permitted him to enter. The two of them seemed of one mind. He stepped to look out at the street. An old woman was moaning as she passed, her daughter supporting her.

He turned back to Maureen and took her arm. The two of them walked back to St. Joseph's Church, then over to St. Stanislaus, back and forth through the mourners, hiding their own emotions in those of the milling crowds. His sorrow was not spent. It seemed deeper and truer, shared with her. Being with her made him, however, more afraid. As long as one was alone and counted on nothing, there was nothing to lose. Happiness was difficult for him to trust.

They did not speak much that day. Together they watched some of the wounded who were able to walk. They saw old women carrying their shoes, walking barefoot back toward the South Side. They watched the neatly uniformed National Guardsmen walking slowly on their patrols. They stopped once as a platoon of mounted cavalry clattered across an intersection in front of them. They saw stable boys leading the hearses back to the undertaker's. They saw two Greek Catholic priests, bearded and in flowing black robes, surrounded by acolytes in lace surplices and by serious-faced laymen. They saw timid miners in plug hats and others in the same peaked mountaineer's cap that Mike Cheslak had worn on the march.

Together they shared a cup of hot black coffee from a street vendor. From time to time, Maureen dabbed another tear. Ben was not happy. Sorrow was everywhere. But for him the afternoon was like healing.

Only alone again, that night, did he warn himself that he might again be rejected by her family. The emotions of the day might have made her vulnerable in a way she would not be again. Still, it touched him that she felt sorrow for his friends.

He didn't know whether he trusted her. He hadn't had much experience with women. Especially not in America.

As he pulled his shirt off in his room in Harwood, he resolved to walk over to McAdoo the next day. He would not be afraid to meet her brother or her father. Not now. Death had somehow made everything equal. John Futa, Steve Jurich, Andrew Jurechek—they were gone now. If life is so short, why be afraid?

The worse things looked, the clearer his mind. He intended to see her often.

Sunday, September 12, 1897

THEODOROVICH'S INVESTIGATION

ON SUNDAY AFTERNOON, as the men returned to Harwood from the funerals of Cheslak and the others, Theodorovich conducted a hearing with John Nemeth acting as notary public. There were to be three further hearings in Hazleton after the big funerals and memorial services of Monday and Tuesday were over, from September 15 to 18. John Andryanski, Andrej Sivar, his father Jacob and his cousin Andro, John Eagler, John Welsh, Michael Malody, Andrew Novotny, Charles Guscott, and others, were all to give notarized depositions. Some of the witnesses were to testify later at the trial, but others would not be called. Before any U.S. official had taken testimony, the Austrian government had the following sworn statements:

Michael Malody, born in Magyaroska [probably Magyarsas], County Zemplén [Zemplín], a Hungarian subject appears and being questioned, makes the following statement:

"I walked on the tenth of September in the front row of the procession with John Eagler, John Pustag, who is now in the Hazleton hospital wounded, with Mike Cheslak and Steve Jurek [Jurich], who were killed on the spot near Lattimer, also with Andro Novotny and Georg Jensco [Jancso]. As we came near Lattimer we met the sheriff with seventy armed deputies. Sheriff Martin came to meet the procession and told the men that they must go no farther. Someone behind me called out 'go ahead' [English] and the sheriff thinking that these words came from me, seized me by the coat and asked me what I had to say, to which I answered that the order to march onward did not come from me. After this answer had been confirmed by my companion Andro Novotny, standing near me, the sheriff seized the latter. About three minutes after, the firing began. I threw myself on the ground and crawled back. The firing may have lasted two minutes. Each deputy fired several times, and I think that each one shot off all the cartridges in the magazine of the guns they were carrying. I saw that all the workmen immediately took flight, like me, at the first fire, while the deputies continued to fire on the fugitives."

Read in the Slovak language, and then the witness asks on account of fear that his testimony may do him harm, to be excused from signing.

Andro Novotny, born in Krusco [Vyšný Kručov], County Šariš, a naturalized American citizen, appears, and, being questioned, gives the following testimony:

"I was at the head of the procession and was not far from Malody whom the sheriff seized by the coat. When the sheriff let him go he caught me by the coat with one hand and with the other pointed his revolver, which he then drew, at my breast. The sheriff asked me, 'Where are you going?' and I answered, 'Let me alone' [English], at the same time throwing off his arm with which he was holding the revolver against my breast. At this movement of mine the sheriff gave the command 'Fire,' and the shooting began. George Jancso, who was near me, helped me out of the hands of the sheriff, and once free from the same I ran until I found proper shelter."

Read in the Slovak language, and the party asks to be excused from signing, lest he may suffer harm from the deposition.

George Jancso, a Hungarian subject, from Visnyó [Višňov], County Zemplén [Zemplín], appears, and being questioned, gives the following testimony:

"I was near Novotny when the sheriff threatened him with the revolver, and I tried to free him from the sheriff's hands, in which I succeeded. The sheriff then caught my coat with one hand and with the other pointed his revolver at my forehead. He did not shoot at me, and I think his pistol was not loaded, for it seemed to me that he snapped it. When he caught me the firing had already begun. I attribute my escape, although I was in the front row, to the fact that my body was protected by that of the sheriff. I think I heard the sheriff call to the deputies, 'Give two or three shots' [English]. At first I thought that the deputies were firing blank cartridges, but when I saw my companions fall wounded to the ground I realized the seriousness of the situation, tore myself from the hands of the sheriff, and ran to a ditch not far away, in which I lay down flat."

Read in the Slovak language, and the party asks to be excused from signing, lest he may suffer harm through the deposition.

John Andryonski, born in Sasó [Šašová], County Sáros [Šariš], appears, and being questioned, makes the following statement:
"I was marching at the head of the procession as we came near to West Hazleton. About three hundred yards from the last-named place, Sheriff J. Martin came to meet us. He had about forty (it might have been more) armed deputies with him. The sheriff leaving the deputies behind him and holding a revolver in his hand, came to meet us and told us to stop. To my remark that we, as well as everybody, had a right to go where we chose, he answered me and those standing by me that we must not go through West Hazleton, but that we were at liberty to go in the public road. I had never seen the sheriff until that moment, nor did he announce himself as such. I must also add that the sheriff did not say a word about forbidding us to go to Lattimer. The word Lattimer was not mentioned during the occurrence I have described. On the prohibition of the sheriff we avoided West Hazleton, and continued our way to Lattimer. The sheriff came to meet us from the latter place, leaving the deputies standing fifteen or twenty yards behind him. I do not know whether the sheriff said anything to those standing in the first row or not, but I can testify that I heard nothing, although I was standing only four yards from the sheriff. The sheriff had only his revolver in the hand, and read nothing aloud. I only saw him tussling with some of those standing in the front row. About two minutes after the sheriff had reached the first row of the procession the firing began. Five men fell dead around me. I flung myself flat on the ground and stayed there about ten minutes. I cannot say how long the firing lasted, as I was very much excited at the time, but I think it was over two minutes. As I lay on the ground I lifted my head and could see that the deputies were firing at my fleeing companions, already about three hundred yards away. The deputies

while they were firing at the fugitives called after them, 'Come back, you son —————,' I lay until things around me were comparatively quiet. When I arose I saw the deputies still standing in the same place, while my companions, with the exception of those who had immediately thrown themselves on the ground, had run far away. I can testify that not one of us had a weapon in his hand. When we left Harwood in the procession we decided to take nothing, not even a stick, in order not to create the impression that we had the intention of committing acts of violence. I am ready to swear to the above statement. I am a Hungarian subject, and not naturalized."

Read and signed.

Andrej Sivar, born in Jaso-Ujfeln [Nováčany], County Abanj [Abov],* twenty-seven years of age, fifteen years in America, not naturalized, appears, and being questioned, gives the following testimony:

"I marched in the procession from Harwood to Lattimer on the tenth of the month. I was about three hundred yards from the front, and could hear nothing of what was said between the sheriff and those marching in the first rows. So it was near West Hazleton, and so near Lattimer. When the firing began near Lattimer I saw everybody run away; I myself bent over so as to partly protect myself, but I could nevertheless see everything. As I stood so bent over one of my fellow-workmen came running to me. I do not know his name, but it seems to me it might have been a Lithuanian. He came running to me, wounded in the right arm, and begged me to help him. I told him I would gladly do so if I did not have to save myself. The firing lasted two or three minutes. I only stayed a short time bent and then ran myself. While we were running the deputies shot at us when we were already about three hundred yards from them."

Read and signed.

---

* The correct Magyar spelling should have been: Jászóújfalu, Abanj County.

Monday, September 13, 1897

MORE FUNERALS

ON MONDAY MORNING at nine, General Gobin received Father Aust and almost a dozen other clergymen and spoke gravely to them of his prohibition against any ceremonial weapons among the marchers.

Even as this meeting was taking place, the funeral procession was forming in Harwood, to escort the bodies of Anthony Grekos, Andrew Mieczkowski and Rafael Rekewicz along the dusty road to St. Stanislaus. An even larger assemblage than the day before joined the march. General Gobin had instructed Father Aust that there was to be no music. The silence, however, was so eerie, accentuating the ominous tramp of feet, that the General quickly rescinded this order.

Thus, ninety men—ten to carry each of nine coffins, in rotating shifts of six—marched slowly to the beat of a funeral dirge from undertaker Bonin's, carrying Broztowski, Chrzeszeski, Czaja, Kulick, Monikaski, Skrep, Zagorski, Ziominski, and Ziemba.* The Italian Band of Bunker Hill led the way, followed by several other groups in resplendent uniforms.

The closed caskets were borne to the platform erected before the altar. The coffins were larger than had been anticipated, and the flowers were too numerous. There was no room for all the dead. At the last minute, therefore, the cortege from Harwood bearing Grekos, Mieczkowski, and Rekewicz was diverted to St. Peter's and St. Paul's Lithuanian Church not far away. At St. Stanislaus, Father Aust celebrated a solemn high requiem mass, assisted by five priests. Most of the victims were Polish. The first sermon was in Polish, but after mass Father Moylan of St. Gabriel's in Hazleton addressed the assemblage warmly in English. The procession to St. Stanislaus

---

* Undertaker Bonin listed a tenth dead man, John Tarnactick (as he spelled it). This was no doubt John Tarnowicz, and it appears that his family came for the body and buried him privately. The stone marker was found in 1972.

Cemetery numbered eight thousand and was, according to the *Daily Standard*, "the largest ever witnessed in this region." Nine men were buried in a single mass grave, and three in hastily dug single graves. The decorum pledged by the clergymen to General Gobin was in somber evidence.

On subsequent days, Jacob Tomashantas and Clement Platek were buried in McAdoo. For each, the UMW formed a silent honorary procession. A long struggle had begun—a struggle that would endure for decades.

September 13–15, 1897

THE STRIKE CONTINUES

ON THAT same Monday, September 13, General Gobin was obliged to report to his superiors that over ten thousand strikers were out. Day by day, the number had grown, although as always some mines would be closed, then reopened, then closed, as the unemployed desperately sought work. The demand for coal was very low, however, and the operators seemed content to let the strike continue.

After the peaceful conduct of the funerals convinced him the time was ripe, Calvin Pardee, Sr., arrived in Hazleton on Wednesday, September 15. His son, Calvin, was of course hiding out in the Traymore Hotel, but Calvin senior was not intimidated by the strike or the strikers. He was disgusted that his superintendents could not get his collieries back in operation, being scarcely able to believe that the foreign laborers had had the wit to incite themselves. He told a group of reporters:

The English speaking element is not in this thing; they have no complaint, except in so far that miners are always dissatisfied. I have been among them for forty years, and I have always said that miners were the greatest grumblers there are.

They were driven from the mines by a mob, stirred up by these agitators, but they will go back to work without getting one cent advance for their trouble. If they will not go back to work for what they were getting, then our mines are for sale, for they will never be started up otherwise.

Pardee was especially scathing about John Fahy. Fahy's own role in the strike was a curious one. He seems at times to have been slippery—as in his initial antagonism against the foreigners, in his support of the alien tax, and in his deliberate absence from the march on Lattimer. Some students of the era regarded him as an opportunist. But perhaps his actions are to be explained by his conservative nature, and even more by his faith that building a solid organization would make a more lasting contribution than violence. If at first he despaired of the foreign miners, he came at last to build his organization on their strengths and their peculiarities, seeing to it that they were well represented among its officers and on its committees. In mid-1897, the UMW *in toto* numbered 30,000 members. The 10,000 added by Fahy in August and September represented a growth of 33 percent. In 1901, the classic observer of the region in that era, the Reverend Peter Roberts, was to write in *The Anthracite Coal Industry*: "It is conceded by men intimate with the situation throughout the coal fields during the last strike, that its universality was more due to the Sclav [*sic*] than to any other nationality. . . . They have been trained to obedience, and when they organize, they move with an unanimity that is seldom seen among nations who pride themselves on personal liberty and free discussion." Unity, of course, is not a famous Slavic attribute, as the word Balkanization shows. But many observers, like Peter Roberts did note a different sort of individualism and sociality among the Slavs than among Anglo-Saxons. The exact name for it could not have been, as Roberts hypothesizes, obedience, for in the long strike of 1897—as many at the time remarked—there were no leaders. An odd consensual system seemed to be at work.

Meanwhile, in the days after Pardee's arrival, restlessness grew. Each day began again to bring news of closings, grievances, meetings, offers. By September 20, Gomer Jones had at last been prevailed upon to resign, and the Lehigh and Wilkes-

Barre Company was prepared to offer a ten-percent wage increase in some categories. Even A. Pardee and Company despite Pardee's words, was willing to get the Harwood and Lattimer men back to work by raising some wages by ten percent. Those most to be thanked for these modest successes were the Slavic women.

September 15–20, 1897

THE SLAVIC AMAZONS VERSUS THE CAVALRY

IN eastern Europe, in cases of social protest, men who were peasants were vulnerable to reprisal. During September 15–20 it was into the hands of their women that militancy passed. On September 15, Big Mary Septak led a band of over two hundred women armed with weapons from the kitchen and household across the mine fields. Dubbed "Hungarian Amazons" by the press and by the military, the women confounded General Gobin's soldiers. They marched to the collieries and washeries, ordering the miners to desist from work, knocking tools from their hands, and shouting orders. From a safe distance, the men and boys egged them on. From time to time, with shamed faces, soldiers with bayonets or cavalrymen on horseback drove the women off. Standing on the slag of a culm bank, "Big Mary" shook her fist at a captain on horseback: "If we had guns," she told him, "you'd pay the devil!"

A large woman with a great Slavic face, Big Mary was once described in *Century Magazine* (April 1898) as "by far the most forceable and picturesque character in all the mining area. In her peculiar way she is queen, and rules things with a high hand." She had had ten children in America and lost nine of them. Of her husband of thirty years she once said: "When I 'way from my man I cry all the time, and when he 'way from me he cry all the time." She struck terror in those who crossed her. It was said that all the men in the mining company's office were afraid of her and gave her a wide berth, that trolley-car conductors trembled when she hailed a car, and that not one of them had ever been known to collect a fare from her except when she felt disposed to pay.

Led by Big Mary, the Amazons struck first in Lattimer. After the massacre, all the men of Lattimer, English-speaking as well as Slavic, refused to work, and at a rally in front of the schoolhouse the next day, all joined the UMW. They named three Slavs, three Americans, and three Italians to present their grievances to Mr. Pardee, and on Tuesday the fourteenth, after the funerals, the Lattimer men gathered in front of the company store, next to Big Mary's boardinghouse, to hear Mr. Pardee's response to their grievances.

The strikers wore their Sunday best. At 2:30, squadrons of cavalry came clattering down the main street of Lattimer, "sabres flashing by saddle, carbine butts showing in the leather boots, revolvers and burdened cartridge belts showing." Not a miner moved in his tracks until the blue-shirted column had swept beyond the crest of a hill.

Voices were silent as the door of the company offices opened. Out stepped Augustus W. Drake, the Lattimer superintendent. He said no to each of their demands except the demand that no one be fired for serving on the grievance committee.

He wanted to be fair, he said, and would gladly have the whistle blown the moment the men decided to go back to work. "You have nothing to gain by being idle," he told them in a matter-of-fact voice. "What do you say, will you come back?" There was a pause. Then in heavily accented voices there came back a thunderous "NO!"

Mary Septak stood on the porch of her boardinghouse, listening with disgust. The next morning she marched with 150 women across the Lattimer strippings. At first the blue-clad soldiers of the Thirteenth did not try to stop Big Mary's brigade. But finally cavalrymen drove the women from the field.

The next day, Big Mary led another contingent of women, some carrying their babies on their hips, ten miles south to McAdoo. They knew that the soldiers had no jurisdiction outside Luzerne County. The women appeared at the Tyler and

McTurk washery, got between the men and their work, and threatened to demolish the place. They did a certain amount of bodily harm to some of the men. The owners telephoned General Gobin. He said they would have to have Sheriff Scott call the governor to permit the troops to operate in Schuylkill County.

Although McAdoo and Audenried were universally regarded as the hotbeds of the strike, Sheriff Scott sent word that he did not want troops in his county; he would go to McAdoo himself. He did not rush to the scene, but got there at 2:00 P.M. and "did his best to have matters amicably arranged." If the women do become obnoxious, he said, he would arrest them equally with men. He left the scene peaceful, having learned, however, that now the Irish, the English, and the Welsh had openly joined their Slavic colleagues. So Sheriff Scott called the governor again and told him that the feeling against the deputies ran so high that the Eighth Regiment, camped two miles away, ought to cover McAdoo and Audenried. The governor said he would need a written request from citizens. The sheriff said no citizens from McAdoo and vicinity would sign it, only coal bosses. The governor said to get their signatures, then.

On September 16, raids by "the Polish Amazons" took place at five separate places, among them the Carson, the Star, and the Monarch washeries at Honey Brook in Audenried. On the seventeenth, they struck again at McAdoo. The women hurled sticks and stones. And when the cavalry appeared, some of them mounted the culm bank, hooting at the mounted officers and throwing coal at them. These women on top of the bank were only a decoy, however. A second group was hidden behind the culm bank and when the cavalry left, these marched out to challenge the whole body of employees, who quit work on the spot. The women closed down Bunker Hill, then Honey Brook. Confusion reigned. Superintendent Lawall demanded action from Sheriff Scott. General Gobin's officers admitted to being "in a quandary over the foreign women's raids," since "the women are worse to handle than the men." The guard "cannot use measures in dispersing them that they could in attacking a crowd of men." The general was afraid that the women would once again incite the men. And then, on the night of the seventeenth, a heavy thunderstorm broke over the soldiers' tents, turning the encampments into deep puddles and slippery mud.

Day after day the guardsmen suffered humiliation at the hands of hooting, jeering, cursing women who had no fear of them. "They know their sex protects them," complained General Gobin. "I thought we had come to Hazleton to fight men." The Wilkes-Barre *Record* denounced their "ill-advised and unwomanly demonstrations."

On September 18, forty or fifty English-speaking miners and another two hundred fifty foreigners went back to work at Lattimer. A thousand men were still out. Big Mary Septak was not about to give three hundred scabs any peace. So at nine o'clock, she gathered eighty women on the railroad tracks between two culm banks at the eastern end of the patch. Colonel Mattes, commanding officer of the Thirteenth, took personal charge and ordered one company of men down the track at double time, to cut the women off from the men working in the open pit and washery. He ordered two more companies to follow in reserve.

Brandishing a crude wooden sword, Big Mary cavorted ahead of the approaching soldiers as if she would battle them alone. On the top of the culm banks, a group of Hungarian and Italian men gathered to watch, beaming at the women. Back and forth Big Mary sallied, the other women standing brazenly behind her, taunting the approaching blue coats, waving clubs, iron bars, and stones. The line of soldiers wavered. Colonel Mattes ordered a halt and commanded the men to fix bayonets. Then he ordered them to form a skirmish line. The women hooted in derision. Colonel Mattes again ordered the line to advance. Big Mary charged the bayonets, then retreated. From above, the men on the culm banks roared with laughter and applauded. This time, however, the soldiers were not to be cowed. Unable to beat the advancing bayonets, the women were forced to disperse.

The revived militance of the week after the massacre brought concessions from the coal operators. Gomer Jones was replaced. Wages were modestly raised. Nearly a month had gone by since the first strike at Honey Brook. The National Guard had gradually squeezed the life out of the strike. Surrounded on every side by armed soldiers, the men started going back to work. Only the actions of the women salvaged the modest gains that could be won by partial organization. Nationwide the UMW were to grow from 40,000 at the end of 1897 to 200,000 by mid-1902. So the picture was mixed. The strikers did not gain most of what they were asking (little enough it was). But they made small gains and now had an organization through which to affect the future.

September, 1897

THE COMMITTEE FOR PROSECUTION
AND CHARITY

ACROSS THE COUNTRY, unionists, socialists, Wobblies, and ethnic fraternals denounced the bloodthirsty sheriff and millionaire owers. A man named Murphy at a rally of Social Democrats in Chicago called for every miner to arm himself and offered the slogan: *"For every miner shot, shoot a millionaire."* The heavyweight champion of the world, James J. Corbett, offered to hold a benefit bout for the families of the victims. But the actual money came in by dribbles.*

There were sixty families to provide for; most of the wounded could not work. There were no such things, of course, as workmen's compensation or unemployment benefits. Beginning immediately after the funerals of the victims, on Tuesday,

---

* Of the approximately 250 contributions received, by far the majority amounted to $5.00 or less; only ten reached $100 or more. Most came from ethnic parishes, fraternals, and individuals. All told, the Prosecution and Charity Committee, with Father Aust as president, collected $4,305.60 for charity. Another $4,761.67 was collected separately for the prosecution fund. By April of 1898, all but $10.09 of the latter fund had been spent on the trial. $2,725.00 had gone for attorney's fees. By January, 1899, the Charity Fund was exhausted, too.

Septeiner 14, Father Aust gave $5.00 to Ella Cheslak and $3.00 each to Mrs. Futa, Mrs. Jurich, and Mrs. Tarnowicz. Thus began his fifteen-month support of fifty-nine adults (widows and cripples) and thirty-eight children (half of them orphans), until the last payment he could make, on January 2, 1899, had exhausted the $4,305.60 treasury of the Charity Fund. One of the saddest gifts was to Mrs. Stefan Jurich, on January 7, 1898, for the funeral of her premature infant. One of the largest single payments went to Hilary Bonin, the undertaker: $94.81 to cover the funeral expenses for ten of the victims.

Father Aust tried to pay his new dependents once a month. After his first grant to Ella Cheslak on September 14, he gave her $12.50 in October, $15.50 in November, $16.00 in February, $20.00 in March, and then $19.00 each month until December 1, 1898. Young Ella went to work immediately and was lucky enough to be married, at sixteen, within the year. Her mother and the four small children moved in with her and her new husband.

September 20, 1897

CHANGE OF VENUE—AND BETRAYAL

ON March 23, 1899, Father Richard Aust was to write: "But it is over, the fight was made and unluckily lost. . . . May God be the father and protector of the poor unfortunate ones: may He be the avenger of the unfortunate victims." There were to be many difficult days to get through before he was to set down those words. The drama of the trial was, if possible, to exceed that of the massacre.

The drama began on the very day of the massive funeral, Monday, September 13. That afternoon, while mourners were still milling in the streets, District Attorney Daniel Fell returned to Hazleton from conferences in Wilkes-Barre and Harris burg and closeted himself with the coal operators, all of whom were long-time friends and associates of J. Gillingham Fell, his father. He also called on General Gobin but would not talk to the press. The *Daily Standard* became suspicious: "No one could ascertain his mission, but he may depend on it that his actions in this important matter will be closely watched."

From the beginning, the strikers' prosecuting committee, composed of John Nemeth, Father Aust, and Matt Long, worried that District Attorney Fell would play a double game. He had built his young career on a strong showing in the Hazleton area and in 1896 had run unusually well for a Republican in the immigrant wards and the outlying mining patches of the South Side. On the other hand, his family connections made him exceedingly vulnerable to the pressures not only of the coal operators but also of the governor's office and the U.S. Department of State. The Austro-Hungarian government was preparing to lodge an immediate formal protest in Washington, and while the State Department was to treat the Austro-Hungarian ambassador with elegant coolness, clearly federal interests were going to be brought to bear on the Commonwealth of Pennsylvania. Having dealt with all the governments involved, John Nemeth, in particular, wanted a clear record drawn up from the very first. Each step was crucial. The first and most important step was a coroner's inquest, on which charges of murder might be brought. To this end, it was indispensable that the district attorney not hold hearings, request indictments, or make arrests until after the inquest. On September 14, meeting with the prosecuting committee, District Attorney Fell gave solemn assurances that he would comply with these wishes.

But in the following days Fell kept up his secret conferences with the coal operators and the governor's office. From the point of view of the operators, the governor, and the State Department, it was imperative that a proper trial be held and that it end in acquittal. Three compelling interests were at stake: to block potential claims of indemnity to its subjects, as would be demanded by the Austro-Hungarian Empire; to protect the future authority of Pennsylvania sheriffs and their posses; and to honor the risk borne by Sheriff Martin and his men for the coal operators. If the latter were to be found guilty, the whole structure of law and order would be threatened. Indeed, that structure was evidently in need of shoring up. The governor and the attorney general set in motion plans to create a state police force, so that the entire burden of enforcing law outside local jurisdictions would no longer have to fall upon sheriff's posses. This represented a major shift in law enforcement in the commonwealth. But, for now, Martin and his men would have to be protected.

The betrayal the prosecuting committee feared became evident on September 20, the Monday after the funeral. There was to be a planning session for the inquest with Coroner Frank S. McKee at three o'clock. As the members of the prosecuting committee waited outside his office, they did not realize that McKee had spent the morning in the Wilkes-Barre courtroom, by prior arrangement, receiving a warrant for the arrest of Sheriff Martin and seventy-eight deputies. But when they saw McKee enter the building with a delegation from Wilkes-Barre and shut themselves in another office, they immediately surmised what was afoot and they were correct: jurisdiction was to be moved from Hazleton to Wilkes-Barre, away from their own close inspection. That the whole business had been centrally coordinated became clear because, at that very hour, Governor Daniel H. Hastings broke the news in Harrisburg: "I consider that the civil authority is now able to protect the sheriff and his deputies, and I have allowed warrants for their arrest to be served from the court of Wilkes-Barre." The district attorney's promise had proved worthless. Imprecations were showered on his head for breach of faith.

Totally ignoring the men waiting outside his office, Coroner McKee, with Detective Isaac G. Eckert, left the building to serve warrants on the sheriff and his men, who "did feloniously, willfully, and of their own malice aforethought kill and murder," as the warrant charged, twenty-four men mentioned by name and wound thirty-five others also listed by name. There were many errors in these lists, as also in the list of deputies. Worst of all, the warrant was global and lodged the most difficult charge to prove: wilful murder, without any distinction among the deputies. That evening, a reporter saw Sheriff

Martin in Wilkes-Barre and was told: "I am not disturbed about the matter." He had every reason to feel reassured. Coroner McKee, meanwhile, told the Wilkes-Barre *Times* that he expected no interference from General Gobin: "I am armed with greater authority than his." His authority came not from the justices who signed the warrants—the general had, after all, refused to honor the earlier warrant issued by a justice in Hazleton—but from the governor.

Indeed, General Gobin now calmly allowed the new warrants to be served on the deputies, and the next day he detailed D Company, Ninth Regiment, to accompany the deputies on the train to Wilkes-Barre. The scheduling of the hearing in Wilkes-Barre, as had been foreseen, prevented many witnesses subpoenaed to tell their side of the story from making an appearance. As the train chugged slowly away from the Hazleton depot, it left at least fifty witnesses who lacked money to pay the fare standing forlornly on the platform. Only a few of the better-off foreigners, like John Nemeth and Father Aust, could afford the trip. At 9:00 A.M., the train pulled into the Wilkes-Barre station. Surrounded by troopers seventy-two deputies marched four abreast on East Market Street to the courthouse. Fifty men of Company D, bayonets fixed, waited at the station. As the deputies walked in rank down the almost empty street, clerks from the stores and a few others called out quietly: "Look at the bums," and "See the loafers." Some pointed: "These are the men who shot down the strikers." As on the day of the shooting, the deputies wore dress suits and plug hats. Some averted their faces.

The deputies were held in Courtroom Number One until the crowd in Number Two was orderly, and then judges Lyman H. Bennett and John J. Lynch called them in. Attorney John Garman, balding on the front of his square-set head, opened for the prosecution by saying with heavy sarcasm that "Dictator Gobin" had refused for ten days to permit this hearing, and that Coroner McKee, a major in the Ninth Regiment, had unfairly provided the deputies with an armed escort and treated them as favored prisoners. But what truly infuriated him, he said, was Gobin's order that the case be removed from Hazleton to Wilkes-Barre. Garman moved that the case be removed to Hazleton, to the jurisdiction of Squire Gorman of that city, where it belonged, and where there was easier access for the witnesses. Attorney McGahren then supported Garman, stressing that the miners were paupers. Whereupon Attorney John T. Lenahan, a feisty infighter, arose for the defense to cry "claptrap" and to protest against these "stump speeches." District Attorney Fell intervened to say he wanted the list of witnesses called, to determine how many were absent. Only one-fourth answered the call. The court ordered Coroner McKee to take the 1:00 P.M. train and bring back the prosecution witnesses while the hearing began with those present.

Garman, McGahren, and Loughran, the three lawyers retained by the prosecuting committee, could see a plot in the trial's having been moved to an area favorable to Sheriff Martin. Moreover, the warrants had been badly formed, making the task of the prosecution almost impossible. Stunned spectators watched as, one after another, Garman, then McGahren, and after a while Loughran, rose to say, "Your honor, I now desire to withdraw from all further connection with this case." Just before leaving the courtroom at the side of Garman, McGahren announced, "We leave the case in the hands of District Attorney Fell, who represents the Commonwealth." Without losing stride, and as if unaware of the sensation that had just been created, Mr. Fell then carried on.

Witnesses were called: John Welsh, school official from Hazle township; Jonathan Lichensberger, a contractor who was at the scene in Lattimer; and Charles Guscott, the schoolteacher. It was almost noon when Fell asked the judges what would be done with the prisoners. After a conference, temporary bail was set at $4,000 for each man. Sixty-four deputies were present. Mr. Joseph A. Sinn, trust officer of the City Trust, Safe Deposit and Surety Company in Philadelphia, posted the bond totaling $256,000. (The prosecuting committee was to be able to raise just over $4,000.) In the afternoon, the court heard John Holden, a butcher who was at the scene; John Merinko, a bartender from Hazleton who went to Lattimer on the fateful day to see what would happen, stood ten feet from the sheriff, and ended up carrying a wounded man to the schoolhouse; George Yeager, another foreigner who worked in a saloon in Hazleton and had come to Lattimer in a trolley just ahead of the marchers and had stood only a yard from the deputy nearest the Craig house; Dr. J. H. Stearns, assistant surgeon at Hazleton Hospital, who described all the wounds, made both by .44 caliber buckshot and rifle balls; Reverend Richard Aust; and Reverend Karl Hauser. Undertaker Philip Boyle described wounds in the backs of ten of the dead and the six gunshot wounds in the face of the eleventh. No cross-examination of the undertaker ensued.

The next morning, Coroner McKee and Detective Eckert showed up in court with forty-six men (some of them in bandages) from among the foreigners who marched at Lattimer, and three women. At least that much had been won for the prosecuting committee. Strangers to an American courtroom, the foreigners seemed restless and out of place. At 9:30 A.M. they were seated. At 9:45 A.M., the deputies were marched in and seated on the opposite side. "Both sides looked at each other rather curiously and some of the strikers smiled grimly." When Sheriff Martin walked in moments later—at six-foot-four and over 200 pounds, an imposing man even under trial—every eye among the foreigners followed him. The prosecution then called the following witnesses: Andrew Novotny; Martin Shefronik; Mrs. Ellen Witchie, Mrs. Kate Case, and Mrs. Weitzel, all of Lattimer; Mattias Czaja, who had been shot in the back, and Anthony Angello, an Italian, both of whom said they had been intimidated by the passing strikers and joined the marchers out of fear ("All I heard the strikers say was, 'Strike, Lattimer.' They were all Hungarians and Polanders, and I am an Italian," Angello said); Hilary Bonin, Andrej Sivar, his father, Jacob Sivar, and a cousin, the second Andrej Sivar: all told the same basic story.

One more important witness that morning was John Eagler. Eagler, clean-cut, handsome, made an excellent impression whenever he told his story. Counting Theodorovich's hearing and the coroner's inquest, and twice at the trial, he was to testify, in all, four times.

First, Eagler identified himself: "I was one of the crowd

of strikers. We were sent for by the Lattimer miners, who said they would quit work if they saw us."

And asked by Fell to tell what happened at Lattimer, he responded, "Well, the sheriff stepped in and got hold of one man and said: 'Stop, you are disobeying the law. Go back!' One of the men said: 'We are not disobeying the law. We have no clubs; we are not going to kill or murder.' Someone said: 'Don't mind the sheriff, go ahead.' The sheriff said: 'Who said go on?' and he grabbed a man. Then he pulled a revolver and snapped it but the revolver did not go off.'"

"Did anybody hurt the sheriff?"

"No, sir; no one touched him. When the firing began I thought the deputies had blank cartridges, but when one man dropped dead beside me I dropped to the ground too. Another man fell on the other side of me, and when I saw him bleeding I got up and ran away."

"What did the strikers do when the shooting began?" asked Judge Lynch.

"They all began to run and the deputies kept shooting after them as they ran."

"How long did the shooting continue?"

"From one to two minutes."

"Did anyone hit the sheriff?"

"No, sir; they did not. They had no arms or clubs."

"They told the sheriff they were going to Lattimer?"

"Yes, sir."

"Did they pass the sheriff?"

"Yes, a lot of the strikers walked some distance past the sheriff when the shooting began."

"Was the sheriff surrounded by the crowd when the shooting began?"

"Yes, there was a crowd around him."

On cross-examination Mr. Lenahan, the defense attorney, asked: "What is your business?"

"I work in the mines at Harwood."

"When did you stop work?"

"The Saturday before."

"Did you not stop many men from working?"

"No, sir; I did not. This was the first time our crowd went out to stop men."

"Are you not a strike leader?"

"I am a kind of a leader."

"Did you not tell the sheriff you would not disperse when he told you to do so?"

"I did not say so; the sheriff pulled out a paper but did not read it; he put it back in his pocket and said we must disperse."

"Did you not have some trouble with the deputies at Hazleton?"

"Yes, I picked up a rock; I thought there was going to be a fight; I saw Cook with a gun pointed and I picked up the rock."

"Did you throw the rock at the deputies?"

"No, sir, I dropped it when I went to talk to the sheriff at West Hazleton."

"Why did you not come up here yesterday when you were subpoenaed?"

"I had no money."

"You say the sheriff clicked his revolver?"

"Yes; he pointed it at one of the men and clicked it."

"Had you been at the Upper Mines that week?"

"No, sir, that was the first time I was out with the strikers."

"Why did you go to Lattimer?"

"Joe Layothic [*sic*; John Hlavatly] came for me and said that the Lattimer miners wanted me to come to give them an excuse to strike."

"What became of the prisoners?" asked Judge Lynch.

"What prisoners?"

"The men who had the guns."

"I don't know. I saw some of them going away with their guns."

"How many had passed the sheriff when the firing began?"

"There was about fifty. I was one of them."

After the Sivars, father and son, had testified, District Attorney Fell told the judges he had thirty-three more witnesses, most of whom would corroborate what was said but not add much that was new. The two justices looked at each other. They conferred. They asked Mr. Fell what he desired. The district attorney moved that the sheriff and deputies be held under bail until trial in the next session of the court. He cited a similar case in 1874 in which bail had been set at $3,000. The judges rejected Fell's low figure. They had heard enough to reply firmly that bail would be set at $5,000 for each man for each count of murder and another $1,000 for each count of felonious wounding, twice as much as Fell had requested and $2,000 higher than the figure they had set for the initial warrant.

Twelve deputies had not yet been arrested. Many were still in hiding in other cities. Still, the sum required of Mr. Sinn had now climbed to $438,000 for the seventy-seven deputies who had signed in on the books in court. The total would reach $510,000 when the remaining twelve had been placed under arrest. As banker for the coal companies, Mr. Sinn signed for the money with no sign of strain. The defense had been eager, Lenahan later told reporters, to have bail set in Wilkes-Barre, so that the men could not be arrested and taken before some other court.

When the actual signature of Mr. Sinn upon their bond at last gave hard proof of support by the coal companies, the sheriff and the deputies breathed a sigh of relief. Long worried that he had been marked to be sacrificed, Martin now felt considerably better. George Ferris explained to him how they had now gained an advantage by being able to hear the stories of the best witnesses for the prosecution. He and Lenahan had seen several weaknesses they could exploit: the evident fear among the Lattimer women; the coercion of Czaja and Angello; slight but multiple discrepancies about whether an order to fire was heard, about numbers, about timing, about virtually every small detail. Everything had happened within five minutes. Hundreds of persons were involved. No two witnesses had precisely the same memory. The simplicity of the miners, and the fact that most of them could not understand other speakers and were obliged to speak through interpreters, would be a mighty asset. The Hungarians would testify in isolation from each other and could not react to the flow of testimony in order to make a cumulative, subtle case. Above all, the key witnesses for the prosecution—Eagler, Sivar, and others— tended to agree that the sheriff had not fired a shot and had not given the order to fire. If all of them had heard the sheriff shout the order—as the sheriff himself had at first confessed doing ("I hated to give the order to fire. . . .")—the case against the sheriff might have been hell to budge.

But this way, Ferris encouraged the troubled sheriff to think, no jury can pin the blame on him. What jury will want to blame deputies who saw their leader in danger and fired to protect him? If the marchers cannot single anyone out, no one can be judged guilty. Not of murder, anyway, and probably not of manslaughter, either.

Father Aust and John Nemeth sat in the courtroom in a state of quiet outrage. The only bright spot was that in two short days an effective case had been made that there had been unnecessary bloodshed. Moreover, some of the witnesses for their side were truly eloquent. The unlearned miners had stood up rather well under cross-examination. Mr. Lenahan had been willing to concede, for the sake of brevity, that all sixty-four deputies then in court had stood in the line at Lattimer with guns. It would not be necessary to find witnesses to identify each deputy. That would have been an almost hopeless task. There was room, then, for guarded hope.

Still, the commonwealth was obviously working hand in glove with the defense. The defense wanted an umbrella indictment covering all the deputies, even those many who apparently did no firing at all, whereas the prosecuting committee had wanted precise indictments alleging various degrees of cooperation. The prosecuting committee wanted to single out at least three deputies who had pursued the marchers after the general firing had ceased and continued to fire in cold blood. They were also working to build up conclusive evidence against eight others who had acted with specific violence. At the end of the hearing, Father Aust was steaming and called the hearing "high-handed." The Pottsville *Republican* recognized that the hearing was "of a perfunctory nature, the outcome having evidently been agreed upon."

THE INQUEST

THE NEXT DAY, many of the witnesses who had been brought to Wilkes-Barre were obliged to appear at Hazle Hall in Hazleton, for a coroner's inquest. Now that the deputies had already given themselves up for arrest and bond, and charges of murder had been formalized, the inquest was no longer decisive and would have been merely a *pro forma* proceeding except for one point: its stenographic record enabled the defense to explore weaknesses in the case against its clients. After two days of hearings, the coroner's jury rendered the following verdict:

That we, the jury empanelled to inquire into the cause and manner of death of the Lattimer victims, do say that from the circumstances of the case and from the evidence offered, the said Clemens Plotack [*sic*] and others came to their death by gun-shot wounds on Sept. 10th, 1897, at the hands of James Martin and his deputies, and in this we do all agree.

And we, Philip J. Boyle, Barton Freas, Thomas L. Thomas and Peter McKiernan, of this jury, do further say that Clemens Plotack, with others was marching peaceably and unarmed on the public highway; that they were intercepted by said Sheriff and his deputies, and mercilessly shot to death and we further find that the killing was unnecessary and could have been avoided without serious injury to either person or property; and we find finally that the killing was wanton and unjustifiable, but in this we, George Maue and F. J. McNeal, of this jury, do not concur, and we, the jury do further say that there was such strong suspicion of unlawful violence at the hands of person or persons unknown to this jury as to make this inquest necessary.

The National Guard now began to withdraw, a regiment at a time. On Tuesday, September 21, at night, a fire had burned the breaker at Beaver Brook to the ground, and General Gobin became alarmed. First reports suggested criminal arson. Investigation proved otherwise. Thus, when the inquest rendered its verdict on the twenty-seventh, the Twelfth and Thirteenth

Regiments went back, said the Pottsville *Republican,* "to the girls they left behind."

By Tuesday, September 28, the dead had been buried, the strike broken, the hearing and the inquest completed, the trial of the sheriff and deputies scheduled, the guard departed, and the first tokens of charity, averaging four dollars each, given by Father Aust to fifteen of the widows.

October, 1897

AUTUMN LOVE

BEN SAKMAR had been as good as his resolve. He walked over to McAdoo the day after the funeral and went directly to the saloon owned by Maureen's father. It was midday and about a half-dozen men were fondling glasses of beer. Ben went to the empty end of the bar. Mr. Kearney, a short wiry man with a blue vest over his shirt, eventually walked down to him, put his fingers on the bar, and raised his eyebrows as if to ask his order.

"Me Ben Sakmar," Ben said.

The Irishman hesitated. Then his manner changed. "It's on the house," he said. "So you're the fellow Maureen's been seeing. Glory be to God," he said, pointing out Ben to the other men. "The young man who's courtin my daughter." Ben felt the man's brown eyes scrutinizing him. Mr. Kearney turned to pick out a glass and turn the tap to fill it with beer. He set it down in front of Ben. "So you're the fellow what's got her heart in a flutter." At last he smiled and held out a hand. "Daniel Kearney," he said. "I suppose you'll be wanting to see her."

Ben was lifting the beer and almost choked. He set down the glass and shook hands. There wasn't much light in the saloon and he felt totally tongue-tied.

"She told me about ye, she did," Mr. Kearney continued.

He was not above an ironic twist. "Come to think of it, so did my boy, Danny. Tough kid," he smiled, making fists like a boxer. "Any friend o' Maureen's a friend o' mine. Drink up!"

Ben took a drink. Mr. Kearney was patient with his English. They talked for a while, as long as they could, and then Mr. Kearney showed him the side door into the family living quarters. Ben was impressed by its polished floors, solid furniture, and lace doilies under the plants. Mr. Kearney called his wife and Maureen. Soon the two women entered the room, and Mr. Kearney retreated to mind the bar. A moment later, Danny entered the room, too. Ben couldn't tell if he was sullen or sheepish. He kept his eyes on Maureen. The silence was agonizing. Maureen introduced him to her mother and took her brother's arm so that in the introduction they would have to shake hands. Ben looked the boy right in the eyes and was grateful for the firm handshake. Then Mrs. Kearney urged him to sit down and busied herself pouring tea. The nearest chair was a straight-backed rocker, the most uncomfortable Ben could have chosen. He had already had to go to the bathroom after his long walk, and then the beer and now the hot tea added to his embarrassment. Maureen set a dish of cookies before him, while her mother chattered on about the terrible killings, the beautiful funerals, the marvelous sermon by Father Moylan. After a decent interval, Maureen and he were able to excuse themselves.

Outdoors, he paused long enough to use the outhouse. Then, behind the bushes, they kissed.

He saw Maureen often after that.

On one of these occasions, a cool Sunday in October, he met her by accident in downtown Hazleton. He had walked up the hill from the valley between Harwood and the city with John Eagler and some of his other friends to visit John Nemeth at the shipping company and to call on Andrew Meyer in the hospital. Ben was sending some money back to his mother and his sister. While he was standing inside Nemeth's place with Eagler, he saw Maureen passing on the sidewalk with another girl. Quickly he went to the door. He knew the others would tease him. He didn't care. He called out to her.

Maureen stopped. The other girl, plump and a little older, put an arm on Maureen and tried to urge her along.

"Ben!" Maureen said. She pulled herself away from her friend and came back to stand before him. Her eyes searched out his. "I was hoping I'd see you." She said the words slowly, pointing to herself and to him.

"Sun-day," Ben said. He pointed to the spot. "Sun-day." Then he pointed toward the sun and again toward the spot.

Her green eyes flashed. Her black hair framed her thin white face. She smiled. She had beautiful teeth when she smiled. She nodded vigorously. Her friend was calling to her, red in the face. Maureen waved to her friend to go on. She reached forward and pressed Ben's arm. "Sunday," she said. "Here. In the afternoon. I'll come alone."

Ben understood clearly that she would come. Her fingers felt cool where she touched his arm.

The next Sunday she didn't come. He waited in the street all afternoon.

But the following Sunday he returned. This time she was with her father. Ben had seen in McAdoo that Maureen got her eyes and chin from him, and that he was a fair-minded man. He shook Ben's hand so hard it hurt. Ben wondered if he had insisted on coming along, or if Maureen had arranged it. She was a direct woman, no doubt of it. It was also plain she was the chief pleasure of Mr. Kearney's life.

"Come along now, Ben," Mr. Kearney invited, or rather ordered, him. The three of them marched along the street together. Ben admired how matter-of-fact Mr. Kearney was. How he seemed to accept Ben without effusiveness. "For the life of me, I don't see how the two of you can talk," the father said. "But there's no reason why you shouldn't walk together." He pulled out a watch and said: "Be good now, the two of ye. I've got appointments to keep. Don't be gettin into any trouble—she's the very devil, Ben. You have to watch her every minute." He winked. Then he waved and disappeared down Church Street. Maureen took Ben's arm happily. Ben wasn't sure what this ritual meant—the father, the watch, her arm in his. But the thought of walking down the streets of

Hazleton thrilled him. He felt like a man. He felt as powerful as anyone in Hazleton.

They walked slowly. Maureen chatted gaily, giving him new words. Meeting her had intensified his desire to learn English. The foreignness began to disappear from the language. Each new word meant a link to her. She taught him sounds he had difficulty with: *th, w* and *wh*. He practiced vowel sounds like the *i* in Vine Street, and the *y* in Wyoming Street. The *-ing* was difficult for him.

At the corner of Church and Broad streets, they passed the gleaming white Pardee mansion. The mansion and its lawns were like a park in the center of the city. To one side was the Presbyterian church, and behind it rose the two towers of the Methodist Episcopal church, one tall, the other shorter. The spacious Pardee building rose for three floors, the bottom floor surrounded by a portico. Trees lined the sidewalks on every side, except for some buildings at the corner of Laurel and Green streets. The leaves were tipped by the browning of autumn. Maureen liked walking around the mansion. They walked down East Broad a block or two, past Hazle Hall and Hazleton House, and around the block past the Edison Electric Illuminating Company and the Eagle Carriage Works. After an hour, Maureen pulled his arm and hurried back to meet her father on Broad Street, near Wyoming. She smiled as she left him. She took her father's arm and laid her head on her father's shoulder as they departed. Her steps seemed light and happy to Ben's eyes, and his own strides on the way back to Harwood, down the hill from the city, were long and loping. Twice he bent over, picked up a rock, and threw it as far as he could, making his shoulder ache. The rocks sailed in the sky and crashed below into the trees.

The next Sunday, late in October, Ben and Maureen walked in the fields near McAdoo. The leaves were everywhere brilliant yellows and reds. Thick white clouds floated across the wind-cleared sky. The sun was hot for so late in the year, but the breeze pulled against their clothes. They were sitting, knees drawn up, on a hill overlooking the sweep of a large wide valley. The most distant range of hills seemed pale, the closer one darker, and the closest one alive with autumn foliage; the hills stood like an army shoulder to shoulder. Ben liked the hills of Hazleton. They lacked the alpine ruggedness of the Carpathian mountains near his home; the sheerness and sharpness, and the climate around them seemed more humid and less rarefied, less pure. But America seemed to him now endlessly fertile, with far more space than anyone could use. In Slovakia, the underbrush was kept cut, and dry firewood gathered every year. The forests were almost like part of the neighborhood garden. They were cared for. In America, the woods were thick with laurel and bushes no one had ever cut. Ben often felt as though he might have been the first person ever to stand in certain places. On this glorious Sunday afternoon on the brow of the hill, he felt totally alone with Maureen. The whole continent, the whole future, seemed untried before them. Ben dug with his toe in the brown earth at the base of a clump of wire grass. Maureen pulled a large clover and sucked on its stem. Both felt restless. Their friendship had advanced. Words were difficult.

Ben reached forward and ran his fingers through her black hair. She shook her head and fell back closer to him. She placed one of his hands on her bosom. Ben was not certain. He felt confusion, almost got up to walk away. Yet the time had ripened. Instead of running he pulled her over on top of him, their bodies making the grass rustle, their hearts echoing each other's pounding. The hillside became very silent. When their passion was spent, they lay in the grass on their backs, watching the clouds blow across the sky, uncertain what now was to become of them.

Things were different between them as they dressed and descended the mountain. Something had been consummated, something altered. Ben was uncertain what was now entailed. That Maureen had been willing he knew clearly. He had not forced himself upon her. If truth be told, he was afraid of an American girl. He wasn't sure what love with her would mean. Her face, afterward, was pale, concerned, lovely, and yet preoccupied. She felt, perhaps, she had something within her of great awe and fearfulness. She said little. When she left him, it was as though to seek solitude, to be alone. He felt strange feelings of joy and fulfillment, and shame and fear, of awe and puzzlement. He had loved a woman. The feelings of it, relived, enkindled passion. Yet a chill descended on him, too. Why such contradictory feelings? He regretted keenly having no one to talk to. The worst part of America was the terrible silence. Walking home this time he threw no stones. By the time he came over the brow of the hill down into Harwood it was dusk and he was sad.

He saw her again often that winter. They stayed away from each other, being careful. But passion was almost impossible to control. How could he marry her? How could he go back to Slovakia if he did? He might win one life, only to lose another. Why such choices? He shrugged it off as another matter he did not understand. He tightened his chest and accepted yet one more limitation to his possibilities. Compressed into so small an area of operation, his courage could overpower any obstacle in its path. Every adversity made him stronger. If tears burnt at his eyes, it was because so much seemed wasted. He concentrated on working so hard that his superintendent could not lay him off, could not afford to be without him. His target was to find work at least three out of every six days.

He knew now that he would marry her. But he did not want to go back into the mines. He loathed every day underground. He began to plan to move west, possibly to Pittsburgh. He could work in the mills. Anything to stay aboveground.

He began to think of himself as an American. His sons would speak English and play baseball and go to school. They would know nothing of the Old Country. They would never be half-men.

DEMOCRACY

THE TRIAL of Sheriff James L. Martin and eighty-seven deputies was postponed into the new year. On the first Tuesday of November, District Attorney Fell, up for reelection, was narrowly defeated in Hazleton and the surrounding mining towns. A man of the same name as the unhappy sheriff, one James Martin, was elected to replace Fell. To give the new district attorney time to prepare his case after taking office in January, the trial was rescheduled for February.

The Austro-Hungarian government expressed disturbance at the long delays. With barely disguised disdain, the State Department explained that the matter fell under the jurisdiction of the Commonwealth of Pennsylvania and not under that of the federal government of the United States. Nonetheless, anxious official inquiries came from Washington to the governor's office. Sheriff Martin had been obliged to file his own official report to the governor.

The final indictment drawn up by District Attorney Fell had named Michael Cheslak as the sole victim of the sheriff and deputies, leaving open the possibility of a later trial for other victims. From the point of view of the prosecuting committee, this indictment was a travesty. How could it be proved which shots, fired by whom, actually killed Michael Cheslak? Besides, the prosecuting committee did not wish to prosecute all the deputies. The defense would try to show, as some newspapers were already saying, that there had been a "reign of terror" held off by a tiny but intrepid band of deputies. The victims were being portrayed as dangerous criminals. Even many of those who disapproved of the killings—and most citizens in Hazleton did—would not wish to see eighty-seven of Hazleton's best-known citizens convicted for crimes not all of them had committed.

Still, Fell's defeat had given the strikers hope for, and some small satisfaction in, the democratic system.

PART FIVE

February 1–March 9, 1898
The Trial

February 1, 1898

THE TRIAL OPENS

ON February 1, 1898, a huge crowd milled about outside the Luzerne County Courthouse, stamping happily and jockeying for position. Despite the cold, thousands had gathered for the trial, the most significant, the papers said, in the history of northeastern Pennsylvania. Women stood on tiptoe to estimate their chances of getting inside the courtroom. Men elbowed one another. Youngsters snaked through the crowd dodging elbows and twisting past legs. The weather was cold enough to see breath frost before one's face. People had been using every ounce of influence they commanded to get inside. When the doors were finally opened, the crowd pushed forward in high spirits. Although every seat was taken, every corner packed, and the aisles overflowing, more were left outside than were allowed in.

The sitting judge, Judge Stanley Woodward, sixty-six years old, was a heavyset man of substantial reputation. His father had been chief justice of Pennsylvania; his brother, a brigadier general, had led union troops at Gettysburg. He was short and chunky and adorned with a walrus beard. Besides the new district attorney James Martin, the attorneys for the prosecution were John McGahren, John T. Garman, and the most distinguished and eloquent lawyer in the area, James Scarlet of Danville. For the defense, the lawyers were Henry T. Palmer, of distinguished family (his father had been sheriff in the

Molly Maguire period and he himself had been state attorney general from 1879–1882), who was widely regarded as the most successful lawyer in the eastern part of the state. He was a rival to Mr. Scarlet and courtroom connoisseurs looked forward with zest to the coming battle. As lawyer for Sheriff Martin, George Ferris was determined that he, too, would play a major role for the defense. Assigned to do most of the cross-examination was the well-known gut-fighter and emotional hell-raiser, John T. Lenahan of Wilkes-Barre.

Those who had managed to elbow their way into the court-room for the "Court of Oyer and Terminer, Luzerne County, Pa., Commonwealth of Pennsylvania v. James Martin and others, Trial of James Martin, Sheriff, and others for the murder of Mike Cheslak," had the air of those about to see a sporting event.

The indictment, by singling out only one victim and at the same time grouping eighty-seven deputies as a single collective defendant, constrained the prosecution and liberated the defense. For the prosecution was now forced to prove: that the marchers were peaceful and unarmed; that the deputies acted with premeditation and malice; and that the deputies did kill Mike Cheslak outside any lawful right. The defense on the other hand had only to cast doubt on the peaceableness of the strikers; to picture a state of riot, danger, and terror; to picture upstanding citizens pushed beyond their limits, indeed beyond the common good—and then to let the case for the prosecution collapse of its own weight. Still, there was some hope that the prosecution could persuade the jury to see the truth as they saw it, and to find some way—if only a charge of manslaughter—to reprimand the sheriff and the deputies for so much bloodshed. Everything depended on the picture in the minds of the jurors.

Still, Sheriff Martin told newsmen several times before, during, and after the trial, that he was certain of his acquittal; and he had reason to be.

All twelve jurors were Americans, most of them farmers or craftsmen from the northern end of the county outside the strike zone; two were from Hazleton, one of whom had worked for several of the defendants. They were: Eli Weaver, a laborer in the railroad in Plymouth, age forty-five; D. R. Shaw, carpenter in Ross township, age thirty-seven; Albert Follman, rope-maker of Wilkes-Barre, age fifty-five; Alfred Stevens, clerk in a department store of Wilkes-Barre and an old soldier, age sixty; Herman Gregory, farmer in Huntington Township, age fifty-three; Ada Laroon, a tinsmith of Sugarloaf Township, age forty-five; C. C. Ransom, a housebuilder at Plymouth, age fifty; B. M. Rood, a farmer living at Bloomingdale [age not given]; Jones B. Oxrider, carpenter living near Carbon, age about forty-five; H. A. Wolfe, a farmer living in Ross Township, age twenty-six; A. W. Washburn, a carriage-maker, living at Freeland, age fifty-five. Of course, none was a "Hungarian." None was a miner. Nearly all were descendants of Yankee farmers, in religion and in politics like the deputies: Protestant and Republican.

All together, the trial was to take up twenty-seven working days, from February 1 until the verdict on March 9. Two days were spent selecting a jury, a third on the opening statement of the prosecution. The commonwealth called more than one hundred witnesses, most of them eyewitnesses, and on the major points of their testimony the defense raised no dispute. This testimony used up just over twelve days and was laden, as Attorney General Palmer put it in his memoirs, "with details which were unnecessary and nauseating."

District Attorney Martin was not familiar with the early hearings, had not been party to the six month's investigation by the prosecuting committee, and by his lack of preparation was an embarrassment to the prosecution. He had not shaped the indictment he was expected to prosecute. In addition, about half of the testimony for the prosecution had to be conducted through interpreters, whose skill in grasping the regional idiom of many witnesses generated, according to Father Aust, many blurred and faulty translations. Delays for translation prevented rapid and lively cross fire in the courtroom.

Many of the deputies who had been wearing beards or moustaches on September 10 now came to court clean shaven, and some of those who had been clean shaven came now in beards or moustaches. Witnesses for the prosecution got confused, and had trouble recognizing individual deputies. The defense attorneys played on their ignorance. Attorney Lenahan, in cross-examination, instructed one poor man to walk across the courtroom to point out the deputy he was mentioning. The miner hesitantly got up and stiffly, in confusion, went and laid his hand on Attorney Henry Palmer, to general laughter.

Even six months after the massacre, some of the victims were in bandages. Some could barely speak because of damage to their throats or their brains. Some had scars and ugly purple holes. Some showed two, three, or even six wounds when commanded to remove their shirts. Tiny Ella Cheslak appeared and seemed frightened half to death. At moments it seemed that the jury could not fail to find the deputies guilty in some degree.

February 4, 1898

THE PROSECUTION'S OPENING SPEECH

THE COURTROOM was crowded for the opening speech of the prosecution, with much coughing and scraping of chairs, and a buzz of conversation. Outside, the weather was four degrees above zero. After the gavel, the court refused a motion that a visit be arranged to the site of the killings at Hazleton. Then John McGahren strode to the front of the courtroom and cleared his throat. "Your honor, gentlemen of the jury," he began. "We cannot fail to realize the importance of this case. It is a case which, possibly, in its importance, has no parallel in this Commonwealth or in this country." He appealed to the conscience of the jury, taking care to describe the coming witnesses: "Their race or creed, their political relations or condition should have nothing to do with your case." He explained the distinguishing features of murder, manslaughter, and other terms relevant to the defendants. "There are two indictments," he stressed, "murder and felonious wounding. You may find them guilty of murder or manslaughter or you may find some guilty of murder first degree, others guilty of murder second degree, or manslaughter, and may acquit others if you find nothing against them." These admonitions were accurate but glossed over the weakness in the prosecution's case. If the prosecution were merely bound to prove conspiracy and manslaughter, the case might have been easier.

McGahren was a stocky man with wavy black hair and a bushy moustache. He was given to holding the lapels of his coat as he talked and wore a thin black-ribbon tie. He spoke calmly and deliberately, announcing that the commonwealth would ask a conviction of the deputies for murder in the first degree. "It is not necessary to show who fired the shot," he was careful to say, since no one could tell whose bullet actually killed Mike Cheslak. "All who were armed, aiding and abetting, are also guilty in the eyes of the law." He pointed to the ragtag miners who were in the courtroom as witnesses and described their grievances and lawful pursuit of justice. They went to Lattimer "in an open, lawful way, candidly and honestly, and they had a right under the law to do so," and they were "carrying American flags for their protection under our laws." He described the roughness of the deputies at West Hazleton, and described how "the American flag the marchers had for their protection was torn into shreds" and how two miners were there ruthlessly clubbed.

The floors of the courtroom creaked as McGahren walked slowly back and forth. McGahren pointed out how "the Burgess of West Hazleton came forward and said he was in authority and made the Sheriff desist." Then he stressed the vicious threats and epithets with which the deputies left West Hazleton to prepare for the scene of Lattimer. He stressed the malice of the sheriff and deputies in the fury of the "horrible massacre" in Lattimer, "worse than an Indian massacre of our early settlers when there was no law" and how it occurred under the eyes of the very sheriff "who should protect these poor fellows. And we will show you, gentlemen, that most of these men were shot in the back, while they were running away." He then spoke with a mixture of disbelief and disdain of the deputies standing armed after the slaughter, smoking cigars, and Hess raising his rifle and threatening to shoot a civilian who complained to him of the butchery.

For the next fifteen and a half days, the commonwealth paraded 140 witnesses through the courtroom. Many of them were still in bandages; others were asked to expose their wounds. Some were carried in on stretchers. Many disinterested citizens were among them. So repetitive and telling was the testimony that, in exasperation, Attorney Henry Palmer rose to object on February 10 that, to save time and spare tedium, the defense was ready to stipulate that certain facts were true and acceptable; viz, (1) that at the meeting at Harwood, September 9, the strikers had agreed to march unarmed; (2) that the marchers were unarmed; and (3) that the deputies did, in fact, fire upon them, killing and wounding those officially listed. The defense did not contest these points, he said.

These stipulations were startling. They conceded almost the entire case made by the prosecution. But, of course, the strategy of the defense was consistent with the whole and open admission of all the salient facts. What the defense hoped to do was to arrange these facts within an exculpating picture. Every move made by the defense was consistent with a tacit admission on its part that its clients were stone-cold guilty; only, they wished to show, the homicides were *justified*. Unaccountably, the case presented by the prosecution did not go directly to this jugular. The prosecution tried so hard to establish the three essential points so effortlessly conceded by Defense Attorney Palmer that its attack was easily outflanked. Attorney McGahren's efforts to contrast the peacefulness of the strikers and their rights under American law with the meanness, hostility, and malice of the deputies went in the right direction. But, as we shall see in tracing some of the drama and high interest in the parade of prosecution witnesses, this point was soon lost from sight.

February 5–20, 1898

WITNESSES FOR THE PROSECUTION

FOR the first week court remained in session until noon on Saturday. Outside, the temperature dropped to just above zero. The crowd at the doors diminished in numbers as the slow grind of justice set in. The first witness for the prosecution was Andro Sivar, followed by Joseph Michalko, the reverends Aust and Hauser, the photographer Henry Dryfoos, the schoolteacher Charles Guscott, Mr. Keller (brother-in-law of Frank Pardee), Reverend Stofflett, Grace Coyle the schoolteacher, and two travelling salesmen at the scene, Messrs. Corrigan and Adams.

Each of the witnesses made good points. Sivar was especially effective, and was described in the papers as the "hero" of the prosecution. A good-looking young man, he spoke with poise and vivid detail about the peacefulness of the march, and was especially effective in testifying about the assurances from Chief of Police Evan Jones in West Hazleton that the men were within the law and could proceed. This last point should again and again have been hammered home at the trial. It was not.

Defense Attorney Lenahan was the shortest and squattest of the attorneys and he walked stiffly up and down, trying to bore in on Sivar's story. The young witness knew English well enough to fend him off decisively. Lenahan scattered shot all over the place, linking Sivar to the Molly Maguires—who had been Irish and had disappeared from the area before Sivar had even been born—and to incidents all over the region for the month before the trial. Attorney Scarlet rose in anger to protest this total confusion of places, events, and persons. But he needn't have worried. Sivar remained calm and unflustered.

Michalko had to have an interpreter—Edward Ujfalusi was assigned the job—and then had trouble understanding Ujfalusi's dialect. Many of the witnesses were to have this difficulty. When Lenahan asked him why he and the others had not taken a mere committee to Lattimer, Michalko said: "I was afraid to go alone with ten men. I was afraid of the deputies. They would shoot us all."

During his cross-examination of Charles Guscott, Lenahan approached the schoolteacher rapidly and with shaking fist. McGahren challenged the defense attorney for this unseemly threat. Lenahan replied sweetly that he meant no intimidation and then provoked a prolonged and loud fight between himself and McGahren and Scarlet. Guscott, watching nervously, got quite confused.

Reverend Stofflett of the Reformed church reported how weary and quiet the marchers had seemed as they neared Lattimer. Miss Grace Coyle, a chubby and pretty redhead, corroborated Guscott's story. Lenahan accused her of colluding with Guscott to coordinate their testimony. He then asked her slyly about her relationship with the secretary to the prosecution committee:

"Did you see Matt Long last night?"

"Yes, sir."

"Was he talking to you about the case?"

"No sir," she blushed, "the meeting was accidental."

"What did he say?"

Hesitation. "He asked me to go to the opera with him."

"Did you go?"

"Yes, sir."

Laughter. Gavel.

Matt Long shouted to Lenahan: "Don't you like it?"

Released, the witness stepped down. Matt Long came forward to take her arm, bowing to Mr. Lenahan, asking his permission.

Lenahan protested to the court.

On Saturday, District Attorney Martin told the judge that through the oversight of his predecessor, bail had not been renewed for the deputies. He requested that they be placed in jail. Alarmed, Lenahan jumped up. Garman said it would be unfair for accused murderers to walk out free. Outside the courtroom, he said, the defense attorneys had been heard to boast that their clients, though accused of murder, were walking free. The lantern-jawed Garman told the judge such conduct was shameless.

"That's false," Lenahan shouted.

"Well, we know the law in the matter," Garman said to the judge.

"If that is so," Lenahan stuck out his chin, "it is the only law you ever knew and I further say that you are a low-down puppy and you don't know who your father is."

Garman ignored him, but Lenahan's language worsened. When he finished his plea to the judge, Garman walked to the table where Lenahan stood and raised his fists.

"You dare not hit me or I'll kill you," Lenahan shouted, "you coward."

Garman quietly picked up his cane which lay on the table. Lenahan uttered a "sulphurous epithet" (which no newspaper dared to print) and excitedly asked Garman if he intended to use it. Very quietly Garman said "No," and walked away as if Lenahan did not exist.

Scarlet was so disgusted with the conduct of the attorneys that he nearly walked off the case that afternoon. Judge Woodward warned Lenahan and Garman that he would tolerate no further behavior of that sort.

Still, Lenahan's outbursts had their effect. Guscott, who should have been an excellent witness (he wrote a clear eyewitness account, together with a hand drawing of the scene, for the New York *Journal* of February 6), fumbled and the good effect created by another strong witness, John Eagler, was clouded by the near-brawl immediately afterward.

The prosecution used twelve more days for loose testimony, spread from Monday, February 7 to Saturday, February 18. The evidence was relentless. The reporters, however, seemed to be yawning a good deal and appeared vexed at the lack of any new sensation. The sinking of the *Maine* had drawn many out-of-town reporters to better stories. On Thursday, February 10, the steam was turned off in the courtroom thanks to milder weather, and everyone found it easier to breathe.

Daniel J. Ferry, a tea merchant who had been standing twenty yards from the sheriff at Lattimer, testified how John

Turner, Edward Turnbach, and William Raught had been aiming their guns and how Bill Raught ran up on the electric railway to get better shots at a man sprinting away.

During one recess, Father Aust demonstrated for reporters how a Winchester automatic could be emptied in a minute and a half.

On the twelfth, a girl who worked as a servant for the Williams family in Lattimer, Mary Kohler, made the prosecution tense when she began to describe how frightened she had been before the marchers arrived, and how as soon as they appeared people in Lattimer started rushing indoors. The deputies began to beam.

Garman asked her, "What caused the fright?"

"Because we heard the deputies were going to shoot."

The smiles disappeared from the one side, appeared on the other. Often, half the courtroom broke into applause or laughter, like spectators at a sporting contest; then later, the other side would do the same.

John Petruska, a fruit peddler and grocer in Hazleton who had ventured to Lattimer, was a powerful witness for the prosecution. He testified that he had stopped in Hazleton to sell vegetables and heard some deputies say they "were going to shoot the miners." He walked to Hazleton, then, because, as he said, "I had never seen anything of the kind." Palmer tried to rattle him in cross-examination, since Petruska stood not four feet from the sheriff at the shooting and fully corroborated the miners' story. But Petruska only repeated: "I was not a striker and I went out of curiosity to see the shooting." The more Palmer questioned him, the more damaging the details he brought out, so Palmer gave up.

At one point, four husky young men carried George Gasperick in on a chair. He was one of those in front of the sheriff when a bullet smashed into his head; it was there still. He remembered Roger McShea giving him two drinks of whiskey while he lay on the road. He was asked to show his head wound to the jury. One juror put his finger into the gaping hole. Gasperick complained that with every step he took he felt something shake in his head.

During these days, Attorney Scarlet seems to have seen most

clearly that something was going wrong with the prosecution's case. He was a thin, intense man who wore frameless glasses on his narrow face and sported a well-groomed thick moustache; he pointed his thin fingers as he talked. Through the testimony of witness after witness, he attempted to open up testimony about the prolonged shooting, the running after the victims, the kicking, and the shooting at those already fallen, in order to demonstrate that such malice constituted murder in the first degree. But since the case before the court was solely the felonious wounding of Mike Cheslak, his every attempt to bring in evidence about the motivations, mood, and actions of the deputies concerning other victims was open to objection. Portly and self-satisfied, Judge Woodward consistently sustained objections against Scarlet's necessary line of attack. He was thoroughly reined in.

Thus, the prosecution did not, or could not, concentrate on making an airtight case against the handful of deputies it believed to be conspicuously guilty. Testimony by eyewitnesses showed that at least twelve deputies actually fired shots: Turner, Raught, Ridgeway, Zeirdt, Hall, Platt, Turnbach, R. D. Jones, Cook, Fritzinger, Frank Clark, and Price; but the prosecution's case never snapped tight on any one of them.

This twelve-day procession of survivors, especially the wounded and mutilated, seemed ultimately to have the effect of hardening, rather than moving, the spectators. The prosecution was relying heavily on pathos, as though its purpose were to put on the record a grisly history of sufferings.

February 21, 1898

FOR THE DEFENSE

ON FEBRUARY 21, George S. Ferris arose to present the case for the defense. Lenahan had badly wanted first position, but Sheriff Martin had insisted that his own attorney lead off. Martin was still worried that the companies, through their attorneys, would abandon him. He was not a local boy from Hazleton, and he wanted to protect himself.

Mr. Ferris was "a man loved and respected by every member at the bar," and began his long and eloquent defense quietly and in a mood of conciliation: "May it please the Court and gentlemen of the jury: It is hardly needful to say that this is probably the most momentous trial that has ever been heard in our criminal courts." He congratulated the "learned counsel for the prosecution" for explaining the law of homicide "fairly and correctly." "But, gentlemen," he added softly, "as you well know, all homicide is not criminal." Then he created a totally new perspective on what had happened on September 10. "The story of the disturbances culminating in the Lattimer riot has never yet been fully told," he said, referring constantly to "the Lattimer riot." He pictured weeks of "riot and outrage" in which "the reign of law had given place to a reign of terror."

The highways were swept by surging masses of armed and desperate men. Peaceful citizens were forced into their ranks. Those who resisted were set upon, beaten, clubbed and wounded—some of them nigh unto death. Those who fled from the fury of the mob were pressured, stoned and fired upon. The sanctity of the home was violated. Dwelling houses were broken into and men dragged out of them—or forced to flee to the woods for their lives. Women were assaulted and threatened with death. Robbery was committed. Buildings were attacked and windows smashed with stones and collieries taken by storm. Men who sought to earn an honest living were driven from their work. The whole community was terrorized. The local authorities were powerless; and law had been supplanted by anarchy. This is no fancy sketch, gentlemen, what I tell you here the witnesses will tell you there, [he pointed to the witness box] and more. But neither I nor they have language to express the horrible anxiety and paralyzing fear in which those people lived.

Such was the condition of affairs when the sheriff arrived upon the scene. He was at Atlantic City when he heard the call to duty, but, like the faithful officer and brave man that he is, he at once obeyed the call.

Ferris spoke softly but all his memories of the anxious days he had spent with Sheriff Martin flowed back to him and gave his voice passionate conviction. "The fatal attack on Lattimer was concocted at two meetings held on the night of Thursday, September 9," he said, "one at Harwood, the other at Cranberry." Then he proceeded to draw a picture of scheming, desperate men deliberately ignoring the sheriff's proclamations posted even at their places of meeting, men who threatened bombings and shootings at every turn. He spoke of the "mob" that gathered the next day, "eight-hundred strong."

They were armed with clubs, iron bolts, bars and revolvers. They freely announced their purpose to be to march upon Lattimer and stop the works. They were warned not to go there, as bullets might be flying. The reply was, "We no 'fraid—we got bullets, too." They said to men whom they ordered to join them, "If you want revolvers, we'll get them for you." They expected to be joined by the desperate McAdoo crowd who had terrorized that whole region on the previous Friday. The McAdoo crowd failed to come and the others growing impatient of delay set out upon their desperate errand. From the start they spread terror wherever they went. They rushed from house to house in Harwood and Cranberry, breaking into them and dragging men out of them and forcing them into their ranks, beating and wounding those who resisted and stoning and firing upon those who fled. The rioters threatened to dash out the brains of a heroic woman who stood on the floor of her own home with a loaded gun in defense of her husband who was hiding from them in the cellar. They fired a shot close to the head of another brave woman who dared to withstand them. They even attacked and threw stones at an old woman aged eighty-two years.

The jurors strained forward in their seats. All their own fears of the foreigners pressed against consciousness. Flooding into their minds were images of the peaceful, bucolic cottages in which the Americans had lived—in peace, as many now nostalgically remembered it—before the foreigners had come to take away their jobs, to drive down wages in the region, and to force honest, hardworking citizens to migrate westward in search of better living. The soft voice of Ferris drew them on. They saw the lonely sheriff and his outnumbered band of deputies try to calm the riotous mob at West Hazleton, and the disobedient strikers gather to plot to outflank the sheriff by taking a hidden route to Lattimer.

Then Ferris introduced a new idea. He began to speak of a mysterious "big Hungarian" on one of the deputies' trolleys out to Lattimer. He described the scene at Lattimer pretty much as had the prosecution, except that he placed the deputies' line almost entirely in front of the Craig house and said that the strikers rushed forward from the road "at the little band of eighty deputies in one furious charge."

"All at once," Ferris recounted, "a revolver shot rang out from the rushing mob—then another—then three close together—then a rattling volley from the guns which lasted a few seconds."

Ferris paused. He walked back and forth directly in front of the jury. "How did the firing begin? We shall show you, gentlemen." Ferris swayed on his toes in a long silence. Only then, speaking in a gathering crescendo and then, finally, very softly, did he conclude:

As the deputies lined up, Welsh, Yeager, and the "big Hungarian" and some others stationed themselves at the entrance to the alley in the rear of the line. When the sheriff advanced to meet the mob and while he was talking to them Welsh, Yeager and the Hungarian, who were in their shirt sleeves, raised their arms and beckoned to the mob to come on—and they came—with howls and yells that mass of furious men came rushing down the road away from the road, across the intervening ground straight at the line of deputies. Then from the charging men a shot was fired, then another, then the big Hungarian in the alley in the rear fired three shots in quick succession from a revolver, one of them point blank at deputy Price who avoided the shot by dropping to his knees. The Hungarian then dashed through the line of deputies to join his friends in front and fell in the rattling volley that followed. The order to fire was given by whom we do not know, but it was none too soon, for the head of the charging column had rushed within fifteen feet of the deputies' line. Many of the men were killed and wounded, while Deputy Treible was shot through both arms by some person in the rear of the deputies. When the rioters had fled, the sheriff and his posse proceeded to care for the wounded and dying. With all possible humanity and tenderness they gave them such as they could. That, gentlemen, is the story of Lattimer as you will hear it from the defendant's witnesses and when you have heard it, and have listened to the charge of the Court upon the law of the case, we shall hope for acquittal—a verdict that will say to the world that these men did no deed of crime, but did their duty as faithful officers and as defenders of that liberty under law which we have received from our fathers and, please God, shall yet hand down to our children. . . .

It was a quietly fiery and very effective opening speech. It threw all the preceding testimony into a quite different light. Mr. Ferris was afterward much congratulated.

February, 1898

BEN'S STORY: WINTRY HARWOOD

THE WIND whipped bushels of snowflakes down Harwood's Old Street, over the cold metal rails of the train tracks, up against the thin board shanties. Inside Ben's room, snowflakes swirled near the crack of the wooden door. Ben blew on his hands before he picked up his great coat. The news from Wilkes-Barre was bad. The men thought that Sheriff Martin —"King Martin" they called him—would be exonerated. They feared that all their friends who had testified at the trial would be barred from further work anywhere else in the region. Three witnesses from Harwood had already been told that they would never again find work in Luzerne County.

Ben pulled his coat up over his shoulders and buttoned his collar before pulling open the door. The wind howled against the house. He had known all along that Sheriff Martin would be acquitted. He did not understand how anyone could doubt it. In Slovakia, his mother's hired hand, who had cared for the horse and ploughed the fields for five years after Ben's father died, had finally claimed the horse as his own, bribed the magistrate, and received a judgment in his favor; he had stolen the horse outright, using the law. Justice is not to be expected in this life, Ben Sakmar had learned early.

Still, Ben wanted to talk to Ishtvan, who had just come back from two weeks at the trial. Maybe in America justice was different. He trudged through the wet snow. Ben had made plans to leave for Homestead once spring came. He planned to find a job and then send for Maureen. He was worried that Pardee & Company might cut him off from work before then. He needed every dollar he could get.

February 21–March 1, 1898

WITNESSES FOR THE DEFENSE

AFTER Ferris's opening speech, the defense called Mrs. Catherine Weisenbaum, Mrs. Glace, Mrs. Rose Gillespie, Mrs. Catherine Brennan, Mrs. Michael Gallagher, Mrs. Charles Mullen, and Mr. Joseph Schultz. The husbands of all these women worked for Pardee and Company (as did Mr. Schultz's wife) and their testimony was to establish that great pressure had been put upon their husbands to join the strike before September 10. This testimony was allowed on the grounds that it explained the sheriff's riot order of September 6.

On February 22, Washington's Birthday, Judge Woodward asked Attorney Scarlet, on account of his fine voice, please to read aloud Washington's Farewell Address for the court before hearing testimony. When Scarlet finished his reading, the courtroom broke into applause.

The witnesses for the defense were apparently called to support the picture painted by Ferris, but actually their role was diversionary. Their testimony was in virtually every case, as one legal observer put it, "vague, inexact, and palpably exaggerated." It was hardly ever furnished with proper names, precise dates, or pointed detail. Mostly, it was testimony to their own fears. As to actual facts, its general tenor was to support overwhelmingly the case for the prosecution. The witnesses pointed to no loss of life, to no serious bodily injury, and to very little damage to property. Their testimony showed persons going about their normal lives at home and at work, with absurdly little actual disruption of routine, not at all under conditions of riot or mayhem. Careless about dates, very few of them had anything of significance to say about events in Lattimer, September 10. But the hidden agenda of this tremendously rapid parade of witnesses—twenty-seven on February 23, thirty-three on February 24—was to keep alive in the memories of the jurors every resentment and fear they may ever have nourished of "the Slav invasion" of the mine fields.

Some examples may convey the flavor of their testimony. Peter Wolfe testified that three or four strikers, who did no other harm, called him "an Irish son of a bitch." Elizabeth Money, testifying to the revolvers she saw among the marchers, admitted under cross-examination that she saw no more than one. Mr. Louder said he was hit by a stone thrown by a striker but also that he continued directly to work. John Beech— brother-in-law of one accused deputy and father-in-law of another—said the marchers carried clubs when they left Harwood but admitted under cross-examination that they made no threats of injury to persons or to property. He also admitted that he himself had warned them not to go to Lattimer "as bullets will be flying there." (It was probably he who telephoned Sheriff Martin about the marchers' destination.) Frank Sherry, a fruit dealer in Hazleton, testified that strikers stole peaches from his wagon. Adam Weir, a store manager in Jeansville, saw "armed" strikers on September 3, but admitted under cross-examination that they were "acting in a lawful manner in every respect."

Some of the journalists from the Hazleton papers were outraged by the way the defense attorneys asked questions of their witnesses in misleading ways, so that events that happened elsewhere on September 3 or 6 or other days were allowed to seem to the jurors as though they had all happened on September 10, and as though all the strikers in the region could be identified with the marchers on Lattimer in one undifferentiated mass. Judge Woodward permitted all this meandering and usually dateless testimony because it might have bearing on the legitimacy of the sheriff's proclamation of conditions of riot. Over strenuous objection, he permitted the sheriff's proclamation to be read to the jury. Conditions of riot were being asserted, the prosecution claimed in vain; they were not being proved.

The tenor of the proceedings was most revealing when Mrs. James Edmundson testified how the "men from McAdoo" were armed with clubs, sledgehammers, and "miner's needles." Thus the defense got a chance to exhibit one of these long flat iron bars as a symbol of fear. Mrs. Edmundson also referred twice to the Slavs as "niggers."

Attorney Garman in cross-examination asked her if she had called them niggers because they had at some time harmed her.

"No, sir," she replied.

"Why do you call them that name?"

"Because other people call them that."

"Is it not out of contempt for them, Mrs. Edmundson?"

"Yes."

No one seemed to be above the pettiest kind of hostility. When Mrs. Michael Gallagher, for instance, told of hearing shots outside Harwood as the marchers of September 10 assembled, Attorney McGahren said, "That was the hunting season."

"Yes, for hunting men," Lenahan called out from across the room.

"Well, you know all about that," McGahren retorted.

Some witnesses seemed as though they might have been called by the prosecution, not the defense. Thus, Sheriff Setzer of Carbon County testified how at Beaver Brook on September 9 he had dispersed hundreds of strikers without any shooting or bloodshed. John Wagner, a member of the deputies' posse at Drifton, told how fifteen hundred strikers at Beaver Meadow were dispersed when he and two others "talked to them in a gentlemanly sort of way." Frederick D. Zerby, superintendent of the Lehigh Valley Coal Company, described how Sheriff Martin with one deputy stopped a crowd in the streets of Hazleton. The defense attorneys did not seem to care if points were scored for the prosecution. In their eyes, it did not matter if they reduced the case for the prosecution to a total sprawl. They wanted the jurors to forget the testimony of the prosecution, and to acquire a picture of confusion and fear.

On February 26, a brave woman stood out from among the other witnesses, Mrs. Elizabeth Harvey, the wife of the company physician in Lattimer, who told how the sheriff halted the men and talked with them a few minutes. "Those from the rear rank kept crowding on the front men. Those front men were then driven on towards Lattimer by those behind, and when they came about opposite the deputies they were fired upon; and they started to run after the volley, backwards, as they came. The shots struck the men when they were running." This testimony flatly contradicted the opening statement of Attorney Ferris. Like others, she maintained that the deputies were never under attack. Mrs. Harvey conceded that up until January, 1898, her husband's pay came chiefly from Pardee and Company through deductions from the wages of the miners.

On February 28, another twelve witnesses unwittingly made clear that the greatest fear among the citizens arose *after* the shooting. Cross-examination of these and other witnesses demolished allegations that the marchers on Lattimer were armed. Indeed, that they were unarmed was one of the points Attorney Palmer had permitted to be stipulated on February 10.

The strategy of the defense, plausible in conception, was shabby in its execution. It was tantamount to a recognition of guilt, covered by a bald attempt to work upon prejudice. Attorney Robert D. Coxe of Philadelphia, the official observer for the Austro-Hungarian government, who began by siding with the sheriff, so characterized for his client the major part of the witnesses: "They are employees of Pardee & Company, and of a different race from the strikers, partaking of the hatred of the Hungarian, which undoubtedly exists to such an extent as to color testimony."

The day everyone was waiting for, however, was March 1: the day Sheriff Martin was expected to take the stand.

March 1, 1898

SHERIFF MARTIN TESTIFIES

A TALL, broad, and yet in some ways meek-looking man, Sheriff Martin lumbered to the witness stand, swore his oath, and was seated. He spoke in a clear voice although the reporters noted that his hands shook. He conveyed a fervent belief in his own words. He began with how he had been in Atlantic City

September 4 when the first telegram reached him. Understandably, he omitted certain aspects of his own behavior. He was on trial for murder. But he was, in the main, both persuasive and likable in the story he told.

The sheriff seemed leaner than he had been. He had a neat curly beard, much in fashion at the time. He was quite frank about the fact that his proclamation of riot had been prepared for him in Wilkes-Barre before noon on Labor Day, September 6. This was before he had even visited Hazleton; only afterward, and then only from representatives of the coal companies, had he "first learned of what had really occurred." The coal company managers told him "the strikers were a regular mob and went about armed with clubs and made threats of violence on life and property." The managers arranged a posse for him. All he did himself was make sure to take "none but American citizens." He claimed not to know where they got their arms.

The sheriff recounted his activities over the next four days in simple narrative sentences. He tried to emphasize the clubs carried by the strikers, their threats, and the fear they inspired, but his vanity—and simple truth—obliged him to conclude each episode by telling how he had single-handedly and peaceably dispersed large crowds. He left out of account that he was able to go home to Wilkes-Barre early every evening but one, and that on that occasion was having a leisurely dinner in Hazleton when interrupted. He spoke of his forays as occasions on which, as he arrived, "people were fleeing for their lives," then, almost magically, "by coaxing, talking, and arguing," he brought calm.

He seems to have invented an incident in Cranberry on September 10, as if he first met the marchers there before meeting them again in West Hazleton, where, he said, "the mob became angry and jeered at me and called me bad names." He described the situation at West Hazleton thus: The strikers "began to crowd around me. It looked so threatening for me that I pulled out my revolver and pointed it in the air, as I did not wish to shoot." It was as though the two scenes— at West Hazleton and at Lattimer—had by now blended together in his mind. He said nothing of the pressures of the coal operaters upon him, and nothing at all about the presence of Chief of Police Jones in West Hazleton or the tearing of the flag and the breaking of one marcher's arms.

Perhaps the sheriff realized that his account was getting away from the written account he had sent to Governor Hastings in October. But if so, he did not show it. He was by now quite rapt in his memories.

"We took up the position that we did," he said of his deputies in Lattimer, "as I was determined to make one more effort to stop the crowd and make the last effort to have them disperse."

Had the sheriff halted his story here, cross-examination might have asked him: "Why do you say 'one last effort'? Last before what?" But if the sheriff worried about the words that now rushed out, he brushed doubts aside and added quickly: "The deputies formed in line along the road. I told them to be very careful, as this was the worst mob we had to contend with so far. The mob carried clubs and revolvers as they passed Farley's hotel."

It may have passed through the sheriff's mind that, in his letter to the governor he had recorded his words to the deputies quite differently: "I said I would go out and stop the mob again and see what they intended to do. *I said if they say they are not going to do anything, I may let them go on and we will go along with them.*" But, in truth, the sheriff was not an introspective type. As he talked, he always believed himself. He knew he had the jury with him. He stole a glance at the judge, too, and was glad to see him nodding in an unconscious gesture of encouragement. He was about to embellish his story—as he had begun to do after his talk with Ferris at the Hotel Redington the night of the massacre, adding new color each time—and he was grateful just now for that encouragement.

When I saw the strikers come I walked down the road a ways and waited for them. When they reached me I walked out and halted them. I demanded to know where they were going, and they all answered, "Lattimer, to get out the men." I begged and pleaded with them not to go any farther, to disperse and obey the law. I told them they were doing wrong, and began to read my proclamation. The head ones halted, when some one in the crowd yelled out in Hungarian to go on and the crowd pushed up around me. Some called me bad names and one tried to grab me by the neck. I arrested him, when a big crowd rushed around me. I pulled out my revolver for protection and held it in the air, as I did not want to shoot. One of the mob tried to grab it, but failed, and in the struggle I and the crowd around me were pushed to one side of the road.

Just then one John [sic] Novotny, one of the mob, struck me an awful blow on the cheek. It staggered me, and I fell down upon my knees. The crowd was yelling, "Kill him," meaning me. Then I tried to defend myself with my pistol and tried to shoot the man that was attacking me, but the weapon failed to go off.

I saw two men in the crowd about me wave pistols, and one had a knife with which he tried to stab me and would have succeeded only that I was pushed away by one of the men just then.

While I was down on my knees, struggling with the mob, and being tumbled and kicked by them, the deputies started to shoot. The shooting lasted only about half a minute. When I got to my feet the mob was running away and then I saw several men had been shot in the crowd around me and were there lying on the ground near me.

The sheriff had spoken without interruption for almost an hour and he was exhausted. Still, the response in the courtroom was excellent. Somewhere a radiator banged. It was plain that his story had been believed. He could feel exhilaration rising in his veins.

Attorney Ferris did not wish to break the silence too quickly. After a moment, at a nod from the judge, he arose without a word and walked to the table of exhibits, and introduced a revolver into evidence. It was a large gun and looked like a cavalryman's weapon, with a ring in the butt by which to strap it to a saddle or to one's wrist. The attorney asked the sheriff if it was his.

"Yes, that is my revolver. I did not fire a shot out of it, and I handed it to County Detective Eckert at the hearing in this city," replied Sheriff Martin, as the weapon was placed in evidence.

When the defense was finished, Attorney Scarlet arose and walked across the courtroom with his head lowered and his chin in his hand. When he stood directly in front of the sheriff, he raised his head and looked him coldly in the eyes. "Sheriff

Martin. Are we to understand that no Justice of the Peace, no officer of the law, no Mayor, no Burgess notified you prior to September 6 that he was unable to keep the peace in his jurisdiction?"

"Mr. Wall called me at my home," the sheriff began weakly. "Mr. Lathrop, superintendent of the Lehigh Valley Coal Company, told me there had been interference at the company's mines around Hazleton, and he would hold me responsible for further interference."

"You got no other information?"

"None, except from the papers. Mr. Stearns, manager of the Coxe estate, also told me he wanted his property protected. When I got to Hazleton, Mr. Platt, Mr. Zerby and Mr. Hall told me some mobs had been marching."

"Did you make any investigation to find out if there was a complaint or cause of disturbance?"

"No, sir, I did not make any."

"Did you see Calvin Pardee, and did he make complaints?"

"Yes, he said it was too bad his men were driven from work by the mob without any cause at all."

"Did he counsel you?"

"No, sir, I took counsel from no one."

"Did you see the Mayor or the Justice of the Peace or Constable of any city or township and ask for help from them?"

"None, except I did see the Mayor of Hazleton once."

"Did you not when Mr. Hall was selecting the deputies tell him not to select men connected with coal companies?"

"That was not mentioned. I did not think it material."

The defense objected. Lenahan rose and cried out: "Men employed by coal companies are as good citizens as any!"

The court held that the commonwealth could not question the employment of the men.

The sheriff resumed, "I did not inquire at the time where or how the men were employed and as a matter of fact I do not know what most of them do."

"Was there any promise of pay or reward for the deputies?"

"No, sir."

"Who provided them?"

"I do not know."

"What directions did you give relative to loading the rifles? Did you ask how they were loaded?"

"I gave no direction and did not ask anything."

"You knew that they contained sixteen shots?"

"So some of them told me."

"Then you did not know whether one shot or the whole sixteen would be fired in the event of a collision with the strikers?"

"I expected no shooting."

"Did you direct your men to shoot in the air or at the legs?"

"I gave no directions at all."

"Then you went out prepared to shoot and kill with each and every shot?"

"We did not want to shoot at all."

"You had 150 deputies. Was each armed with a 16-shooter?"

"All except a few, who had buckshot guns."

Changing his tone, Mr. Scarlet asked: "Did you read your proclamation to the strikers?"

"Yes, sir, in English."

"You did not have a Polish or Hungarian interpreter?"

"No, sir."

"Were there any instructions to your deputies when the posse was organized about arresting anybody?"

"Yes, if we found them destroying property."

"Then you would not arrest them if they were marching on the public highway?"

"No, sir, not if they were doing nothing."

"Then you did not intend to shoot at Lattimer?"

"No, sir, decidedly not."

"And you instructed your men to attempt to arrest the strikers before shooting?"

"Those were my general instructions, yes."

The sheriff was asked if he arranged his line of deputies so that the strikers would be struck by an "enfilading fire."

"No, sir," he replied.

During the cross-examination the sheriff said the deputies were joined at Lattimer by some twenty-five men armed with rifles and shot guns.

"Were these men sworn in as deputies at once?" demanded Mr. Scarlet.

"Some were and some were not," replied the sheriff.

"Who were the men at Lattimer with you at the time of the shooting?"

"I could only name them from the list or perhaps point them out by sight. I do not know that I could tell all of them."

The sheriff looked over the list and named the following: "A. E. Hess, Rob Turner, A. M. Eby, A. P. Platt, T. M. Morris, Frank D. and J. Potter Clark, Alonzo Dodson, William Raught, John Turner, Thomas Hall, Thomas Marsden, S. B. Price, A. W. Drake, J. W. Bornheiser, Rich Jones."

"Can you point out any more?"

"I do not think I could."

Speaking of the shooting, the sheriff said, "My thoughts were that if they passed me and insisted on going to Lattimer then the strikers had been sufficiently warned."

"Did you tell this to your deputies?"

"No, it was my own thought."

"Did you unfold the proclamation and try to read it to them?"

"Yes, sir."

"You got angry when that man called you a name?"

"No, I did not then. I wanted to arrest him because he urged the crowd on."

"Where did they strike you?"

"All over the body."

"Who struck you in the face?"

"Novotny, I think he was on the stand here."

"You gave the order to fire?"

"No, sir, I did not. I'm quite sure of that."

"What was the signal for the shooting?"

"None, we did not expect any shooting."

"Did you say anything about them not shooting when a man is running away?"

"Yes, I said that if a man is running away he is dispersed and they should not shoot."

"Did the shooting last half a minute?"

"Well, hardly that."

"Were you in the line of fire?"

"Yes."

"He must have been," laughed Lenahan. "He was standing with the strikers."

Scarlet's face was grim: "You might have occasion not to laugh so gaily." Then he looked full at the sheriff: "Did you ask who gave the order to fire?"

"Yes, I asked Price and Hall. They said they did not know who gave the order or who fired the first shot."

"After the shooting did you find any dead or wounded near the schoolhouse?"

"Not myself, but I heard some were found there. I could hardly believe it."

"Were there any beyond the railroad?"

"Yes, several. I went over and saw them. I did not see any dead there, all were wounded."

"What time did the deputies get to Hazleton?"

"About 6 o'clock. I left them for home and got there about 7 o'clock."

Cross-examination was soon concluded. Scarlet had been surprisingly gentle. The sheriff was warmly congratulated by his lawyer, the deputies, and many in the courtroom. He had shown himself to be a man of feeling.

Scarlet knew as he sat down that he had not pounced on the glaring contradictions in the sheriff's testimony. In a wholly neutral courtroom, the sheriff's story might have collapsed of its own weight. In that courtroom that day, the sheriff had too much credibility. A direct challenge might have seemed like persecution. Intelligent as he was, Scarlet knew that the sheriff was boldly lying—about the "knife" aimed at him in the crowd, for example. If the men had pummeled him, as he said, he should have arrested them for resisting arrest and assaulting an officer. Martin said Novotny struck him, but he did not arrest Novotny on the spot or file charges later. Moreover, Sheriff Martin offered no corroboration for the preposterous episode of "the big Hungarian" woven into the story by Ferris. Martin's tale, except for the heightened drama of his own struggle, matched in its essentials the tale of the marchers. He was, of course, now saying that he had *not* given the order to fire.

One reads the testimony of Sheriff Martin, even from a distance of eighty years, with sadness and a pity close to affection. Not so the testimony of others among the deputies on subsequent days.

Wednesday–Friday, March 2–4, 1898

DEPUTIES ON THE STAND

IN February, the defense had boasted to the press that not a single deputy would be called to testify. But in the final hours of the trial, the defense did call Samuel Price, Ario Pardee Platt, Alfred E. Hess, Thomas Hall, John L. Salem, and Charles J. Haen. Of these, Haen was the only deputy willing to admit that he had fired a shot—one shot, a "sort of excitement thing," he explained. He was not willing to admit that his shot had actually hit anybody (He was also the only deputy to testify that "he thought he was shot at.") None of the others who testified would admit to having given the order to fire, to having heard such an order, to having fired their weapons, or to having heard or seen anyone else fire—notwithstanding the fact that the defense had stipulated that the deputies had in fact fired upon the marchers; and notwithstanding the more fundamental fact that the very bullet wounds had been shown in the courtroom.

Samuel B. Price, chief deputy from Hazleton, was a building contractor who had just won the contract to build a new breaker at Harwood. He testified that at West Hazleton he had walked through the ranks of the marchers and felt in the hip pockets of "about fifty of them." He estimated that he felt "25 pistols and maybe fifteen to twenty stones." In their hands, he said, they were carrying clubs, irons, and mining needles. "I went to an alley and heard a shot," he went on. "I saw a big Hungarian with a revolver, pointing it at me. I dropped to the ground as he fired. The ball went over my head. Then I heard the volley of shots." The three deputies that Price said were with him in this alley were not called to the stand to corroborate his story.

Price, Platt, and Hess insisted that the sheriff's life had been in danger. Yet they conceded that they themselves had neither run forward to help him nor fired a shot. Hess observed that the curve of the road brought the line of strikers closer and closer to the deputies, so that while those at the rear were a hundred feet from the right flank, those at the front were only fifteen feet from the left flank, at Mrs. Craig's house. He said he was afraid that those nearest the front would rush the deputies and seize their guns. Thomas Hall, who had selected the Hazleton deputies for the sheriff, supported the picture presented by Mrs. Harvey, that the rear of the strikers had pushed forward upon the front, seeing no reason to stop, and that the sheriff and the knot of leaders around him had been drawn off toward the deputies.

Under cross-examination Hall was asked about West Hazleton: "And the strikers made no attempt to interfere or resist arrest?"

"No, sir."

"Why did you anticipate more trouble at Lattimer?"

"Because the strikers were determined to go and the sheriff was determined to stop them."

Ario Pardee Platt, Jr., was particularly belligerent on the stand. He made no effort to conceal his contempt for the foreign horde. If the deputies had thrown a line across the road, he said, they would easily have stopped the marchers cold. When he was questioned about the flag he tore up at West Hazleton, he pulled a torn flag from his pocket and offered it in evidence. It had only a few yellow, red, and white stripes; the field of blue with its stars was missing. It looked very little like an American flag.

The next day, March 4, Andrej Sivar and John Eagler, called to rebut, denied that Platt's cloth was the flag they had carried.

Attorney Palmer tried to trick Sivar and Eagler in various ways, without success.

Fred Williams, a witness at Lattimer, testified that the marchers did not leave the public road until fired upon, and then not on the deputies' side but away from the deputies. In all, the defense had called 130 witnesses. Rebuttals were brief. The closing speeches were ready.

Monday, March 7, 1898

THE END OF THE TRIAL

AT 10:10 A.M. on Monday, James Scarlet was called from his seat to give the summation for the prosecution. Every seat was taken. The aisles were jammed and around the walls spectators stood on each other's toes. Several score ladies in colorful winter coats had been admitted to reserved seats through the side doors, while several thousand persons stood outside still clamoring to get in.

Scarlet pensively stroked a hand down his long face, lifted his glasses, replaced them, and then walked to a place in the room directly opposite the jury box. He gestured toward the jurors in a clear signal that he knew exactly what his target must be. "Gentlemen of the jury," he began, offering a brief word of congratulations for their work. Then he set the stage: "No jury ever sat in a box in which so many defendants are on trial. . . . No jury ever sat in a box in which the eyes of the whole nation were upon it, in such a way as they are upon you." It took him, then, only moments to come to the theme to which he would return again and again: "American freedom has not come by the blood of Americans alone. It was achieved by the blood of Englishmen, Irishmen, and of every race. Therefore I say this to you . . ." and here he lingered for a very long moment. He was talking quietly. He walked all the way over to the jury box. When he at last picked up the thread of his sentence, he could have said it in a whisper, so still was the room: ". . . to charge you, that you are expected to try this case without prejudice." He held the jury in his glance until he had looked each man in the eye.

Then Scarlet walked back to the center of the room, directly in front of the judge, and began to set forth the salient events of September 10 in the most matter-of-fact manner he could muster. He wished to break the spell of emotion around the jury. But he found he had to plead with them, and expert that he was, he could feel the strain. Despite himself, urgency kept coming into his voice. "These same deputies," he said, "who stopped the crowd at West Hazleton, could have stopped it again anywhere on that weary march." That was his first point. A little later, he wanted another point to sink in: "At Lattimer, the deputies were thrown across"—he lingered on the word—"the road, but were taken from that position and lined diagonally with the road." His hands showed the line of deputies and the public road veering down to the corner of the Craig house. "Is there anything significant in that?"

After a pause, he reminded the jurors how the deputies had previously halted the marchers by standing athwart their path. This time, instead of stopping them again, "the deputies form to deliver an enfilading fire." He reminded the jurors of specific witnesses who had described the marchers at this point as unarmed and peaceable.

Then Scarlet described how the sheriff stepped out in front of the crowd "to provoke anger and give a cause for the shooting." He bore in, then, on the decisive point:

The formation of that line of deputies plainly indicates that it was a prearranged plan to murder. The whole mass of testimony points to but a plain fact. There was no riot, there was not even a rout. . . . And as to the firing itself, it is shown absolutely that there was not one volley. There was a series of shots. All of them effective.

Scarlet then for a moment became carried away and rapidly went through the testimony of a variety of witnesses. Then, once again, he showed surprising gentleness toward the sheriff: "Oh, gentlemen, the only human man there, if I must say it, was the Sheriff, who raised his arms as the firing continued, as much as to say, cease, stop." Matching his own words, Scarlet stopped and let silence deepen. Scarlet pictured the sheriff standing with arms erect.

"What is there in this?" he finally asked. "The Sheriff was not shot; he was not knifed; and, according to witness Ryder, he was not even bruised." Then Scarlet walked toward the place where the sheriff was seated and pointed him out. "No man was more surprised at the firing than the Sheriff himself and no man more horror-stricken." Again, a pause, while the attorney turned and walked back to the center of the room. "But, what are the deductions?" He looked to the jury while pointing to the sheriff. "He was brought there as a tool, to further the purpose of the deputies organized to crush that strike."

Scarlet had made his main points. He lingered for a while on how all but five victims had been shot in the back, and how many of them had fallen at great distances on the far side of the road. None, he said, could ever have stumbled so far without running first, before they were hit, "for the shock from a .44 calibre is such as to cause suspension of the faculties." He ended by recalling how often sheer persuasion had been effective during the strike, and could have been effective at Lattimer but for malice and hostility. "I will not appeal to your prejudices," he concluded. "I believe that you are determined that there shall be no more slaughter of the innocent in this Commonwealth."

Scarlet had spoken for an hour and a half. In the time before noon, tousle-haired Lenahan was called for the defense. Rubbing his hands, the feisty bantam sprang from his chair and paced quickly up and down across the polished floorboards and with his booming voice quickly changed the mood. "We expect to show you that there is no guilt," he almost shouted. Then, suddenly, he paused and gestured to the portraits high on the walls. His voice became deep and passionate, a Fourth-of-July voice. "We stand on historic ground and within these walls have been historic deeds. On these walls hang the pictures of men who were cultured and refined." His eyes swept slowly over the witnesses for the prosecution, newcomers, their poverty obvious, some of them unable to comprehend English. "Men who fought, some of them, in two wars." Then he abruptly walked over to the jurors, as Scarlet had, his finger pointing toward them, his voice menacing: "And we today are battling, not alone for the honor of our country—" his left hand gestured toward the flag at the judge's side, and his voice then changed pitch to a note low and reverberating—"but for the honor of the county of Luzerne." Then he walked away, as if in despair, speaking quickly, his hand on his forehead: "When we shall be gathered with our fathers, this case will be handed down as the greatest in the history of the world. Oh, I cannot discuss this case dispassionately." His hand now covered his heart: "This is the county I love. I am jealous of its honor among its sister counties."

There was much more of this. Lenahan tried to frame the legal question—was there a riot?—but kept being overwhelmed, for effect, by the horrors of the materials he had to deal with: "It is true that this crime, this riot, was done under that flag, that flag that was drenched in the blood of patriots. . . . It is for that flag that you bared your breasts to rebel bullets—to protect that flag." It was too much. He choked. "They would desecrate it." He spread his hands: "Shall it be?" He pounded his fist into his hands again and again: "Oh no! Oh no!"

It was nearly the lunch hour, but Lenahan was only warming up. "Shall this brave officer suffer for suppressing this foreign band?" he asked, letting his hand sweep across the witnesses for the prosecution. "This mob, inspired by no tradition of ours in the past, or hope in the future, was lawless. The law throws around all its protection, but it demands in return he shall give submission to it!" With sarcasm he added, "It was contended by these strange people we should take them into our bosom."

Lenahan hated to be interrupted just now but Judge Woodward halted him in midstream and promised that he could resume at one. At lunch, Lenahan was warmly congratulated but he told his friends they hadn't seen anything yet.

In his afternoon speech, which lasted four hours, Lenahan talked throughout with a long, ugly miner's needle in his hands, making menacing blows in pantomime, creating a feeling of threat. "That lawless horde," he began to stress, "that came down from the steppes of Asia has found its way here, and by *them*," his lips curled, "the High Sheriff of this county, pledged to duty, is here charged with murder!" Having stirred patriotism, he now concentrated on contempt. "The history of the Hun and Slav in the old country is that of mischief and destruction. And they marched, under Attila, ruthlessly over Europe. No home was too sacred," he warned the jurors, "or virgin too pure, for their assault."

Mr. Lenahan's blood, according to a reporter, "was thoroughly up. He warmed to his task. . . . His powerful voice rang like a clarion. People sat there amazed at the power of his utterance, the force of his logic, his marshalling of testimony and his clear-cut logic."

Mr. Lenahan all but exhausted himself. He ended by saying, almost in a whisper: "The evidence failing to identify the persons who shot Mike Cheslak, there can be no conviction under the indictment." It was nearly five o'clock, and by this time mere matters of fact seemed irrelevant.

The next morning, former Attorney General Henry W. Palmer conducted the second summation. Wealthy, distinguished, aristocratic, scion of one of the oldest and most established legal families in the region, Palmer nevertheless regarded this day as one of the most significant in his life.* "Mr. Palmer," wrote the Wilkes-Barre *Leader*, "was prepared for the occasion and it is an event in his life not soon to be forgotten by either that gentleman or the audience that listened." One expected Lenahan to use brass knuckles, but it was breathtaking, actually, to hear

---

* By far the largest single section of his autobiography, *Fifty Years at the Bar and in Politics* (1913) consists of clippings about and documentation from the Lattimer trial (214 pages in all). The verbatim transcript of speeches and fragments of cross-examination suggest that Palmer (or his editor) had at his disposal the now missing stenographic record of the trial. In his autobiography, Palmer reprints without comment a summary of his speech by the reporter for that evening's Wilkes-Barre *Leader*. The tone of this lengthy summary is quite different from the tone of the full text of Palmer's speech, which was reprinted in the *Leader* the following Sunday (March 13). The printed speech is intelligent, logically organized, effectively argued. In the actual courtroom presentation, Palmer may have departed from the text and presented what the reporter of the day recorded. Perhaps the reporter caught the emotive signals and neglected the full logic. I have followed the reporter's version, by and large, while also including the main points of the written text.

Palmer, from his first words, take the high road of elegantly hung Victorian periods, while masterfully employing every weapon of sarcasm and invective. First he attacked "certain journals that disgrace civilization" for distorting facts and making Lattimer a "rallying cry for socialists, anarchists, and haters of organized government."

Bitter and seething was his denunciation of "the barbarian horde" that, "unless throttled now, will rise up in rebellion against our government to tear down the stars and stripes and fix over the highest places the red flag of riot and confusion." Palmer then denounced "the pastor" of the prosecuting committee, a priest dedicated to peace, who was now helping "this band of assassins and cutthroats," and Matt Long, and Garman, and McGahren. He bowed to the "learned gentleman from Danville, the eloquent gentleman from Danville," who would "also aid the assassins." He sneered at "the curled and scented Adonis of the bar, the prosecuting attorney, Mr. Martin." He called them—said the reporter—"the lowest of the low, the meanest of the mean." "Anarchists all," Palmer said with withering scorn, "and fire brands who would nurture and give comfort to fire brands."

Some spectators gasped. The prosecuting attorneys could hardly believe their ears. Palmer moved elegantly on. Tall and dignified, bearded in the Viennese fashion like Sigmund Freud, Palmer was now saying that John Fahy is "like all the other foul birds of prey called labor agitators, low, brow-beating villains who are crawling over the country." And then he was on to "the foul-mouthed Gompers" whose work is "lies and slander" and whose aim is "red-handed murder."

District Attorney Martin could barely control himself and rose to protest. "It is unfair to deal in prejudice and to inject prejudice into the jury box."

But Palmer regarded him icily and pushed on to his major surprise. The defense had all along seemed to concede almost everything. Now Palmer asserted that no conviction in this case was possible. Why? Because there had been presented absolutely no evidence concerning the one question that mattered: Who killed Mike Cheslak? "No one but God can tell that," he said. "Who that man is, no one knows. No one pretends to know. There is not one syllable of evidence identifying or tending to identify that man. The man who did the deed is not himself conscious of it."

In short, the indictment drawn by former District Attorney Fell had been carefully designed to prevent conviction. The prosecution had walked into a beautiful trap. The single case before the bar was not a case that anyone could prove. The trial was a sham.

Palmer then took every theory of the prosecution and offered five or six reasons why each was unsustainable. Indeed, he turned the prosecution's case around. The innocent marchers became the highly moral deputies. The unlawful posse of murderers became the unlawful rioters. The failure of the deputies to try peaceful persuasion became praise that they had finally taught a lesson to a small group, before the whole region exploded in bloody civil war. If the sheriff were not now upheld, he said, the next time no one would have protection from a mob, and every mob would know that no sheriff could halt it.

Palmer's deportment seemed designed to let the jurors know how deeply the better class of people in the area felt about riotous conditions. He praised "the noble deed at Lattimer," the "brave deed," the "deed of duty and honor." He praised the witnesses for the defense. He praised the deputies. "The deputies—were they to wait until they saw the Sheriff's blood flow before they shot? Were they to wait until they saw his mangled corpse brought to them before they fired?" He turned and faced the jurors as though they were his equals. "What would *you* do?" he asked. He waited until the jurors were almost ready to leap out of their seats with frustration at not being able to answer. "I am sick of this sickly sentimentality!" he exclaimed. "I want, and *you* want,"—placing them and him on an equal plane—"men brave enough to do just what the deputies did: stand up for honor, for homes, and for the lives of the peace officers." He pointed with scorn at the prosecutors: "They say that the deputies fired too long and too much and that too many men were killed. . . . The Sheriff and his posse there at that moment were the sole judges of the amount of force necessary to quell this awful tide of hot, riotous rebellion."

Palmer then disposed of objections that the strikers were shot in the back, that some were six hundred feet away from the scene when fallen, that sympathy with labor might infect the jury box. "At the erection of the Tower of Babel there was a strike and that has been going on ever since." He saved his best till last. The Wilkes-Barre *Leader* offered a summary: "The peroration was a brilliant effort on the rights of American citizenship, and the danger threatened by the lawless Slav."

On that note, the defense rested. The day had been consumed. The defense presented Judge Woodward a list of sixteen propositions to guide his judgment and his charge to the jury, wherewith court was adjourned until the morrow. The linchpin to the sixteen propositions was that no one could prove who killed Mike Cheslak.

The final summation for the prosecution lay in the hands of District Attorney Martin. He began Tuesday morning by quoting Thomas Jefferson's appeal for "equal justice to all, of whatever race, religion, or persuasion." He asked the jury not to be led by any ties of their own, or any prejudice, but to extend their concern to all men. He corrected Lenahan's history of the Slavs; they do not, he said, descend from Attila. And for some time—continuing into the afternoon—Martin defended the racial characteristics of the Slavs. He praised revolutionary war heroes, defended Father Aust and the prosecutor, and, in general, replied as though from a mental checklist to each point made by the defense. He called Sheriff Martin a "stool pigeon" for the mine operators, and blamed him for "carelessness that savored of a wicked disposition" for choosing as deputies men whose interests lay with the operators. It was easy, he said, to color the testimony of the defense, by speaking of patriotism and loyalty to flag and country. He pointed to signs of intention, motive, and malice on the part of the deputies. He asserted that the shooting was prearranged, and recalled evidence that the deputies were out of temper. He cited by name those deputies who threatened violence before the actual hour. He complimented the jury for their patience. He went into the law concerning malice. He meandered back and forth, and at last sat down.

Relieved, the judge then called for close attention and asked the jury to focus on one paramount question: had the posse become an unlawful mob by deciding to disregard the law and commit a crime? The judge had the clerk read a long portion of Sheriff Martin's testimony, which he supported thus: "We say to you now that the testimony of the Sheriff himself as to what occurred at Lattimer after he went forward to meet the strikers is not, in any material particular that we can discover, contradicted by the evidence on the part of the Commonwealth."

After this ringing endorsement of Sheriff Martin's testimony, the judge then read to the jury the sixteen propositions presented for his guidance by the defense. He affirmed seven of them outright, modified three only slightly, affirmed two only in part, and declined to affirm only four.

At 5:30 the court recessed. When the jury did not announce a verdict after dinner, the judge decided at 8:30 upon an adjournment until the next morning at 10:00. Outside the courthouse, reporters could see the lights in the jury room. They could plainly see the jurors through the windows, so they knew that deliberations for the night were at an end. What they were to learn the next morning was that in fact the verdict had already been reached in the jury box and that by now the jurors, with no method of getting home at night, were simply enjoying one another's company and exchanging comments on the case.

Wednesday, March 9, 1898

THE VERDICT

PROMPTLY at 10:00 A.M., with the usual crowd in attendance and a larger one outside, Judge Woodward was in his seat. At 10:05 a tipstaff led the jury to their seats at the judge's right. Chairs squeaked in the painful silence as the roll of jurors was called and the twelve male voices, one by one, replied "present."

"Clerk," intoned the judge. "Take the verdict."

Clerk Jeffries called out each name and a sealed verdict was handed up to the judge who glanced at it without surprise and passed it to the clerk, who shouted out: "Gentlemen of the jury. Harken to your verdict as the court has recorded it. You and each of you do say that in the case of the Commonwealth against James Martin and others, for the killing of Mike Cheslak, you do find the defendants *not guilty*. And so say you all."

Each juror nodded his head and one or two in the audience made a feeble gesture of applause, and then immediately a great buzz arose and the crowd went out. Some of the deputies stood, but others motioned them to stay. Mr. Lenahan came and shook many of their hands, and then went to the jury box on the left where the wives were seated and shook the hands of Mrs. Turnbach, Mrs. Hall, Mrs. Morris, and others. Attorney Wheaton moved that bail be forfeited, and after some rustling around for papers the district attorney consented. The deputies were totally free. "It was easy to see that all were happy that the agony, for the time, was over."

In the courtroom and outside, Sheriff Martin was pressed with handshakes all around. "On every corner and every shop in the city, the verdict was discussed with much vigor," wrote the Hazleton *Daily Standard*, "and although a verdict of acquittal had been expected by nearly all, the conduct of the trial was condemned by nearly every person. Judge Woodward was censured by a good many for what was considered his partiality all the way through, and particularly his charge to the jury yesterday, which left the prosecution without any hope as to the final outcome." Some newspapers had learned the verdict the night before, and early editions had cautiously announced it. During the morning, it was learned that the jury had taken a ballot immediately at their first meeting at 7:30 P.M. and were unanimous even before discussion, but decided to wait until morning in order to be properly paid, at two dollars per day, seventy-six dollars for thirty-eight days, plus three dollars for travel.

Father Richard Aust was bowed: "I am not surprised at the verdict, as I expected it, but we will have another trial. One more and it will be tried differently." Indeed, the prosecuting committee had learned that one of the jurors had boasted to friends that he would get on the jury in order "to liberate Sheriff Martin and his deputies." Before the trial this same juror had gotten into a public fistfight defending the latter's innocence—by itself grounds for a new trial. But a new trial was not to be. The $4,600 raised by the committee had been depleted.

Although a few papers like the Scranton *Times* and the New York *Evening Journal* deplored the verdict, most—like the New York *World*, the Philadelphia *Ledger*, the Springfield *Republican*, and the Elmira *Gazette*—welcomed it. The Philadelphia *Press* called it "a triumph for order and civilization," and the New York *Sun* said that "the result proves that American civilization is safe under the protection of law." A few, like the Hartford *Courant* and some papers in Wilkes-Barre and Hazleton, sympathized with the legal acquittal, but felt that, in moral terms, the sheriff and deputies still bore unmet responsibilities.

The deputies left Wilkes-Barre on the 1:00 P.M. train, some with their wives beside them. On the same train were many of the marchers, whose air of defeat was as profound as the jubilation of the deputies. Two of the witnesses from Harwood had lost their jobs because of their part in the trial. The others were now afraid. Most were determined to blot out all trace of the event, so that it might never again be held against them.

When the train pulled into Hazleton, many of the deputies went directly to the Old Hazle Brewery on the South Side to celebrate. They drank beer, told stories, and slapped one another on the back in renewed congratulations. Word of this gathering was later published in a neighborhood newspaper, Patrick McGarvey's *Truth*, and from then on Hazle Beer came to be known as "Deputies' Beer." Many in the surrounding country refused to drink it. Within six months, the brewery closed.

1898–1962

BEN AND MAUREEN

BY THE TIME the trial began in Wilkes-Barre, Ben and Maureen had decided that they could not live without each other. Mr. Kearney gave his approval for their marriage. In April of 1898, in St. Patrick's Church in McAdoo they were wed. Ben withdrew his savings from Mr. Nemeth's care.

Ben had paid as little attention to the trial as he could; it was too painful. He had promised Maureen that he would leave the mines, for he had come to loathe the darkness underground, where in the pitch-blackness the pallid faces of his dead friends sometimes shone at him with looks of irrepressible bewilderment.

In May, he went west to Pittsburgh to look for work. Then he came back to take Maureen to McKeesport. They lived there for the rest of their lives. Ben never went back to Slovakia. His mother died just after the turn of the century. Anička wrote from time to time, less frequently after she married. Ben wished he could see her and her children just once. He longed to see again the cross they had built together in the roadway with the vistas of the distant mountains and the deep valleys. He kept her letters, neatly written in a thin, tall hand on thin paper, in a little brown wicker basket with a blue and red cross woven into its top. But he never went back. Soon he seldom even looked back.

He told his children little of the past. Their world was not his world. His grandchildren would remember him on his knees in the corner of the sitting room-kitchen where he kept his "prayer basket," with a rosary, a book of Slovak prayers, and other sacramentals of his boyhood. As an old man, he would pray for long hours on his knees.

And in his undemonstrative way he continued to love Maureen very much. They quarrelled openly, and shouted and yelled with the best. They never dreamed of being apart, although each stated often the sheer impossibility of living with the other. Their children inherited a mite of Irish wit from their mother. One of the granddaughters had a nose and a smile so uncannily like hers that Ben thought he was seeing in her the childhood of Maureen, the only part of her life he had not shared. One of his sons played American Legion baseball on a championship team, and his grandchildren, after the family had covered the long stretch of the Depression and World War II, became the first members of the Sakmar family to enter college. One of them went to law school.

Before he died in 1962, Ben lived to see a Catholic president and a Polish postmaster-general. His home in McKeesport was an old frame house, not at all like those featured in *Better Homes and Gardens*, but in his eyes it was a great mansion, many miles and many long hours beyond the wooden cottage on the hill, past which the spring rains rushed in torrents, on the stark hillside below the line of firs in the distant Tatras.

EPILOGUE

AUTHOR'S REFLECTIONS

BY THE OPENING of the ninth annual national convention
of the UMW at Columbus, Ohio, on January 11, 1898, the
15,000 members John Fahy had enrolled in the Hazleton district made his region the second largest in the country. The
lessons learned and now taught by John Fahy led that union,
in Pennsylvania at least, to organize chapters for all cultural
groups, and to have officers from each group. In 1898, John
Mitchell became the national president of the UMW and in
1902 led a major national strike. The strike of 1887 had been
broken easily, and that of 1897 in Hazleton had been only partly
successful. By 1902, the union was able to hold out against the
operators on a national front and to swing President Theodore
Roosevelt to their side. During 1901 and 1902, fourteen miners
were shot. In the settlement of 1902, the miners won the right
to organize, to negotiate, and to hold some authority in the
industry.

The Coal and Iron Police continued in existence until 1935.
But the experience of Sheriff Martin led the Commonwealth
of Pennsylvania to form the Pennsylvania State Police in 1905.
This was the first such state force in the nation. Its main mission for its first thirty years was to keep order among laborers,
particularly in the mining areas. The miners called the new
mounted force in their gray uniforms, astride black horses,
"the Cossacks."

Epilogue   243

The guns of Lattimer exploded in tragedy through flaws in both sides which led to an outcome neither fully intended. The marchers, most of them not speaking English, were unsure of the role of the deputies. They may have thought that the sheriff's men were simply in the pay of the coal operators. No one among them seems to have imagined that the deputies would shoot. They lacked experience with an institution like a posse and were no doubt too aggressive in their resolve to go forward. Their language toward the sheriff was probably provocative.

In the minds of some of the deputies, on the other hand, the foreigners were by reputation anarchic, lawless, violent in their personal habits, fatalistic, and not quick to understand language or manners. Stories abounded about fights and killings at weddings and over weekends, when the foreigners had been drinking heavily. It may have seemed to the deputies that force, not reason, was all the foreigners would understand. Anglo-Americans share with other cultures, more than is usually recognized, a strong belief in the efficacy of force, hidden under an admirable respect for law and free institutions. This belief in force is never far below consciousness, whether among the wealthy like Calvin Pardee or among farmers and tradesmen like those on the jury. The deputies truly believed that American institutions were uniquely free; that the foreigners were not prepared for them; and that the foreigners, having been "brought up under the lash," respected only the lash, so that it might be the duty of good Americans to give them their own kind of lesson.

Perhaps at the moment when his command to halt was ignored and his person insulted, the sheriff's hand showed more anger in its rough seizure of Malody's collar than he intended. Then when he drew his pistol, or raised it (if it was already drawn), and Novotny grabbed it firmly and twisted it away, anger turned to panic. The deputies may even have had certain fantasies about the invincibility of the foreigners, and in seeing the sheriff thrown off balance may have been swept by the instinct to protect themselves. Their rifles were already at their shoulders—itself an ominous sign of their intentions—and when one shot rang out other fingers moved as if by command.

Instructions had not been given to fire a warning shot first. Anxiety about the need to hurry led some to fire point-blank. Some probably did feel exhilaration in the sudden bloodshed and continued to fire until their chambers were empty.

In rational terms, there was no reason for the confrontation to have reached such a point. But the form of reason under which each side was living prevented it from seeing the reasoning of the other. What is quite moving in the sands of evidence the historian is obliged to sift is that, on both sides, there were men of considerable decency, good humor, flexibility, and patience.

Human beings like to believe that they are rational, not primitive, and this desire breeds self-deception. Modern societies spill blood for ritual purposes just as primitive societies do, but in less conscious ways. Before native Americans in the Hazleton region would accept other races as brothers, they first submitted them to ritual bloodshed to "teach them a lesson," and then in subsequent waves of guilt those who taught the lesson also learned one.

Our nature is a dual one, rational and animal, and both its sides require special tutoring. We are by nature sacramental. More than an enlightened age would like to imagine, moral advances cost blood, not metaphorical blood, but the blood of individuals with families and friends. Mere bloodshed is insane, chaotic, meaningless. But reason, glacial under prejudice, is sometimes broken open by the heat of symbolically spilled blood. At Lattimer on September 10, the deputies arranged themselves for ritual slaying. The dread logic of what they were about had revealed itself in jest and speech all that morning long, and when the exploding rifles flashed the action was already ripe.

The guns of Lattimer, therefore, dramatized the place and weight of the ruling race in the Commonwealth of Pennsylvania. It was not a case, merely, of capital versus labor. Not only social class was at stake, so also was race. The members of the jury were of the working class, as were many who sympathized with the defendants and feared the strikers. The truth is a painful one, and not many Americans like to hear it, because its springs are irrational and deeper than glib enlightenment. It has become easy in recent years to recognize racism with respect to colored peoples. It is more difficult for rational persons to admit to racial feelings concerning other, "white" cultures, even when painful facts require such recognition.

In his imaginative collection, *The Pennsylvania Sampler* (1970), Paul B. Beers of the Harrisburg *Patriot-News* reports that in 1893, the Pennsylvania legislature voted as follows: "Resolved, that we recognize in the constant influx of an ignorant and vicious class of immigrants a great and growing evil and highly injurious to American workingmen and dangerous to American institutions." The Know-Nothings in the 1850s and the Ku Klux Klan in the 1920s and 1930s received substantial support in Pennsylvania. In the 1844 anti-Catholic riots in Philadelphia, 13 persons were killed, 50 wounded, 30 homes damaged, and 2 churches burned. In the railroad riots of 1877, 32 were killed and 1,600 railroad cars and 126 locomotives destroyed. At Homestead in 1892, 16 were killed and 60 injured. In 1902, 14 were killed in the anthracite strike, and 13 in the steel strike at McKees Rocks in 1909. All these killings fell with severest weight upon "foreigners." "Religious bias was coupled with anti-labor and ethnic opposition," Mr. Beers concludes. "It can be argued that Pennsylvania has been a melting pot, but a slow one."

The tragic destiny of America is hidden in its virtue. Its founders, so noble and enlightened in countless ways, suffered from racial blindness in the largest sense: those of northern European culture have imagined themselves to be superior to other races of any color, including white. Moral in so many ways, they have found reason even in their moral virtue for feeling superior. Every other race feels this whip. Were it no longer denied, such a flaw could be overcome.

Since 1897, indeed, the descendants of those who labored in mining patches, under conditions in some ways worse than those of Southern slavery, have had a chance to use intelligence, imagination, and desire. America has yielded them the one significant form of equality: not love, and perhaps not even respect, but at least room to work. Given this gift, they could break free from centuries of serfdom. Of those killed and wounded at Lattimer, the descendants are spread now to the winds. For all we know, they or their children may surpass in talent and achievement the children of the Markles and Pardees, the Martins, Hesses, Turnbachs, and Platts, who in 1897 represented privilege.

The earth moves. The generations come and go. Power and wealth rise and fall. A few things endure: a passion for life, a thirst for justice, courage against established power. These are the legacy of simple, weary men, blown back by a sudden explosion on a hot September day.

A NOTE OF THANKS

THIS BOOK could not have been completed without the help of many persons. The details of the story were scattered; early accounts were full of conflicting or simply erroneous mentions of time, place, identification, and spelling. The sheer volume of detail seemed overwhelming. Without extraordinary assistance, I would have had to give up.

This project was first conceived in 1971, when I read a brief account of the Lattimer Mines massacre in Victor Greene's *The Slavic Community on Strike* (1968). A forty-page pamphlet, *Lattimer Massacre* (1950) by Edward Pinkowski, next awakened my curiosity and my desire to learn more. Both authors encouraged me. I asked Ginny Perrell to begin researching this "most forgotten episode in American labor history" at the New York Public Library. In 1972, Ellen Walsh, a native of Scranton, scoured the mine-field area for valuable leads. Kathleen Kennedy of Harrisburg, a longtime friend, began mailing me photographs and documentary materials from the Pennsylvania State Library and, in addition, interviewed several key witnesses from that period. John Bodnar, director of the ethnic archives at the Pennsylvania State Library, was of consistent help. Mrs. Eileen Zanar then performed the herculean task of preparing index cards and careful handwritten notes, including a chronology of dates, places, persons, deeds, and statements which, typed up, gave me a manuscript of over two hundred pages to build from. Other work—the presidential campaign of 1972 and my duties at the Rockefeller Foundation—prevented me from reviewing my reading and broadening my investigations until 1976.

Yet I am not a historian. Professor George A. Turner of Bloomsburg State College, not far from the site of the massacre at Lattimer Mines, has devoted years of precise research to the subject. Since at least 1973, we have nourished each other's work. Beginning in 1977, I was fortunate to benefit by Professor Turner's two published essays, even, as an editor, to publish one of them. He generously shared with me, as well, many of the items of evidence he had collected, and gave me several fruitful leads to follow up. I was happy to share some of my finds with him; but the debts are mostly mine.

In 1976, Lisa Lilienthal, granddaughter of Margaret Bonin (who at nine had tearfully watched ten bloody victims of Lattimer being carried into her father's undertaking establishment), spent some one hundred hours conducting other interviews and following other leads at the scene. Jack Palance, the actor, was born in Lattimer Mines, and a conversation with him at the banquet of the Ukrainian Research Center at Harvard University in 1976 added perspective. Like many others born in the region, he knew few details about the dread events. Local amnesia has been thorough.

In 1977 Kathleen Kennedy discovered that a new photographic collection just given to the Pennsylvania archives included a picture of the marchers at Lattimer, and she again began mailing me files of the newspapers of 1897 and 1898. From this mass of material Louise Zanar helped me to organize precise details to add to the first full draft I prepared that summer. Her efforts, like those of her mother, were crucial and were performed with excellence. A research grant from Syracuse University for the summer of 1977, inspired by Professor Ronald Cavanagh, my departmental chairman, enabled me to hire Michael Mooney to visit Hazleton several times that summer in pursuit of missing detail. Michael proved to be a discerning and inventive researcher, who won the confidence of many, turned up invaluable materials, and saved me from many errors. Professor George A. Turner again passed on to me some invaluable documents and many important leads. All of us searched assiduously for the families of survivors, for the official court transcripts (which disappeared mysteriously sometime around 1905, as nearly as we could determine), for photographs, and other forms of evidence. Librarians at the newspapers, public libraries, and historical societies of Wilkes-Barre, Scranton, Philadelphia, Utica, Hazleton, and West Hazleton gave advice and assistance of indispensable value. The family

A Note of Thanks

of Mike Cheslock [Cheslak], especially Veronica Gasper; John Roslevich, Jr., of the West Hazleton Historical Museum; James Reinmiller of the Hazleton Public Library; and George C. Brandau, who permitted us to draw upon his father's magnificent collection of photographic plates, must be singled out. Like the strike that summer of 1897, this has been a collective effort.

A constant quiet excitement gripped me and those who helped me as we tried to resolve inconsistencies and contradictions, to put fragments together, and to dig for missing pieces. (For future researchers, our whole collection of newspapers, documents, notes, and letters has been entrusted to the Stonehill College Library, North Easton, Massachusetts.) The sheer detective work of hunting for texts and making them speak yielded countless pleasures. Each new cache of newspapers was like a child's Christmas. The glow lasted for hours. My colleagues join me in hoping that readers enjoy the task as much as we did. So many fragments of American history, like this one, are yet to be discovered, polished, and restored before the national portrait will be complete.

Finally, I thank the following persons, who read this book in manuscript with care beyond any bond of duty and suggested hundreds of detailed corrections and improvements: Paul Beers, George A. Turner, and Mark Stolarik. Robert Paul Magosci of Harvard and Msgr. John Tracy Ellis of Catholic University also offered helpful corrections and comments. I would also like to thank Lori Hudecek for preparing the first draft of the maps in this book. But the greatest of all my debts is to my editor, Midge Decter, whose painstaking line-by-line attentions helped me free the last draft from the rough marble she first saw. Rarely does the writer experience an intelligent and sympathetic editing such that almost every suggestion helps to further his intention; from her I did.

A NOTE ON PROPER NAMES

IN LISTING THE NAMES of the dead and wounded at
Lattimer, Konštantín Čulen in his two-volume *History of the
Slovaks in America* (1942) was obliged to add: "Some of the
surnames were garbled to some extent; most likely they happened to be misread in the course of years that had passed
since the massacre itself." The insouciance of newspaper accounts from that period concerning Slavic names is now a
formidable obstacle. Published spellings varied so wildly that
at times one can scarcely tell if one, two, or three different
persons are intended. Part of this difficulty lies in transliterat-
ing Slavic sounds into English letters. Part of it lies in the
discretion used by priests, civil servants, officials, teachers, and
others who kept public records. Even Slavs of the period, like
Father Richard Aust of Hazleton or Dr. Theodorovich of the
Austro-Hungarian Consulate in Philadelphia, used inconsistent
spellings. In addition, there are significant orthographic varia-
tions in each of the dozen or more eastern European languages
then and now spoken around Hazleton. To compound these
difficulties, immigrants themselves, for multiple reasons, sometimes accepted irregular spellings of their own names. Thus,
even their fellow immigrants might be uncertain of the desired
spelling, and different branches of the same family might settle
on different spellings.

Father Aust regularly spelled the name of Mike Cheslak,
Cheslyak, whereas Dr. Theodorovich sometimes gives it as
Ceslak (but more often as *Cheslak*), and the commonwealth
in its official papers as *Cheslock*. It was the last spelling, it
appears, that came to be used by Ella Cheslock, young wife of
the victim, whose English was limited, and by her children,
who were very young at their father's death.

American typography of the period did not supply the ac-
cents and diacritical marks that guide oral pronunciation of

eastern European names. One misses, especially, the (ˇ) that softens a c or an s so as to give it the sound of ch in chess or the sh in ship. Reporters used their ears and their inventive skills as best they could.

The young Slovak scholar Mark Stolarik points out (in a letter to the author, December 13, 1977) that the Slovak language was not codified until 1846. Until then, names were spelled at the whim of officials. But even after this codification and its subsequent revisions in the nineteenth and twentieth centuries, not everyone knew the rules or observed them; the average peasant certainly didn't know the rules. Moreover, Slovakia was ruled by the Magyars of Hungary, and Magyar officials often Magyarized the spellings of names and places; just as American officials later Americanized them. Analogous forces affected each of the other eastern European populations both in Europe and in America. As Professor Stolarik notes, there was and is a proper way to spell all Slovak (and other) names. I have followed Professor Stolarik's advice, by supplying at least once the proper spelling for each name as it occurs.

For most of the text, however, I have followed the principle of adhering as closely as possible to a readable English form of the original, particularly if that form is found often in the historical record. With Stolarik's assistance, I have supplied the proper Slavic form, in English transliteration, where the sources use inconsistent or plainly erroneous forms. For example, a distinguished Slovak in Wilkes-Barre at the time, whose name appears in variants like *Edward Effalusi* or *Ufalosi*, is well known enough to historians to permit his name to be recorded accurately as Edmund Ujfalusi. Since the original Slovak would almost certainly have been *Českok*, I have rendered the name of the principal victim of the massacre as *Cheslak*, its nearest English equivalent.

On Polish spellings—and it must be noted that most of the victims in this story were Polish—Edward Pinkowski's pamphlet was a valuable guide. The official report by Dr. Theodorovich to the Austro-Hungarian government provided a check on newspaper spellings, although, naturally enough, its own tendencies follow official policies of Magyarization. Father Aust's public report on the distributions of modest funds to the families of the victims was also of assistance.

Still, I confess to many doubts. As best I can determine, one man is referred to as Ulrich, Urich, Yurich, Jureck, Juric, and Jurek. I have used *Jurich*. Yet another is referred to as Jurecek, Jurasek, Yurechek, Yuracek, Yuracheck, Jurezest. I have rendered it *Jurechek*. I have written Mary *Septak* rather than, as some sources have it, *Septek*. A nest of ambiguities also surrounds *Kislewicz*, as I have it, a name attributed in various texts both to an Anthony and a Martin. Some sources have *Kislavicz* for Anthony and *Grenkavicz* for Martin. Others give both men the same family name but spell it in various ways, as though from spoken sounds: *Kascavage* or *Kaskavach*. A payment to a Mary *Kizclewicz* from the Charity Fund led me away from the latter direction. My apologies in advance to any of the families whose names I may have unwittingly distorted.

Professor Mark Stolarik has provided a list of the correct spellings for the following names: Thomas Bell, Tomáš Belejčák; Mehalchik, Michalčík; Annitska, Anička; Josef Kinshilla, Jozef Kinčila; John Eagler, Ján Engler; John Nemeth, Ján Németh; John Fota, Ján Futa; Andrew Bartosh, Andrej Bartoš; Joseph Mehalto, Jozef Michalko; Mary Septak, Mária Septaková; John Glavati, Ján Hlavatý; Thomas Racek, Tomáš Raček; Sebastian Gasperick, Sebastian Gašpárik; Mike Kinaski, Michal Kniasky; Michael Kuher, Michal Kuchar; Martin Shefronick, Martin Šefránek; Andro Siver, Andrej Sivár; John Slobodnik, Ján Slobodnik; John Bonko, Ján Banko; Michael Srocach, Michal Srokáč; Thodorovich, Theodorovich; Anthony Grekas, Anton Grekoš; Edward Efalusi, Edmund Ujfalusi. The short familiar form of Andrej is Andro and is often found in its place. The reader will have noted that two cousins both shared the name Andrej Sivár.

THE DEAD AT LATTIMER MINES*

(WRITTEN)	(PRONOUNCED)
Broztowski	Bross-toff-skee
Česlak (Cheslock)	Chess-lock
Chrzeszeski	Chri-zes-zeskee
Čaja (Czaja)	Tchaia
Futa (Fota)	Foota (Fota)
Grekoš	Greckoss
Jurič (Jurich, Jurek)	Yourich (Youreck)
Jurašek (Jurechek)	Yurashek (Yourechek)
Kulik (Kulick)	Koolick
Mieczkowski	Mietch-koff-skee
Monikaski	Money-kas-kee
Platek	Plateck
Rekewicz	Re-keff-itch
Skrep	Schkrep
Tarnowicz	Tarnowitch
Tomašantas	Tomashantas
Zagorski	Za-gore-skee
Ziominski	Tsio-min-skee
Zicmba	Tsiemba

* The marked grave of John Tarnowicz was discovered only in 1972, although his name had appeared (in many variants) on some earlier lists of the dead. Lists made in 1897–98 show many discrepancies in numbers, persons, and spellings. Often they confused the hospitalized wounded with the dead or dying. The above list is based upon known gravesites.

APPENDIX

Mr. Martin to the Governor of Pennsylvania

Sheriff's Office, October 18, 1897

In reply to yours of the 13th, and also the communication addressed to you by the Hon. John Sherman, Secretary of State, asking for facts and information about the conflict that took place at Lattimer in this county on the 10th day of September, 1897, between myself and deputy sheriffs and a mob of strikers, I respectfully submit the following:

On Friday, the 3d day of September, there was a mob of about 2,000 men who went around the different mines in that region about Hazleton and drove the men from their work and compelled them to join the ranks of the mob, and if they refused they were clubbed and beaten and made to join. On Saturday, September 4, 1897, the Lehigh Valley Coal Company notified the sheriff's office—I being away at Atlantic City at the time—that they would hold the sheriff responsible for any more interference at their mines. My attorney, Mr. Ferris, told my chief deputy, Mr. Wall, to wire me at once, which he did, and I came on Sunday the 5th of September. On Monday morning, September 6, Labor Day, Mr. Lathrop, superintendent of the Lehigh Valley Coal Company, sent for me to meet him at his office, which I did at 9 a. m. I also met Mr. Stearns, superintendent of the Cross Creek Coal Company, and Mr. Lawall, superintendent of the Lehigh and Wilkesbarre Coal Company. Mr. Lathrop and Mr. Stearns then notified me that they would hold me responsible for any more interference with their mines. My attorney, Mr. Ferris, was present at the time, and he and I agreed that, under the circumstances, it was my duty to go to Hazleton and see that there were no more violations of the laws of the State. I left for Hazleton on the 10.15 train, and on arriving at Hazleton I met at the depot Mr. Zerby, assistant superintendent of the Lehigh Valley Coal Company, and Mr. Platt, superintendent of Pardee & Co., and from them I learned the state of affairs, and that the mob that caused all the trouble on Friday, the 3d, were from Schuylkill and Carbon counties, so I had telegrams sent to Sheriff Scott, of Schuylkill County, and Sheriff Setzer, of Carbon County, to meet me at Hazleton Monday afternoon. We all agreed to issue a proclamation and have it printed in the Hazleton papers. Our proclamations were published in the Hazleton Sentinel on Monday evening, September 6, 1897, and in the Plain Speaker and Standard, Tuesday morning, September 7, 1897, and we also had a lot of handbills printed, which were posted around the mines on telegraph poles and in every conspicuous place in the neighborhood.

On Monday evening, just before I went to supper, I received word that a number of men had watched and beaten a Hungarian laborer while returning from work at Cayle's strippings. The man was so badly beaten that he died in a day or two at the hospital.

That afternoon I saw some good citizens and told them that I wanted a number of good citizens to act as deputy sheriffs in assisting me in maintaining the peace, and to protect life and property, and also to see that every man who wished to work would have the privilege of doing so.

So Monday night I made arrangements to meet them and as many more as they could recommend to me in a storeroom on Broad street, Hazleton, about 8 o'clock. When I arrived there, being accompanied by Sheriff Setzer of Carbon County, there were 87 men who were willing to act as deputies, and I swore them in as such. There was a report that evening that a mob was going to start out for the purpose of stopping any mines that were working.

So I ordered the deputies to report at 5 o'clock on Tuesday morning. At 5.30 a. m. I went to the storeroom and a number of deputies were there, but nothing occurred until about 8 a. m., when I received word that a mob was forming at Crystal Ridge Colliery for the purpose of stopping the men that were working at the strippings there.

Myself and Mr. Platt and Mr. Hampden, superintendent of coal and iron police, and Mr. Eby took a special train and ran up to the mines. When we got there, there was a mob of about 150 men who were just commencing to throw stones at the men in the strippings. I ordered them to stop, and read the riot act to them and ordered them to disperse. They all had clubs from 3 to 5 feet long and looked very threatening. After I had them dispersed I went among them and explained who I was and what my duty was, and told them that they were doing wrong, and breaking the laws by interfering with the men at work. One young man said that they would stop the men anyhow. I told him if I heard him say that again I would arrest him and put him in prison, and he did not say any more in my hearing. That afternoon I left for Wilkesbarre at 2 p. m. After I left, a mob went to Lattimer and started to drive the men from their work, when the deputies arrived and drove them away.

On Wednesday morning I went to Drifton and swore in a number of deputies for the purpose of protecting the property of the Cross Creek Coal Company and other property around Drifton, Freeland, Jeddo, Eckley, and Stockton, and also to protect those who wanted to work. After that was done, I went to West Hazleton and made some inquiries in regard to the situation. I was not known there and I went into a barroom and there I met an old Irish gentleman from McAdoo, and from him I learned that a mob was coming from there that afternoon for the purpose of stopping the works. He also told me that he had come to West Hazleton as he did not want to go with the mob, as he was afraid there would be trouble. He also told me that his boys had left home so that they would not be compelled to march with the mob. He also said that all the English-speaking people were hiding away in the woods, or else left for some other place through the night. They were afraid to stay home, as the foreigners had announced their intention that they must go along with them.

After dinner Mr. Samuel Price, one of my deputies, came and told me that the mob was marching to Stockton, so I told him to get a train at the Wyoming Street Depot, and I and the deputies took the train for Stockton. When we reached Hazleton shops there was great excitement, and the people were running in all directions. I ordered the train stopped, and I got off and asked some workmen who were gathering up their tools why they were so excited, and they said that the mob was coming, and, not knowing who I was, told me that I had better get out of the way or they would take me along with them. As soon as the workmen gathered up their tools they would run off so as to be out of the way of the mob, so great was their fear. Rhone Trescott was with me, and I said to him that I did not feel it my duty to stop the mob if they were within the city limits, but the mayor's. We telephoned the mayor, but he was sick. I had Mr. Trescott point out the city line to me, and as they had not yet got to the city, we went to the city line, about 100 yards from where we were, to meet them. Just as we got there we met the mob. I ordered them to stop, and read the riot act and ordered them to disperse. While we were talking to them the chief of police and one or two of his men came. We finally got them turned for home. Then Mr. Trescott, Mr. Blanchard, and I walked around the outskirts of the city, and when we came to the main road a gentleman told me that the mob was going to stop the work at Crystal Ridge Colliery. Mr. Trescott and I cut through the woods and arrived at the colliery before the mob. I had sent word to the deputies to go to Crystal Ridge. After I arrived there I waited about ten minutes for the mob to put in an appearance.

I went up to the railroad to meet them again, and I ordered them to disperse. They refused to do so right away, but wanted to go ahead. One young man had gone to the breaker, and he came back and told them that they must go back as there were too many deputies there for them that day, but they would come tomorrow and stop the works. I told them it was wrong for them to do so, but they said that they did not give a damn, they would do so anyhow. I then warned them that they had better not try.

On Thursday morning I was notified that the mob intended to march again, and that they were going to stop Beaver Meadow mines first, so I took the deputies over there. While there I met Sheriff Setzer, and we got word that a mob was forming, and that they intended to march. We waited until about 11 A.M., when the report came that the mob was coming. The mob got to Beaver Meadow before they were stopped and turned back. One of the mob had a gun, and some of the deputies ran to catch him. The man ran, and as he ran he turned and fired a shot at us, then some of the deputies fired some shots, but I don't think they tried to shoot him. There were about 300 men in the mob. After that we waited around there all day, expecting that they would come back, but they did not. That evening I went to Wilkesbarre.

On Friday, September 10, I went to Drifton, where I met the deputies. We took the train and went to the lumber yard, so that we could be in easy communication with any part of the trouble. We stayed there till about 1:20 P.M., when I received a dispatch saying that a mob was at West Hazleton stripping, and had driven the men from their work. I ordered the train stopped, and we got to West Hazleton about 1:40 or 2 P.M. I was unable to get to the head of the mob, but struck it well toward the rear. I ordered them to halt behind where I met them and read the riot act, but they kept on shouting "Come on," and kept waving their hands. I also heard a man say, "No stop, s—— b——," so I arrested him. I then hurried along through the mob and kept ordering them to stop, but they paid no attention to me, but kept right along shouting and waving their hands to everyone they could see. When I got to the head of the mob I ordered them to stop again. Some ran on both sides of the road, but I got them stopped. I then read the riot act again, and by this time the deputies had caught up to me. They then told me that we could not stop them; that they were going to Lattimer mines to stop it. I had to call several deputies with their guns to assist in keeping them back. I thought then that there would be serious trouble, as some of them had picked up stones, and it looked as though they intended to strike me or some of my deputies. We were there about half an hour. I tried to get them quiet, so that I could talk to them. I went among them and asked them who could talk English. When I found a man who could talk English I would explain what was my duty, and would tell them that they were breaking the laws of the country, and that we could not allow them to do so, when he would try and explain it to the rest of them. I could hear them say, "Him be a ————, and we stop Lattimer mines." I told them that they must not do so. I told them that I could arrest them for what they had done and what they were doing and for what they had declared their intention of doing, but that I did not want to do so.

I begged them to go home and not cause any more trouble. I think that some of them wanted to do so, but it looked to me, by the way they acted and talked, as if the majority wanted to keep on and stop Lattimer mines at any cost. They also told me that to-morrow they would all bring guns along, and we would see whether we would stop them then, and that if we shot they would shoot, and called me and the deputies all the vile names they could think of. I left them there, but warned them that they should not undertake to stop any more mines. We went on up the street, the deputies and myself, and then some one reported that they were marching again. I said that I could not help it as I was tired out and was not able to meet them again. I then ordered the deputies to take the car and we would go to Lattimer and meet them again. When we got to Harleigh, about 2 miles from Hazleton, I ordered the car stopped until the mob came along to see which way they would go. When they arrived at Harleigh they halted. When they saw the car with the deputies they got off on one side of the road, and some of them sneaked away through the woods, and I saw some that were trying to leave the mob get called back, and when they would not come back some of them would run after them and bring them back to the mob. We waited on the hillside at Harleigh to see which way the mob would go, and when we saw them start up the Lattimer road I ordered the car to proceed. When we arrived at Farley's hotel we got out of the car and walked up the railroad toward one of the Lattimer breakers. There I met a number of deputies who had been placed there to see that the men who were working there would not be interfered with. We stood on the railroad expecting that the mob would come that way; when they saw us they went up the wagon road toward Lattimer village and another breaker at Lattimer. I then ordered the deputies to take the car again to head them off before they reached the other mines, which we did. When the car arrived at Lattimer village we left the car again and I told the deputies to stand on one side of the road and to keep cool and not get excited. I said I would go out and stop the mob again and see what they intended to do. I said if they say they are not going to do anything I may let them go on and we will go along with them. I then started out to meet the mob, and I took the riot act out of my pocket, and I walked out between 40 and 50 yards away from my deputies to meet the mob. When we came close together the front column walked slow so that the back column closed close together with it. I ordered them to halt and asked them what they were going to do, and a number shouted out: "We stop Lattimer mines." I then started to read the riot act and they kept pushing ahead and against me, when a young man back in the fourth column said: "Go ahead; him ————; him no good; we stop Lattimer mines." I then reached my hand and caught him with the intent of placing him under arrest, and when I did, some seven or eight of them took hold of me; some of them struck me with their fists, while two of them pulled revolvers, and one of them made a dig at me with a knife. I then pulled my revolver, when one big fellow gave me a blow on the cheek and knocked me on my knees. I would have been knocked down on my back but the crowd was too close around me, so that there was no room for me to get down, and while we were struggling I heard a shot followed closely by a second and then a number of shots together. Those who were attacking me were shot, and I was then unable to recover myself, and there is no doubt in my mind that if the deputies had not shot just when they did I would certainly have been killed. While I was struggling with part of the mob on one side of the road in the ditch where they had pushed me, the part on the other side of the road with a whoop and a yell rushed on toward the deputies, who, no doubt fearing that their lives were in danger and that I was about to be killed, fired, the result being that 18 men were either killed or mortally wounded, and a number of others wounded, all of whom have or will recover. Some of the men that were killed were from 5 to 8 yards from the deputies, and a large number of the mob had passed me by at least 25 yards toward the deputies. The mob numbered about 700 or 800. The number of deputies was 80. When I recovered myself, I raised my hands and shouted to the deputies to cease firing, which they did. The whole firing lasted less than one minute. A few of the men were shot in the back but this can be accounted for by the fact that they were circled around me and had their backs toward the deputies. The mob was composed of desperate men who, in my opinion, would halt at nothing to further their ends. The deputies were all good, reputable citizens, most of them being property owners. They were men who had good, sound judgment, and possessed no desire to shed blood but were compelled to take life to protect their own, and we had no desires or intentions whatever to wantonly kill or wound any person. Most of the mob lived at Harwood and Cranberry, about 6 miles from the scene of the shooting.

The reason I stopped the mob before they came to the breaker and mines was that I was notified by the superintendent, Mr. Drake, that they would hold me responsible for any interference with their mines. I knew very well that if the mob got to the breaker they would surely attempt to stop it, and then if we undertook to arrest them that there would be serious trouble, and I have no doubt that some innocent blood would have been shed, and there is no doubt in my mind that the loss of life would have been greater.

Another reason was that I thought I could get them stopped, and that I would have a chance to talk and reason with them, and that I might possibly get them to turn back and go home; but I saw as soon as I met them that they had no intention of allowing themselves to be stopped. I most positively deny that there was any wanton and malicious killing of anyone, and I further say that I do not know whether those who were killed were American citizens or subjects of a foreign country. What I do know is that they were a mob who were violating the laws of the country; and further, their friends have seen fit to have me and the deputies arrested for murder, and we are under heavy bail for the same. I would think that if any foreign country thought that any of its subjects had been killed unlawfully that it would wait to see what the decision of our courts would be before taking action in the matter. I feel that the Austrian Government is rather premature in the matter. I do not think it right and fair for any foreign country to be allowed to try and prejudice our case at the present time; and furthermore, if our act and actions were wrong, our courts and the American people are the proper parties to say so, and they will not be afraid to do so, without the interference of the Austrian Government.

Respectfully submitted.

JAMES MARTIN,
Sheriff of Luzerne County, Pa.

Appendix

BIBLIOGRAPHY

Books

Abramson, Harold J. *Ethnic Diversity in Catholic America*. New York: John Wiley and Sons, 1973.

Adamic, Louis. *Dynamite: The Story of Class Violence in America*. New York: Chelsea House Publishers, 1958.

———. *Laughing in the Jungle*. New York: Arno Press, 1969.

Aurand, Harold W. *From the Molly Maguires to the United Mine Workers: The Social Ecology of an Industrial Union 1869–1897*. Philadelphia: Temple University Press, 1971.

Balch, Emily Greene. *Our Slavic Fellow Citizens*. New York: Charities Publication Committee, 1910.

Baratz, Morton S. *The Union and the Coal Industry*. New Haven: Yale University Press, 1955.

Barton, Josef. *Peasants and Strangers*. Cambridge: Harvard University Press, 1975.

Beers, Paul, ed. *The Pennsylvania Sampler*. Harrisburg, Pa.: Stackpole Books, 1970.

———. *Profiles from the Susquehanna Valley*. Harrisburg, Pa.: The Stackpole Company, 1973.

Bell, Thomas. *Out of This Furnace*. Pittsburgh, Pa.: University of Pittsburgh Press, 1976.

Bernstein, Irving. *Turbulent Years: A History of the American Worker, 1933–1941*. Boston: Houghton Mifflin Co., 1970.

Blum, Jerome. *Lord and Peasant in Russia from the Ninth to the Nineteenth Century*. Princeton, N.J.: Princeton University Press, 1961.

Bodnar, John E., ed. *The Ethnic Experience in Pennsylvania*. Lewisburg, Pa.: Bucknell University Press, 1973.

Bradsby, H. C., ed. *History of Luzerne County*. Chicago: G. B. Nelson, 1893.

Brophy, John. *A Miner's Life: an Autobiography*. Madison: University of Wisconsin Press, 1964.

Byington, Margaret F. *Homestead: The Households of a Mill Town*. 1910. Reprint. Pittsburgh, Pa.: University Center for International Studies, 1974.

Cahn, William. *A Pictorial History of American Labor.* New York: Crown Publishers, Inc., 1972.

Čapek, Karel. *Hordubal.* Translated by M. Weatherall and R. Weatherall. London: G. Allen and Unwin, 1934.

Carnes, Cecil. *John L. Lewis, Leader of Labor.* New York: R. Speller Publishers, 1936.

Corlsen, Carl. *Buried Black Treasure.* Bethlehem, Pa.: Published by the author, Box 1364, 1954.

Čulen, Konštantín. *Dejiny Slovakov v Amerike.* Bratislava: Nakladel'stvo Slovenskej Ligy, 1942. Chapters on Lattimer translated by Sister Martina Tybor in *Slovakia* 27 (1977): 44–61.

Culin, Stewart. *A Trooper's Narrative of Service in the Anthracite Coal Strike, 1902.* Philadelphia: George W. Jacobs & Co., 1902.

Demarest, David P., ed. *From These Hills, From These Valleys.* Pittsburgh, Pa.: University of Pittsburgh Press, 1976.

Evans, Christopher. *History of the United Mine Workers of America from the Years 1860 to 1890.* Indianapolis, Ind.: United Mine Workers of America, 1914.

Foner, Philip S. *From the Founding of the American Federation of Labor to the Emergence of American Imperialism: History of the Labor Movement in the United States.* New York: International Publishers, 1955.

Gambino, Richard. *Vendetta: A True Story of the Worst Lynching in America, the Mass Murder of Italian-Americans in New Orleans in 1891, the Vicious Motivations Behind It, and the Tragic Repercussions That Linger to This Day.* New York: Doubleday, 1977.

Gendral, Fred. *Luzerne and Its Miners.* Master's Thesis. Incompletely identified fragment; deposited with other materials at Stonehill College, 1946. Michael Novak collection, Lattimer files.

Glück, Elsie. *John Mitchell: Miner, Labor's Bargain with the Gilded Age.* New York: John Day Co., 1929.

Greene, Victor R. *The Slavic Community on Strike: Immigrant Labor in Pennsylvania Anthracite.* Notre Dame, Ind.: University of Notre Dame Press, 1968.

Gutman, Herbert G. "The Workers' Search for Power." In *The Gilded Age,* edited by H. Wayne Morgan, pp. 38–68. Syracuse, N.Y.: Syracuse University Press, 1970.

Handlin, Oscar. *The Uprooted.* New York: Little, Brown, 1952.

Hofstadter, Richard, and Wallace, Michael, eds. *American Violence: A Documentary History.* New York: Alfred A. Knopf, 1970.

Hollander, J. H. *Studies in American Trade Unionism.* New York: H. Holt and Company, 1907.

Holmes, Joseph John. *The National Guard of Pennsylvania, Policemen of Industry, 1865–1905.* Ph.D. dissertation, University of Connecticut, 1971.

Jordan, John W. *Encyclopedia of Pennsylvania Biography.* New York: Lewis Historical Publishing Company, 1916.

Juergens, George. *Joseph Pulitzer and the New York World.* Princeton, N.J.: Princeton University Press, 1966.

Korson, George. *Coal Dust on the Fiddle: Songs and Stories of the Bituminous Industry.* Philadelphia: University of Pennsylvania Press, 1938.

———. *Minstrels of the Mine Patch: Songs and Stories of the Anthracite Industry.* Philadelphia: University of Pennsylvania Press, 1938.

Kuritz, Hyman. *The Pennsylvania State Government and Labor Controls from 1869–1922.* Ph.D. dissertation. Columbia University, 1953. Ann Arbor, Mich.: University Microfilms, #6653.

Lantz, Herman R., and McCrary, J. S. *People of Coal Town.* New York: Columbia University Press, 1958.

McGovern, George S., and Guttridge, Leonard F. *The Great Coalfield War.* Boston: Houghton Mifflin Co., 1972.

Palmer, Henry W. *Fifty Years at the Bar and in Politics.* Williamsport, Pa.: Snyder & Bischof, 1913.

Parton, Mary Field, ed. *Autobiography of Mother Jones.* Introduction and notes by Fred Thompson. 3rd ed., rev. Chicago: Charles H. Kerr & Company, 1976.

Pinkowski, Edward. *John Siney, The Miners' Martyr.* Philadelphia: Sunshine Press, 1963.

――――. *Lattimer Massacre.* Philadelphia, Pa.: Sunshine Press, 1950.

Poliniak, Louis. *When Coal Was King.* Lebanon, Pa.: Applied Arts Publishers, 1970.

Ponicsan, Daryl. *Andoshen, Pa., a Novel.* New York: The Dial Press, 1973.

Quinby, E. J. *Wilkes-Barre and Hazleton Railway.* Fredon, N.J.: Model Craftsman Publishing Corp., 1972.

Roberts, Peter. *Anthracite Coal Communities: A Study of the Demography, the Social, Educational and Moral Life of the Anthracite Regions.* New York: The Macmillan Co., 1904.

――――. *The Anthracite Coal Industry: A Study of the Economic Conditions and Relations of the Cooperative Forces in the Development of the Anthracite Coal Industry of Pennsylvania.* New York: The Macmillan Co., 1901.

――――. *The New Immigration.* New York: The Macmillan Co., 1912.

Smith, Timothy L. "Lay Initiative in the Religious Life of American Immigrants, 1880–1950." In *Anonymous Americans: Explorations in 19th Century Social History,* edited by Tamara K. Hareven, pp. 214–249. Englewood Cliffs, N.J.: Prentice-Hall, Inc., 1971.

Stein, Howard Finn. *An Ethno-Historic Study of Slovak-American Identity.* Ph.D. dissertation. University of Pittsburgh, 1972.

Stevenson, George F. *Reflections of an Anthracite Engineer.* New York: Hudson Coal Co., 1938.

Stirling, Perry. *Bootleggers, Breakers, and Beer.* Summit Hill, Pa.: American Printing Co., 1974.

Stolarik, M. Mark. *Immigration and Urbanization: The Slovak Experience, 1870–1918.* Ph.D. dissertation. University of Minnesota, 1974.

――――. "Immigration, Education, and the Social Mobility of Slovaks, 1870–1930." In *Immigrants and Religion in Urban America,* edited by Randall M. Miller and Thomas D. Marzik, pp. 103–116. Philadelphia: Temple University Press, 1977.

Taft, Philip, and Ross, Philip. "American Labor Violence: Its Causes, Character, and Outcome." In *Violence in America,* edited by Hugh Davis Graham and Ted Robert Gurr, pp. 281–395. New York: F. A. Praeger, 1969.

Thomas, William I., and Znaniecki, Florian. *The Polish Peasant in Europe and America.* 5 vols. Boston: 1918–1920.

Tyson, Mary Siegel. *The Miners.* Pine Grove, Pa.: Sweet Arrow Press, 1977.

Bibliography

Warne, Frank Julian. *The Coal-Mine Workers—a Study in Labor Organizations.* New York: Longman, Green & Co., 1905.
————. *The Immigrant Invasion.* New York: Dodd, Mead and Company, 1913.
————. *The Slav Invasion and the Mine Workers.* Philadelphia: J. B. Lippincott Co., 1904.
Williams, Bruce T., and Yates, Michael D. *Upward Struggle: A Bi-Centennial Tribute to Labor in Cambria and Somerset Counties.* Johnstown, Pa.: Johnstown Regional Central Labor Council, 1976.

Articles

Accursia, Sister M. "Polish Miners in Luzerne County, Pennsylvania." *Polish American Studies* 111 (1946): 5–12.
"The Acquittal of Sheriff Martin," *The Literary Digest* 16 (1898): 335–337.
"Aftermath." *United Mine Workers Journal* 7 (1897): 2–3.
Aurand, Harold, and Hanzely, John E. "Lattimer Massacre." *Program of the 75th Anniversary Banquet,* United Labor Council of Lower Luzerne and Carbon Counties, AFL-CIO and UMW, September 10, 1972.
Bell, Thomas. "Slovak Wedding Day." *Jednota Annual Furdek* 17 (1978): 41–45.
Berthoff, Rowland. "The Social Order of the Anthracite Region, 1825–1902." *The Pennsylvania Magazine of History and Biography* 89 (1965): 261–291.
Brooks, John Graham. "An Impression of the Anthracite Coal Troubles." *Yale Review* 6 (1897): 306–311.
Čulen, Konštantín. "The Lattimer Massacre." *Slovakia* 27 (1977): 44–61.
Gibbons, William Frethey. "The Adopted Home of the Hun: A Social Study in Pennsylvania." *American Magazine of Civics,* September 1895, 315–323.
[Gompers, Samuel] "Lattimer Tragedy—Wilkes-Barre Farce." *American Federationist* 5 (1898): 11–14.
Greene, Victor R. "A Study in Slavs, Strikes, and Unions: The Anthracite Strike of 1897." *Pennsylvania History* 31 (1964): 199–215.
Gutman, Herbert G. "Protestantism and the American Labor Movement: The Christian Spirit in the Gilded Age." *American Historical Review* 72 (1966): 74–101.
————. "Two Lockouts in Pennsylvania." *Pennsylvania Magazine* 83 (1959): 307–326.
Harris, Herbert. "Why Labor Lost the Intellectuals." *Harper's* 228, June 1964, 79–86.
Lane, Ann J. "Recent Literature on the Molly Maguires." *Science and Society* 30 (Summer, 1966): 309–319.
Lovejoy, Owen R. "Coal Mines in Pennsylvania and Child Labor." *The Annals of the American Academy of Political and Social Science* 37 (1911): 133–148.

————. "The Slav Child: A National Asset or a Liability." *Charities*, July 1905, 882–884.
Maclean, Annie Marion. "Life in the Pennsylvania Coal Field: With Particular Reference to Women." *American Journal of Sociology* 14 (1909): 329–351.
Nichols, Francis H. "Children of the Coal Shadow." *McClure's* 20 (1902/3): 435–444.
"Public Concern in the Coal Strike." *The Outlook* 71 (1902): 1035.
Roberts, Peter. "The Sclavs [sic] in Anthracite Coal Communities." *Charities* 13 (1904): 215–222.
Rood, Henry. "The Mine Laborer in Pennsylvania." *Forum* 14 (1892): 110–122.
————. "A Pennsylvania Colliery Village: A Polyglot Community." *Century Illustrated Monthly Magazine* 55 (1898): 809–821.
Ross, Edward Alsworth. "The Slavs in America." *The Century Illustrated Magazine* 88 (1914): 590–598.
Sayles, Mary Buell. "Housing and Social Conditions in a Slavic Neighborhood." *Charities* 13 (1904): 257–261.
Schooley, Harry B., III. "The Lattimer Massacre and Trial." *Slovakia* 27 (1977): 62–79.
Spahr, Charles B. "America's Working People: VI. The Coal-Miners of Pennsylvania." *Outlook* 62 (1899): 805–812.
Turner, George A. "The Lattimer Massacre and Its Sources." *Slovakia* 27 (1977): 9–43.
————. "The Lattimer Tragedy of 1897." *Pennsylvania Heritage* 3 (1977): 10–13.
Valetta, Clement. "Italian Immigrant Life in Northampton County, Pa., 1890–1915." *Pennsylvania Folklife* 14 (1965): 36–45, and 15 (1966): 39–48.
Warne, Frank Julian. "The Effect of Unionism upon the Mine Worker." *Annals of the American Academy of Political and Social Science* 21 (1903): 20–35.
————. "The Real Cause of the Miners' Strike." *The Outlook* 71 (1902): 1053–1057.
————. "Some Industrial Effects of Slav Immigration." *Charities* 13 (1904): 223–226.

Public Documents

Luzerne County, Pennsylvania. *Court Docket*. Commonwealth of Pennsylvania No. 791. September and November, 1897; February and March, 1898 sessions: pp. 338–383. (Photocopy of longhand record from the prothonotary's office.)
National Prosecuting and Charity Committee of the Lattimer Victims. "Report." Freeland, Pa.: Slov Pravda, 1899.
Pennsylvania. *Annual Report of the Adjutant General of Pennsylvania. Transmitted to the Governor in Pursuance of Law for the Year 1897*. Doc. 13. Harrisburg, 1898.

Bibliography   **269**

————. "Immigrant Labor." *Annual Report of the Commonwealth of Pennsylvania* (1884), pt. 3, pp. 63–71.
————. "Industrial Statistics." *Annual Report of the Secretary of Internal Affairs of the Commonwealth of Pennsylvania*, vol. 25, pt. 3, pp. 424–435.
————. General Library Bureau. State Library of Pennsylvania. Pennsylvania Department of Education. *Pennsylvania Newspapers and Select Out-of-State Newspapers*. Harrisburg, 1976.
————. Pennsylvania Historical and Museum Commission. Ethnic Studies Program. *An Ethnic Profile of Pennsylvania's Population*, by John Bodnar. Harrisburg, 1973.
————. *The Legislative Record for the Session, 1897*. Vol. III. Harrisburg, 1897.
————. *Report of the Bureau of Mines of the Department of Internal Affairs of Pennsylvania*. (1897). Harrisburg: William Stanley Ray State Printer, 1898.
Powell, H. Benjamin. "Brief Annotated Bibliography." Submitted to William W. Richards, Director of the Bureau of Museums, and Michael J. Winey, Field Curator for Museum Commission. Harrisburg, January, 1972. (mimeographed).
U.S., Commissioner of Labor. *Third Annual Report of the Commissioner of Labor; 1887: Strikes and Lockouts*. Washington, D.C.: Government Printing Office, 1888.
U.S., Congress. House. *Congressional Record*. H 8202–03. 11 September 1972. "Lattimer Mines."
————. House. *Report of the Industrial Commission on the Relations and Conditions of Capital and Labor Employed in the Mining Industry Including Testimony, Review of Evidence, and Topical Digest*, H.R. 181, vol. 12, 57th Cong., 1st sess., 1901.
————. House, Select Committee on Existing Labor Troubles in Pennsylvania. *Labor Troubles in the Anthracite Regions of Pennsylvania, 1887–88*. Report 4147, 50th Cong., 2nd Sess., 1889.
————. Senate. *Immigrants in Industries*. Senate Document 633, 61st Cong., 2nd Sess., 1909–1910.
U.S., Department of Labor. Bureau of Labor Statistics. "Collective Bargaining in the Anthracite Industry," by Edgar Sydenstriker. In *Bulletin of the United States Bureau of Labor Statistics*, No. 191, March 1916.
U.S., Department of State. Consular Service. U.S. Consul Reports. "Austria-Hungary," by James R. Weaver (Consul General for Austria-Hungary). In *Labor in Europe*, pp. 1212–1287. House Executive Document 54, 48th Cong., 2d Sess., 1885.
U.S., Department of State. *Document No. 244* (Appointment of John Nemeth). August 17, 1898.
————. *Papers Relating to the Foreign Relations of the United States with the Annual Message of the President Transmitted to the Congress December 5, 1898*. Washington, D.C.: Government Printing Office, 1901.
Virtue, G. O. "The Anthracite Mine Laborers." *Bulletin of the Department of Labor*. No. 18, pp. 718–765. November, 1897.

Interviews

Gasper (Cheslock), Veronica. Interviewed by Michael Novak, August, 1977.
Johnson, Roy E. Interviewed by Michael Mooney, July, 1977.
Kotch (Bonin), Margaret. Interviewed by Lisa Lilienthal, June, 1976.
Moye, John. Interviewed by Kathleen Kennedy, March, 1973.
Sonderschafer, George and Stabert, Anna. Interviewed by Ellen Walsh, summer, 1973.
Swank, Beatrice. Interviewed by Michael Mooney, July, 1977.
Turnbach, Rev. Edward. Interviewed by Lisa Lilienthal, June, 1976.

Newspapers

The author consulted the following newspapers for accounts of the events in Lattimer and Hazleton from September, 1897, to March, 1898:

Allentown, Pennsylvania, *The Morning Call*
Ashland, Pennsylvania, Ashland *Advocate*
Bethlehem, Pennsylvania, *Star*
Harrisburg, Pennsylvania, *The Evening News*
Hazleton, Pennsylvania, *The Daily Standard*
Hazleton, Pennsylvania, Hazleton *Plain Speaker*
Hazleton, Pennsylvania, Hazleton *Sentinel*
Mahanoy City, Pennsylvania, *Black Diamond*
New York *Journal*
New York *Times*
New York *Tribune*
New York *World*
Philadelphia, *The Evening Bulletin*
Philadelphia, *The North American*
Philadelphia *Press*
Philadelphia, Pennsylvania, *Public Ledger*
Pottsville, Pennsylvania, *Chronicle*
Pottsville, Pennsylvania, *Daily Miners' Journal*
Pottsville, Pennsylvania, Schuylkill *Weekly Republican*
Shenandoah, Pennsylvania, Shenandoah *Herald*
Utica, New York, *Saturday Globe*
Wilkes-Barre, Pennsylvania, *Record of the Times*
Wilkes-Barre, Pennsylvania, Wilkes-Barre *Times*

In addition, these newspapers provided recent accounts of the Lattimer shootings:

Freeland, Pennsylvania, Freeland *Press*, September 9, 1932.

Bibliography   *271*

Harrisburg, Pennsylvania, *Sunday Patriot News,* June 19, 1977.
Hazleton, Pennsylvania, *Standard Speaker,* October 10, 1966; September 27, 1969; September 9, 1972; September 9, 1975.
Hazleton, Pennsylvania, *Sunday Times,* September 1, 1937; September 10, 1937; October 22, 1951; January 17, 1956; February 19, 1967; September 10, 1972.
Hazleton, Pennsylvania, Hazleton *Vigilant,* September 9, 1932.
Hazleton, Pennsylvania, *Voice of the Valley and Hazleton,* July, 1971.
Lansford, Pennsylvania, *Valley Gazette,* July, 1973.
Pottsville, Pennsylvania, Pottsville *Republican,* August 19, 26; September 2, 9, 16, 1972.
Shamokin, Pennsylvania, *The Citizen-Shopper,* April 10, 1974.
Wilkes-Barre, Pennsylvania, *Sunday Independent,* June 20, 1937; May 15, 1977.

INDEX